THE DEFENSE
OF
WESTERN EUROPE

By

DREW MIDDLETON

APPLETON-CENTURY-CROFTS, INC.

New York

Copyright, 1952, By
DREW MIDDLETON

PRINTED IN THE UNITED STATES OF AMERICA

Foreword

This book is an attempt to assess the progress that
the United States and the other powers of the North
Atlantic Treaty Organization have made toward the
defense of Europe and to estimate their prospects of
averting, through strength, the third and final world
war.

As much of the material as was possible was gained
at first hand through interviews with generals, politicians and soldiers in the field. Some has been sent me
from various headquarters accompanied by the re-
quest that the source of the information remain secret.

Because the overall picture of Europe's defensive
structure changes from day to day, I have not attempted to give any final analysis of what that
strength will be in the future. But I hope the reader
will find here the outline of what the NATO powers
are trying to do, how this affects Europe and the
Soviet Union and finally, the mental and physical
preparedness of Europe for the great contest, in
peace or war, with the Soviet Union.

The opinions expressed are my own.

DREW MIDDLETON
Bad Godesberg, Germany

Contents

1. Towards Peace or War?

All day the little brass clock on the mantelpiece ticks merrily. The big man who sits at the desk across the room glances at it occasionally, strips off his glasses and rubs his eyes. Then he returns to the mass of memoranda on the glass-topped desk: production estimates, conscription figures, orders of battle. The man is Eisenhower, the room is his office at SHAPE (Supreme Headquarters Allied Powers in Europe) and the time is the most critical.

SHAPE is more than a headquarters for the defense of Europe. It is, quite plainly, the physical embodiment of an act of faith. For as General of the Army Dwight D. Eisenhower will tell you, "All these reports are meaningless unless there is the will and the spirit to translate them into something tangible, something we can get our hands on. It's beginning to move, and it's the will, the spirit, the faith, if you like, that's moving it."

No nation or man ever tackled so difficult a task. There have been coalitions in the past. The English coalitions under Marlborough and Wellington to fight Louis XIV and Napoleon. The alliances of the two World Wars. But those were born of war. This is born in peace and of peace. This is being built to deter, and if necessary, defeat future aggression.

The nature of what the United States and its allies are doing for the defense of Europe is easily mis-

1

understood. It is easy to be carried away with the
military aspects of the problem; to say, "If they do
this, then we must do that with this corps and that
air group." There will be much of that in this book,
because if the most favorable outcome of what we
are attempting in Europe is not attained, it will be
terribly important.

But what the West is doing, what it *must* do is to
put itself in a position which will deter a Russian
attack by military means and make it impossible for
the Russians to use their principal politico-military
weapon, the Soviet Army in East Germany.

This weapon has been with us since the autumn of
1945 when the vast armies built up in Europe by the
United States and the British Commonwealth melted
away, leaving the Soviet Union the principal military
power on the European Asiatic land mass.

The Soviet Union has used that weapon with sur-
passing skill. For half a decade the diplomats of
Russia, relying on the presence in eastern Germany
of twenty-five to thirty divisions of the Soviet Army,
invoked the presence of that army to frighten and to
cow the nations of western Europe.

"You have a vast industrial power and great technical skill," the late Jan Masaryk said to me once.
"But in Germany you have less than two divisions.
The Russians are here. Anyone in Czechoslovakia
can see them. Anyone in Poland or Hungary or
Rumania. What was the story about the G.I.'s wife
who wrote asking what the French girls had that
she didn't have and he answered, 'Nothing, darling,
but they have it here.'

"Well, the Russians have it here. When Molotov

gets up to speak the people that listen so closely are not listening to him. They hear the noise of thirty Russian divisions."

Thus an intelligent, a great, European in the days of western military impotence.

A Europe in what General Bradley likes to call "a proper posture of defense" can take that weapon away from the Russians. A Europe that has divisions and air groups of its own and that is united in a common agreement to resist both political threats based on the presence of the Soviet Army in eastern Germany or, if the worst comes, an attack by that army, is the only independent Europe.

But the job is not only physically difficult. It is immensely complex and intricate. The western nations are breaking new ground and with every inch the plow drives they will touch on national aspirations, economic, military and political, guarded for centuries and only released, and that temporarily, under the stress of war.

France's apprehension over German rearmament, even as an ally—an indispensable one, some think— in the defense of Europe is a case in point. Less well understood is the Norwegian fear lest the extension of the North Atlantic Treaty Organization convince the Soviet Union it is being attacked and force it into war. There is the fear of the British people that rearmament, which is being loyally carried out, will end the social gains of the Labor movement.

Finally, and this is the root of the matter, there is the difference in opinion about the intentions of the Soviet Union. There is no basic agreement on what the Russians will do. In 1949 and 1950 the United

States and British estimates of Soviet capabilities and intentions differed widely. They still do although the difference is narrower.

One thing must be kept in mind. In reaching such intelligence estimates, the size and power of the countries involved is not the governing factor. It is quite possible that an unknown Greek may reach a truer estimate than all the high-powered thinkers in Washington. Far-flung intelligence nets and pompous officers with many stars on their shoulders failed signally to estimate that once the United Nations forces adventured into northern Korea, they would be attacked by the Red Chinese.

If, as the army defense runs, the G-2 at a major headquarters does not concern himself with such questions, what *does* he concern himself with?

If we take the most favorable view, the rearmament of western Europe against the Soviet Union has two objectives. The short-term one is to deter the Russians from attacking. Later we will discuss what the chances are.

The long-term objective, the second of the two, is to so strengthen western Europe, physically and morally, that never again will it be open to military blackmail by the Soviet Union. If this state is reached, then the job of Eisenhower, indeed the job of the military forces of the United States in Europe, is over. And the United States will have won a victory in peace as great as any it has gained in war.

Such a victory is in the future, ten or fifteen years hence. We are an abrupt and hasty people and winning such a victory will demand from us more restraint, more good judgment and more sacrifice, without the compensation of military victories, than we ever have had to show in the past. But if the United States is now reaching political maturity in the international field, as it should be, the victory can be won.

We must, I believe, prepare ourselves psychologically to answer the question: What happens if nothing happens? If there is no Soviet attack by the end of 1952, then the United States will find itself in a position without precedent in its history.

It will be armed to the teeth at the head of a large and populous collection of states. Americans will be paying out more dollars than ever before for an army in garrison, an air force on the airfields of half the world and a navy scattered from Brooklyn to Bangkok. To reach this state of rearmament the people of the United States will have had to forego many of those luxuries which they regard as necessities. The normal rhythm of life in the American family will have been disrupted by conscription.

It is then that Americans, in and out of government, will have to display to the world a self-control and political wisdom they have never before been called upon to exhibit. For there will be many times, given the Russians' heavyhandedness and political ignorance, when it will seem better to the keepers of the armed peace, the Americans, to wage war than to rely on the tremendous advantage, expressed over a long period, that their rearmament will give them.

Personally, I have no doubt that if this situation develops, the United States, using sufficient restraint, will begin to exert upon the Soviet Union political

pressure great enough to bring about the internal
crack-up of the second Russian Empire.

If this situation develops. . . . At the moment this is
written, in January, 1952, my impression after six
years of watching the Soviet Union and Russian communism, both inside Russia and from the vantage
point of Berlin and western Germany, is that it is
more probable that there will be a third World War
started by the Russians.

Peace is always sought by the great mass of man-
kind. There are those now, just as there were in 1935–
1939, who profess to see the Russians sated with their
gains in eastern Europe and the Far East, ready to
reach an accommodation with the West, an uneasy
truce. Now, as then, these prophets fail to take into
account the basic conflict between the democratic
and totalitarian ideologies.

To me the argument that the Russians, having con-
quered so much, will wish to sit still and digest is
particularly foolish. It is attractive. Anyone studying
the almost limitless economic possibilities of the empire stretching from the Elbe to the Yellow Sea is
struck by its promise for the future. All the Russians
have to do, it is suggested, is sit still and all will come
their way in the end, attracted by the magnet of this
formidable economic-political complex.

So men reasoned when Hitler had Austria and
Czechoslovakia in his hands. But this most recent
lesson of history teaches us, as indeed all history
teaches, that success in conquest, political or military,
leads only to a greater appetite for conquest.

We must consider too that from the winter of 1945–
1946 onward the United States, with the British Com-

monwealth a close second, has been the object of constant, virulent propaganda by the Soviet government and the governments of the satellite states. Such propaganda is another form of armament. Eventually it clamors for use. If one reads *Pravda* and *Izvestia* day after day, one gets the impression that the Russian people are being prepared for an "inevitable" war.

It is terrifying to realize that day after day, week after week, the United States is being portrayed as evil, grasping, warlike and rapacious by the Russians. Such propaganda organizes moral forces which only war can implement. We will be blind if we allow the external propaganda about peace to fool us. Within Russia there has been a six-year build-up of the United States as the enemy, the successor to "Hitlerite Germany." And, at the same time, there has been an internal propaganda campaign devoted to building up admiration for the warlike characteristics and the military machinery.

Whenever I meet those earnest folk who explain their signing of one of the Soviet "peace" proclamations or appeals by saying, "After all, the Russians are peaceful people," I want to reply: "They *were*." But six years of wooden guns for the moppets in the schools, six years of lectures for youngsters of ten and twelve by Heroes of the Soviet Union in uniform, six years of parades, six years of lectures on the glorious Red Army and six years of unbounded boasting about Russia's supposedly singlehanded triumph in World War II—all these have dispelled and driven underground the people's will for peace. We are in the presence of total rearmament, moral as well as physical.

If we were dealing with Hitler's Germany rather than Stalin's Russia we would be at war now. The military influence in Germany was far stronger than it is in the Soviet Union. One of the basic tenets of the communist faith is the inevitability of political victory. But we will be wise not to overestimate the influence of this tenet upon the Political Bureau today. In other words, let us not think of Stalin's Political Bureau as though it were the group, strong in faith but weak in resources, that gathered around Lenin.

Today's rulers are, I believe, far more impressed with the purely physical advantages of Russia than were those of twenty years ago. They may still believe that victory will come to them in the end through the dissolution of the capitalist system in the West. But the capitalist system has shown surprising toughness and foresight in the United States, and it has displayed an ability to alter itself to circumstances in Britain, Norway and elsewhere.

No western statesman or student can say with certainty that the Russians consistently will avoid war in favor of political methods. What can be said is that if the Russians are impelled by the purely military aspects of the problem, they will attack before 1954; that is, before the immediate penalty for aggression is so great that the cost is prohibitive. Before the end of 1953 there will come a time when Russian military preparations are in balance as far as the Soviet General Staff is concerned; or as much in balance as such things ever are.

That is the time when the Soviet Army retains its qualitative and quantitative superiority over the western ground and air forces immediately available, when the supply of Soviet atomic bombs is sufficient to deal paralyzing blows to the industry of the West and when, above all, the air defense of the Soviet Union has reached the state of readiness that convinces the government that retaliatory bombing by the United States can be dealt with before Russian industry is crippled.

Such an attack is the ultimate crisis toward which all the efforts of General Eisenhower, the North Atlantic Pact and Supreme Headquarters Allied Powers Europe are directed. It may be—and we may pray God this is true—that that day will never come; that Europe will emerge strong enough to deter aggression, standing united against Soviet threats.

So we come to the other great question: If something happens, what happens? And what is *something*?

In the preparation of this book I talked with soldiers, sailors and airmen from many nations about their ideas on Russian war plans. Unanimously they discussed operations far greater in extent than those usually contemplated by the layman. To them Soviet aggression would not be confined to western Europe as we usually think of it, that is between the Baltic and the Alps, but it also would encompass Scandinavia, the shores of the Mediterranean and Yugoslavia as well.

"Even then this immense front will only be part of a far larger front," one Frenchman remarked. "Russia is in a central position globally. Germany was not. There will be operations controlled by a single command everywhere from Kamchatka to Berlin. They will be important, they will cost lives, but never forget that the decisive operation will be here in Europe."

If the Russians attack in the next two years, what will they be after? The headlines of the last war emphasized cities and river crossings as the objectives for both sides. But the first Soviet objective will be the destruction of the Allied armies in Europe. The peculiar nature of the Soviet economy today makes this inevitable.

Beyond that lie the geographical prizes. The first of these is the Ruhr. The capture of the Ruhr, intact if possible, is vital to the Russians if they are to fight a long war with the United States and its allies. The Russians will try to destroy the Allied armies before the latter can destroy the Ruhr or they will try to seize the Ruhr and the crossings of the Rhine with the eight or more airborne army corps which form part of the Soviet Army.

The Russians understand that the United States cannot be defeated merely by seizing western Europe or by the first atomic bombing raids. They count on a long war in which political and social factors will influence the United States as much as military ones. Therefore their second objective will be the capture of the Norwegian and French and Iberian coasts as suitable bases for intensive submarine and bomber war against Allied shipping.

Finally the Russians have read the lessons of World War II. One of these is the scandalous indifference of Hitler and his generals to the importance of the Mediterranean.

No one who has studied the campaigns in the Mediterranean from 1940 until 1942 can fail to miss the point that with a slightly greater expenditure of men and material in the Mediterranean, Hitler could have laid the foundations for victory. Lately, General Eisenhower has been much concerned over his "open" Mediterranean flank. My guess is that the Soviet General Staff in Moscow is equally concerned with that flank and has its own plans for turning it.

When a writer discusses war in peace, even as uneasy a peace as this, he is a pessimist: just as he is an optimist if, in war, he discusses peace. Lest I be unduly accused of pessimism I cite a paper written recently by Charles Mast, a retired general of the French Army. General Mast is a man who deserves well of his country but has been ill treated for a single mistake. That is another story, but Americans should remember Mast as the one French general officer who, when the United States Army scrambled ashore on the beaches of Oran and Algiers, half-trained, uncertain and confused, risked his life to give them aid and support.

The first point made by General Mast is that although our present concepts of Soviet power are based on the peacetime strength of the Russian military, naval and air services, we should be confronted, after a partial mobilization, with 250 divisions of ground troops, 20,000–30,000 aircraft and more than 300 submarines. After three months of full mobilization there would be 350 divisions; this figure would rise to 500 divisions by the end of the first year of war.

This is the basis, General Mast points out, on which the West must make its calculations if it wishes to avoid, in an infinitely more important arena, the underestimates made at the beginning of the Korean war.

Although this book is concerned principally with

Europe and its defenses, it is worth quoting General Mast's appreciation of the direction of the Soviet attacks in time of war. He lists them as:

1. A naval, air and ground attack in the Arctic aimed at the capture of Alaska and Iceland.*

2. An air-ground attack in the Middle East aimed at the occupation of Persia, Iraq, Saudi Arabia and the Isthmus of Suez.

3. An air-ground attack on western Europe and North Africa aimed at the conquest of all Europe and the elimination of western military power from the entire North African shore of the Mediterranean.

4. A harassing action in East Asia (Korea and Japan) accompanied by indirect action, carried out by China, in Southeast Asia.

5. World-wide naval action by submarines against the seaborne transport of the anti-Soviet coalition.

It is General Mast's contention that the Soviet Union will be capable of undertaking all these operations simultaneously. He divides the forces allotted to these operations as follows:

Alaska and Iceland, 3 to 6 divisions and 1,500 aircraft.

The Middle East, 40 to 60 divisions and 5,000 aircraft.

The Far East, 20 Soviet divisions and 5,000 aircraft plus Chinese reinforcements.

For the European Theatre of Operations, General Mast divides the effort in this way:

* Since General Mast wrote his appreciation the United States has begun to prepare the defense of Iceland.

Scandinavia, 15 to 17 divisions and 1,000 aircraft.

Western Europe, 120 divisions, initially, gradually increased to 180–190 divisions plus 10,000 aircraft.

The Balkans, 35 divisions plus 1,500 aircraft plus the armies of the satellite states. These latter we will discuss in detail later.

Thus a general officer of the highest professional qualifications. The numbers seem like figures in a nightmare, rising and falling before one's eyes. Yet they represent the capacity of the great power complex with which we are now faced.

When I read such figures my mind's eye goes back to the scenes at the end of the war, in Moscow on the great days of celebration, and in the cities and villages of Russia, where I saw the Soviet Army. Behind the numbers I see the long stretch of solid blocks of riflemen with impassive faces and a rigidity as great as a Pomeranian Grenadier marching through the Red Square. Out of the smoke of the burning cities of Germany sweeps the power of the Soviet Army with its tanks and guns in the fore and behind it the great mass of hungry soldiery.

Beside the road we took from the airfield at Zaporoshe to the guest house near the great dam over the Dnieper was a soldiers' exercise ground. On the morning that we drove into the town the area was filled with solemn young soldiers. Never, even at the Guards depots in England, have I seen such rigid dedication to duty. And in the evening when we departed they were still there, their uniforms black with sweat, going through the same machinelike evolutions.

One day, as we stood in his office looking out on the masses of troops gathered for Kalinin's funeral,

General Walter Bedell Smith said, "There's a lot of power out there, boy." There is. It's still there.

There is so much, that it is easy to understand those who desire to take the easy way out. Pull the troops out of Europe, build a tremendous air force and navy. Sit tight in our continental island. Don't try to match the Russians on the ground. Let Turkey go. Let Norway go. Let France and England go. Forget the squareheads, the frogs and the limeys. The idea has a certain last-century charm. No one begrudges those who would return to the security of their youth, but such fancies are liable to end, if translated into practical, or rather impractical, politics, with the defense of Tacoma or the line of the Mohawk and Hudson rivers.

The persistent questioning in the United States of why western Europe must be defended, by the United States and its allies, indicates that the immense importance of this area to us still is not clear.

First, there are the primarily military considerations. If we retreat into our American shell, leaving the rest of the world to the Russians, the shell is in for some hard knocks. How much security will there be for the cities of the eastern seaboard, for Detroit, Chicago and Cleveland if the Russians hold Iceland, Norway and the British Isles?

These are important considerations. But ultimately in the great struggle for world power they are less important to Americans than the economic and industrial benefits to the Soviet Union resulting from the conquest or annexation of these areas.

The economic strength of the Soviet Union has benefited greatly from the addition of Czechoslovakia and eastern Germany to the satellite nations. It will benefit even more if it is able to add, by military or political conquest, the economies of western Europe to the new Russian system.

Of the great industrial areas of the world the Soviet Union now possesses only two, the complex in the Soviet Union itself, stretching from the Donetz Basin to the Urals, and that in Manchuria.

It is within the military capacity of the Soviet Union today to seize two other great areas of industrial production, those of the Rhine Basin, including the Ruhr, and the English midlands.

There is a good argument that says the Russians would win these two areas before they were destroyed and there is always a reference to the Russians' own scorched-earth policy in 1941 and 1942. The impression is conveyed that either United States bombers or the inhabitants themselves would destroy the areas and the Soviet Army would occupy only ruins.

Barring the possibility that the Russians might be able to seize at least the Ruhr intact through a gigantic airborne operation, it is extremely doubtful whether the United States would bomb these areas to bits or that the people in them would destroy them.

To anyone who has lived long in Europe, it seems obvious that the second destruction from the air of the means of livelihood of millions of people, who also happen to be our allies, would be disastrous to the political aims of the United States in a long war with Russia.

Nor can we expect the people of those areas to

submit tamely to a program of demolition carried out by the United States Army or their own forces. It is unlikely that they will do it themselves.

Whenever this question of a scorched-earth policy arises I remember a conversation I had in 1946 with L., then the engineer in charge of the reconstruction of the great dam across the Dnieper River, one of the proudest achievements of the Soviet Union between the first two world wars.

L., a great bull of a man, sat fondling a string of amber beads and talking of his work. I remarked that it must have been a terrible duty for the Russians in 1941 to destroy the dam that meant so much in national pride. He laughed.

"We didn't destroy it," he said, "the Germans did."

I forebore to say that the destruction of the dam had been heralded throughout the world by the Russian propaganda service as an example of the Soviet Union's intention to destroy everything in the path of the Russians. I asked what had happened.

"The Germans blew it when they were retreating," he said. "They put five hundred tons of explosive in it and exploded all but fifty tons. When we retreated in 1941 we blew fifty meters out of the top of the dam so the Germans couldn't use it as a bridge. They had the hydroelectric plant in full operation a month after they got here."

The industrial output of these two great areas is important to the Soviet Union. But the skilled manpower that makes that output possible is even more important. In the event of the conquest of the Ruhr, for instance, and its subsequent bombing by the United States, the Russians would transport to central Russia hundreds of thousands of its workers. The same would be true of the French industrial areas of Lorraine and the Saar. The Germans did pretty well with slave labor in 1939–1945. The Russians need it more and might do better. Certainly they would be equally ruthless in its use.

It is possible that we place too much emphasis on the purely economic reasons why western Europe must be held. In the long run it may be that the continued freedom of its political democracy will play as important a role in the settlement of the great world struggle in which we are now engaged as its economic strength.

Since 1945 it has been apparent, I believe, that as long as western Germany, France and Italy—the United Kingdom always was out of reach—could be kept independent of the Soviet Union and free to continue their political development along national lines toward a greater democracy, the Soviet Union was bound to fail to extend its political influence in the area of greatest political and economic reward.

From the standpoint of the Kremlin, however, it was worse than a temporary check in western Europe. The freedom of those states, with their traditional cultural influence in eastern Europe, has retarded the complete communization of the satellite states. In the last series of East European purges, like its predecessors designed to produce a Communist party in each satellite completely subservient to Russia and the aims of Russian imperialism, thousands of well-tried and loyal party members were thrown out, not because of their ties with the American or British "imperialists" but because they were influenced or had been influenced in the past by German, French, or Italian friends and teachers.

It is foolish to think of the new Russian Empire as a solid mass of communist-led peoples controlled by the Kremlin and their respective governments, in that order, and unaffected by other experiences and outside events. This is what the Russians would like us to believe. That is what they are trying to achieve by terror and propaganda. Actually as long as western Europe remains free, the consolidation of the satellites into the system will not be swift.

Wars, hot or cold, are not won by guns or the threat of guns. The truth has taken quite a beating all over the world, but it remains a potent weapon. In many ways the truth, spoken by the people of free Europe to the people of slave Europe, is more effective than when it is spoken by the United States.

The cultures to which freedom is speaking are not American or British in background. The cultural leaders of peoples of the East, even the survivors of the postrevolutionary intelligentsia in Russia, look to Rome and Paris and the great universities of Germany more than to London or New York. And although it would be hard to convince some Congressmen of the fact, these centers of civilization have given quite as much to the world, quite as much ammunition for the war being fought today, as Oak Ridge or Los Alamos.

It would be witless to believe that the moral appeal could be made without the inclusion of the great American and British gifts to political development. But it would be foolish to discount and not use influence which the western half of the continent has exerted on the East in the last one hundred years. As we have seen, the Russians are busy in Sofia, Bucharest, Budapest, Prague, Warsaw and East Berlin rooting out this influence.

If there is to be an international army of troops, there certainly should be an international array of truth. No one country has a monopoly on the latter.

Beyond that, Americans need Europe in so many ways. Here lie the foundations of our own civilization. The export of new ideas from the cultural centers of Europe continues to be enormous. Not all of them are good. Not all of them fit our own concepts. But they bear the tool marks of long and earnest thought, and in our present dilemma, faced with a world we never made, we too often are prone to substitute action for thought.

Europe certainly needs us. But in this great struggle for the minds and souls of men, we need Europe.

2. Is Russia Prepared to Fight?

"Make ye no truce with Adam-zad—the Bear that walks like a man." So wrote Kipling half a century ago. We are learning the truth of his words, the hard way. If the years since 1945 have taught us anything, it is that although it is not difficult to make a truce, an agreement or a treaty with the Russians, it is absolutely clear that the pact will last as long, and no longer, than serves the purpose of the Russians.

It is this factor which should make us wary of those who believe that it is possible to strike a balance with the Soviet Union and live, under arms, at peace. Whether the war is fought with words and political trickery or with tanks and bombers it will go on. In our discussion of what is going on in the Soviet Union, of the state of its industry and agriculture and its armed forces, we should never forget that to the rulers of Russia *we* are the enemy.

A deeper understanding of this fundamental of Russian policy—the Russians for centuries have looked on the people of the West as enemies, and expansion at their expense as a legitimate right of Russians—helps us to avoid falling for Russian "peace" propaganda. Until the outbreak of the Korean war, it was difficult for many to reconcile predictions of the Soviet Union's intention to continue to expand with the persistent bleating about "peace" by the communists and their tools and stooges all over the world.

The Korean war dealt a mighty blow to that propaganda. But as a starting point for an estimate of the Soviet Union and its satellites today, it is essential to understand that whatever the propagandists of the Kremlin have done to the word "peace," there remains among the older generation of Russians, the group that has known a long and terrible war and years of poor diet and overwork, a real desire for true peace. The Communists can whip up enthusiasm for "the heroic defense of the Soviet motherland" among the young, they can arm the orphans with wooden guns as soon as they can walk, but the desire for peace among simple folk of thirty and over is very great.

This desire for peace leads us to one of the most hotly debated of all the questions about Russia: How great is the resistance to the government in the Soviet Union? And this leads, inevitably, to a second question: Is there enough disaffection to justify the hope that because of it the Kremlin will not dare to go to war?

Obviously no one, probably not even the Political Bureau, has the answer to the first of these questions. But an attempt must be made to answer them both. For there is a tremendous amount of wishful thinking linked to them.

Drawing on what I have learned from refugees from the satellites and from the Russians I have talked with in the last two years, I would say that although there is widespread disaffection in the Soviet Union and even more widespread disaffection in the satellite nations, this disaffection is, at the present time, passive, without compulsion to revolt or even to sabotage and, moreover, face to face with the most massive police machinery in history.

Almost since the Red Army overran eastern Europe at the end of the war there have been highly colored accounts of guerrilla fighting against the Soviet forces and the local communists in almost every country east of Germany. There is evidence that there was anti-Soviet activity including armed uprisings in the Ukraine, the Baltic States and Moldavia, in the Soviet Union, between 1945 and 1948; and that armed resistance—never on a large scale but resistance nonetheless—continued in East Germany, Poland and Hungary until 1948 and early 1949.

The rebellion of Tito, certainly the most important thing that has happened to communism since 1917, gave the Russians the excuse to repress such resistance with more than their usual severity.

In no case, however, was the resistance to the Russians on a large scale. Small groups, deserters from various armies, homeless farmers, a few patriots, took to the woods and lived by brigandage. They shot and killed Russian soldiers when they could. They also shot and killed their own countrymen collaborating with the Russians. In the end the bands were hunted down by the Russian security troops and liquidated. So much for the active resistance which has provided so much bright copy for reporters unacquainted with the mechanism of a police state.

The application of the word "passive" to disaffection within the Soviet Union should not make us discount it too much, if war comes.

Nor should we be impatient with the Russians because they do not arise and throw off this monstrous tyranny. Even if the tyranny were not so well armed, even if it did not have at its command hordes of informers and spies, rebellion would be a development totally out of keeping with the psychology of the Russian people.

I am not suggesting that the Russians *like* tyranny. I do suggest that tyranny is not unusual in Russia or to the Russian people. I do suggest that they have had no experience in political revolt and no idea on earth of how to begin one. The revolution of 1917 was made by a few hundred thousand people and whatever revolutionary ardor it inspired in the masses was stamped out by the terrible repressions of the G.P.U., the N.K.V.D. and the M.V.D.

The disaffection lies today, as it did under the Czars, with the daily life of the people. There is not enough—in the lifetime of most ordinary Russians there never has been enough—food, enough heat, enough housing, enough clothes and enough rest. But this will not make a revolution. It will not lead to anything more damaging to the regime than a cynical shrug of the shoulders when the May Day orators tell the Russians how lucky they are to be living in the socialist paradise.

Such disaffection is not dangerous. And there seems to be at least a possibility that it would be submerged in a great wave of patriotism if Russia were to be involved in a war.

The place to look for help in the Soviet Union is not in the masses. It is in the disgruntled and the downcast of the Communist Party, the army and the government. The German people didn't try to kill Hitler. The officers did. Mussolini was cast from power by a combination of military men and monarchists.

How is it possible to believe that the Communists, the group that runs Russia under Stalin's, and the Political Bureau's, guidance, could be disaffected, could entertain ideas of revolt? There are many disappointed souls among the Communist Party, just as there are in every group that believes that because it is in power it will be happy and prosperous and then finds, when power comes, that happiness and prosperity still elude it.

Of course, this will not be the reason advanced by the disaffected for their disaffection. I remember one Russian communist who told me, with eyes full of tears, "We thought we were making a palace for the people and they have turned it into a prison."

This, of course, is true. But I suspected then, and I suspect now, that the basic reason for the anger of this old revolutionary was that the victory of communism had meant, not a good job, power and relatively good living conditions, but a one-room apartment, a minor job and poverty. This is the lot of millions upon millions of Russians. But in most cases, they have no idea that they deserve or could have more. This communist did. More, I would say that there are tens of thousands, perhaps hundreds of thousands of army officers, civil servants and party functionaries who are bitter at the insufficient rewards their industry, loyalty and sacrifice have brought them.

But this must be balanced by Russian patriotism. This is different from communist patriotism and it was one of the great morale factors of the great Russian resistance in the early years of the war. Stalin called it into being then, just as every Russian leader has had to do in national crises, and it is a mighty force. Imbued with it, men fought tanks with bottles full of gasoline and armed themselves from the dead. It ran through the great city of Leningrad whose people lived in ghastly heroism through one of the most terrible sieges of history.

Since the start of the cold war we have been guilty of underestimating the Russians in some respects and overestimating them grossly in others, particularly their political know-how. One thing that should never be forgotten is the heroism of the Russians during the first eighteen months of the war. This sprang from the basic patriotism of the Russian people, and when the bookkeeping of history is done it will prove, I believe, to have been as great a factor in repelling Hitler as it was in repelling Napoleon a century and a quarter before.

But it is not the sort of factor that appeals to a general staff. Too intangible. Yet wars are won by such intangibles as often as by machines.

Will this patriotism be a factor in a war between Russia and the West?

If we attack Russia, as Hitler did and as Napoleon did, by land invasion, certainly.

We can also be sure that every effort will be made by the regime to rally this patriotism behind an aggressive war of its own making. The policy of the western powers gives the communists occasional help.

The rearmament of the Germans, a subject which we will discuss in detail later, is an instance of a democratic policy which can be used adeptly by the

Political Bureau and its propagandists to arouse Russian patriotism.

Among the many things we have forgotten about World War II is the amount of damage the Germans did in Russia. Mr. Molotov helped us forget with his reiteration of interminable lists of destruction at every postwar conference. The Russians, and particularly the peasants, have not forgotten however.

Today the propaganda line in the thousands of villages of Russia that were damaged or destroyed by the German armies is the same. It runs:

"The Americans are arming the Germans again. It was the Germans who killed your son, who raped your daughter, who burned your house, who stole that cow you had worked so hard to get. The Americans want to send them here again. We must make the Soviet fatherland strong. More tanks, more guns, more wheat. If necessary, we must help our communist friends and workers in the nations of western Europe to throw off the yoke of the Americans. We must build a strong base for peace as far from your village as possible."

This is the sort of simple appeal that hits a Russian peasant who is just beginning to recover from the effects of the war. We should not halt German rearmament because of it, because German rearmament is part of the defense of Europe. But we must make it very clear why we are arming the Germans. We must emphasize our sincere intention not to allow the Germans, or anyone else, to begin a war of aggression against the Soviet Union.

The second World War was unique in Russia. It was the first war in which the country had engaged

since the defeat of Napoleon which really mobilized
Russian patriotism behind the government. The reason is that it began with an invasion of Russia on a
large scale. I think we can argue that neither the
Crimean war nor the Russo-Japanese war aroused the
same passionate patriotism precisely because they
were fought on a narrow front at the extremities of
Russia.

No consideration of the morale factor as it applies
to Russia's preparedness to fight a third World War
should overlook what happened in the Ukraine in
1941–1943. Indeed, the danger is that we may overestimate the importance of events there in those
years and, by wishful thinking, come to believe that
the political climate of the Ukraine today is similar
to that of 1941.

In World War II, the German Army's invasion of
the Ukraine was welcomed by a large proportion of
the people of the region. The greatest percentage
were peasants who were promised by the Germans
that their lands would be returned to them. This was
done and the German Army, conscious of Germany's
need for the wheat of the Ukraine, also brought in
hundreds of agricultural machines. Some of them
were still there and still in use in 1946 and 1947.

During 1941 and most of 1942 the German lines of
communication across the Ukraine were relatively
undisturbed by partisan action and, as I have noted
above, the "scorched-earth policy," about which the
communist propagandists made so much fuss, really
was not carried out in the Ukraine to the extent pictured in the propaganda.

The encouragement of Ukrainian nationalism by

the Germans produced a Ukrainian National Army which at one time numbered seven divisions and which fought well. Here, as in so many instances, the Wehrmacht was doing well, until Hitler interfered. Counseled by Alfred Rosenberg, Hitler instituted a program of mass deportation of workers from the Ukraine, a program carried out with terrible cruelty against people who a little while before had thought of themselves as allies of Germany. Resistance was punished with great severity.

Moscow, aware of what was going on, began to parachute saboteurs and partisan leaders into the area. The German lines of communication no longer were at peace. Convoys needed strong guards. German soldiers were murdered in the streets of villages where, a few months, even weeks before, they had been friendly guests.

When the Germans retreated across the Ukraine they herded the remainder of the Ukrainian National Army before them and destroyed the cities, the towns and the villages. Thus ended, in blood and fire, one of the great German opportunities of the war in the East.

The lesson to be derived from what happened in the Ukraine was that there existed in the Soviet Union one known area ready to help an invader against the communist regime. This was the lesson of 1941–1943. But it is not a lesson for 1951 or 1952, no matter how loudly exiled Ukrainians shout that the same thing will happen again or how intensively they bombard western politicians and ingenuous newspapermen with colorful stories of "resistance armies" in the Ukraine.

For the Ukraine of today is not the Ukraine of a decade ago, either physically or politically.

Tens of thousands of those who aided the Germans were killed in the war or deported to the labor camps of the Arctic and Far East. Their families and friends were hunted down and imprisoned or shot. Kharkow, a center of Ukrainian resistance, was subjected to a mass investigation and, subsequently, to mass arrests and deportations.

Late in 1946 the Moscow government carried out a complete purge of Communist leadership in the Ukraine in an effort to eliminate the "unstable" elements who had come up to the top in the period 1943–1945, when the chaotic conditions in the Ukraine gave an opportunity to what *Pravda* called "people of insufficient political maturity" to win the important party jobs.

Almost from the start of the postwar period there has been a steady movement into the Ukraine of Great Russians—those people of the plain that extends eastward from the Polish frontier to the Volga and includes ancient Muscovy. Technicians from the Leningrad and Moscow areas predominate in this influx. They provide skilled labor for the factories and the Machine Tractor Stations and, what is more important from the standpoint of the Political Bureau, lace the population with people of proven loyalty to the regime.

As a result the Ukraine is not today the potentially rebellious area which the events of a decade ago indicate to many optimistic strategists. There remain, undoubtedly, some elements of Ukrainian nationalism and there is, as there is all over Russia, widespread grumbling over the harshness of life. But it is unwise, I believe, to plan on any such support.

Before we turn to the Russian fighting services today, we must consider the industrial and agricultural potential of the Soviet Union for war. These with the various aspects of the political potential, the patriotism, the grumbling, the fear of the Germans discussed above, make up the Russian home front.

Oddly enough, we probably know less about the industrial and agricultural situation in the Soviet Union than we do about the Soviet Army as it is today or the Soviet Air Force. Everything Russian, of course, is veiled in secrecy—it also is hobbled by red tape—but for over a decade the armed forces of Russia have been in a position where they could be observed by foreigners: Germans, British, Americans principally; but Poles, Yugoslavs and other East Europeans as well.

We do not know much, but we know a great deal more than we do about such, to an American, relatively nonmilitary matters as railroad mileage and tractor production.

Whenever possible it is best to approach the Soviet economy without undue emphasis on statistics, not only because Russian statistics are usually represented in terms of percentages of prewar and even prerevolution production figures but because they tend to obscure certain principles and problems of the Soviet economy which we do know about and which are a better guide to understanding than, for instance, the figures for the shoe industry.

One principle which should ever be in our minds is that of direction, direction of Soviet industry and agriculture in accord with the policy of the Political Bureau, direction of the output of industry and agriculture in keeping with its aims.

It is this principle of direction which should modify our easy confidence that the fact that the United States can outbuild and outproduce the Soviet Union means that Russia cannot contemplate war. Of course the United States can, but even in wartime a fantastic amount of its production goes to meet the needs of a people with the highest living standards in the world. In wartime in the Soviet Union almost everything goes to the war effort.

In the event of a great war the Russian people will be expected to work long hours under poor conditions on a diet that would produce strikes and riots in the United States. What is more, the trickle of consumer goods that has reached them in the past three years will be shut off abruptly, housing construction will end and a tight rationing system will be introduced.

There remain tremendous untapped resources within the Soviet empire. There are grandiose and ambitious plans for using these resources in the Russian economy. But I think we can safely ignore these plans in the event of war. There will not be the time or the labor or the machines to develop them and simultaneously fight a war.

Another principle to be kept in mind in studying the Russian industrial and agricultural potential for war is the extreme centralization of the Soviet system. The decisions are made in Moscow and nowhere else by the Political Bureau, a group whose existence as leaders depends on winning any war the Soviet Union fights.

No one worries about what the regional authorities in Kazakistan or the Ukraine will say about the latest ukase. The authorities in the hinterland will utter nothing but praise. This centralization plus a single-minded concentration of the objectives of the Political Bureau is an asset in war.

Of course it also can be a liability. The destruction of the Political Bureau and the apparatus of control in the dozens of ministries of the government in Moscow would have the effect of cutting the head off a snake. The body writhes and twists but without direction. A people long accustomed to having the smallest details of their jobs fixed by a remote authority in the capital could not be expected to suddenly think for themselves, and the industrial machine which is the unique triumph of the regime would sink into chaos.

Anyone who reads *Pravda, Izvestia* and the technical publications of Russia understands that behind the picture of smoking factories, flaming furnaces and expansive farms given us by the propagandists of communism there exists a multitude of problems. Indeed, the constant reading of editorials dealing with these problems is liable to give the foreigner in Moscow the impression that the whole business is about to fall apart, a dangerous theory.

One of the principal problems is that of manpower. The average American thinks of the Soviet Union as having abundant manpower. And so it does—in the raw. But from the nineteen-twenties, when the task of bringing the industrial revolution to Russia began, the government has been dogged by the problem of skilled manpower. For the Kazak or the Mongol or the Ukrainian peasant can be trained into a fair soldier—not, the Russians say, as good as the Great Russian, the Byelorussian or the Siberian—but it is a long, difficult and frequently costly job to turn him into what in Russia amounts to a skilled workman.

The rulers of Russia could see their way clear on this problem late in the nineteen-thirties. True, they did not have enough skilled manpower. But the vast training system of the Labor Reserves, which takes boys and girls on their graduation from grade schools and gives them intensive training in industry, promised that the technicians and artisans would be available in the future.

But the future held the second World War, the most costly ever fought by Russia. Into the battle went the carefully trained young men who were as necessary to run tanks, guns, aircraft, transport, to bridge rivers and plan fortifications as they had been to run the growing industry of the Soviet Union. Into the battle went the youngsters of the Labor Reserves. From June 1941 until the end of the battle of Stalingrad early in 1943, Russia was fighting for its life, and to fight well it had to spend the best trained of its young men and many of its young women.

The end of the war brought the start of the first postwar Five Year Plan and new emphasis on the terrible shortage of skilled manpower. For a time German prisoners helped fill the gap. In 1946 and 1947 in Moscow, the Ukraine, the Donetz Basin and Byelorussia I saw German prisoners, the bulk of them noncommissioned officers from technical units, filling jobs that before the war would have been done by young Russians graduated from the technical schools.

So great was the need for technical skill in industry that it was the untrained Russian victors who were the hewers of wood and drawers of water and the vanquished Germans who directed their labor and ran the machines.

Since then the supply of Russian-trained manpower has increased. But it is startling, and comforting, to see how slow has been the rate of increase.

For six years the Soviet Group of Armies in East Germany has been under constant surveillance by the West. Its officers and men, at present about 400,000 in number, afford American and British intelligence services a unique opportunity to study Soviet man outside Russia. And the Group of Armies' role as an occupation force among a population largely hostile insures a steady flow of information westward.

Not all of this information is accurate, of course. But a great deal of it is, and one of the most interesting things it has revealed is that the shortage of skilled manpower in the Soviet Union still is almost as acute as it was immediately after World War II.

Here is an army that includes some of the finest Soviet Guards and Shock divisions. We must assume that, if war came, this force would be the spearhead of any Russian attack across Europe. Yet critiques of training and maneuvers reveal shocking mechanical ineptness even in the crack tank units; failures in staff work, especially in supply, traced to bureaucratic obtuseness and the shortage of trained men; and a general inability, according to one Russian report, of the average soldier and underofficer to realize the role that "precisely the most simple machine" plays in modern warfare.

The opening weeks of the summer training and maneuver period of 1951 demonstrated not only that there were deficiencies in machinery and instruments, especially in the communications field, but that the Russian officers had spotted a far more serious deficiency in the failure of the supposedly well-trained non-com and private to use correctly even the newest and best machines.

Despite the security risk, the tank parks of the Soviet Group of Armies are filled with German workmen. Parts for tanks, guns and planes, electronic precision instruments and many other pieces of equipment are turned out in East Germany. Many explanations are offered. But always we return to the shortage of skilled manpower in Russia.

Ever since the danger of war with the Soviet Union appeared, we have been regaled with pictures of Russia's industrial weakness compared to that of the United States or, under the most favorable conditions, that of the United States, Britain, France and West Germany.

Even if we accept the most pessimistic intelligence estimates of Soviet industrial strength, usually presented to the public when one of the service departments wants some more money or our rulers decide that what the American people need is a good scare, that strength is far less than our own.

Compare the Soviet Union's scheduled output of coal in 1950, the last year for which a reliable estimate exists, of 250,000,000 tons against over 900,000,000 tons by the United States and the United Kingdom. The Russians will do well in 1951 to produce 25,000,000 tons of steel. The United States' output alone will be over 90,000,000 tons.

A word of caution. We must always remember that in the event of war—indeed, now, during the period of intense Russian armament—a far higher percentage of heavy industrial output flows directly into armament than in the United States, even allowing for that industrial production directed to the extensive capital reconstruction which has featured the Soviet economy since 1945.

Before we become too confident over our production advantage over Russia, we also should take into account that in the Soviet Union production is directed by a single-minded dictatorship, that there will be no popular interference with government production allocation policies and that the driblets of consumer goods released to the population which seem so small to us represent a definite improvement of living conditions to the average Russian.

Similarly although there are serious and recurrent deficiencies in the Soviet food supply, especially in food storage facilities, in the event of war the slogan of "everything for the fighters' front and the workers' front" will be reapplied and there will be no difficulties with indignant housewives or manufacturers of dime candy.

We also tend to forget that between 1941 and 1945 Soviet industry, although it received tremendous help from the United States and considerable assistance from Britain, was responsible for prodigies of labor. Russian tanks, Russian field guns and Russian planes in that war—and I think we can expect in any other war—were of a much higher quality and quantitatively surprising, compared with the general level of Soviet industry.

In the end we must weigh the industrial supremacy in quality and quantity of the United States alone or the United States plus its allies against these factors: a single-minded devotion to the needs of the front; a concentration of technical skill upon weapons; and a population accepting, under certain circumstances, living conditions of unbelievable hardship by western standards.

These are not enough to outweigh the western superiority in quality and quantity of production or the obvious shortages which the Soviet economy faces. But they do reduce that superiority to a considerable extent.

Moreover, the plans made by the State Commission for the Five Year Plan at the end of the war laid tremendous emphasis on the sudden increase in industrial production resulting from the utilization of the capital construction planned under the first postwar plan.

There is also the probability that in its fumbling, uneconomic way the Soviet Union has tapped hitherto unknown resources in the last few years. Their development will be slow mainly because there are not now, nor will there be for years to come, enough skilled workers to do all the jobs required. But both the use of postwar capital construction and the gradual development of new resources, especially coal, iron and oil, will affect our present industrial predominance.

The industrial revolution in Russia is just getting into stride.

3. Russia's Armed Strength

We can comfort ourselves with the thought that there is one mistake we are not making in our appraisals of Russian strength. We are not underestimating the potential enemy's army. In the two years preceding World War II, a great many observers in Europe laid the foundations for their own ridicule by constant disparagement of the weapons, training and personnel of Hitler's new Wehrmacht. One heard all sorts of stories about touring Americans whose cars, colliding with German tanks on maneuver areas, escaped damage because the "tanks" proved made of cardboard. Similar tales were told of the lack of discipline and general unrest in Hitler's army and of the industrial sabotage which limited the efficiency of its weapons.

Today, in our assessment of the Russian army and air force we seem to have gone almost too far in the other direction toward a gross overestimate of the Russian forces. Partly this is because our rulers are obsessed with the idea that the American people must be frightened out of their wits before they will buckle down to the realities of rearmament. But it also is due to the profound ignorance of most of us concerning the Russian army today and the Russian army during the war.

Before we deal with the Josef Stalin tanks, the massed armies and the *MIGs*, let us take a better look at Ivan Ivanovich, the Russian private soldier, the essential ingredient.

He is not a formidable physical specimen as an individual, although like all soldiers he becomes more impressive in mass. His hands are broad and strong, his legs usually slightly bowed. He is not tall. He is young, between seventeen and twenty-four.

The face is broad, almost square, with the blunt Russian nose and the blue eyes. There is always a lot of "terror talk" about the Mongols in the Russian army, but the truth of the matter is that our potential enemy in the field probably will be one of the Great Russians.

It was the Great Russians plus the taller, broader Siberians who held Leningrad and Moscow at fearful cost and fought and won at Stalingrad. It is the Great Russians and the Siberians who make up the majority of the *corps d'élite,* the Guards Armies who man the tanks and the field guns and build the bridges of the Soviet Army. If you are looking for Kazaks or Mongols or Tadziks, you will find them in the second-string divisions or doing the donkey work for the army along the line of communications.

Returning to Ivan Ivanovich: to begin with, the Russian infantryman is a country boy, although with the progress of industrialization since the last war the percentage of rural conscripts probably is slightly smaller today than in 1941. And a country boy in Russia means a boy from an environment a great deal harsher than in the rural United States. It means a boy who almost from birth has been inured to great cold, accustomed to meager, sometimes primitive living conditions and, during the peak periods of work on the collective farm, to day after day of ceaseless toil in the fields.

Ivan Ivanovich never had any luxuries in the village and he gets along on very little now that he is in the army. His uniform and equipment, skimpy to the eye of the overloaded American soldier, is to him more than adequate. Why, in winter he even has a greatcoat! His food is coarse, ordinary fare to us. To him it is good because there is always enough. He does not want the Russian pastries, which make so brave a show in Moscow and almost nowhere else in Russia. He wants his black bread, his *kasha* or cereal, his potato soup, fish and sometimes meat, and he gets it. And always enough, with no fear that the supplies of the village won't last the winter.

The primary condition of the last war for the Russian soldier was the invasion of Mother Russia by the Germans. In those circumstances, he performed prodigies of courage and endurance.

"When I went back to the army in 1941 when the Germans were nearing Smolensk," an elderly major told me in 1946, "we had one rifle to every four men. I should say boys, for that is what they were—children almost. Yet they marched along through the bitter cold singing songs about Stalin. Most of them did not know much about Stalin. But they knew that Russia was invaded and that Stalin had summoned them to fight for her and that was enough.

"The Germans cut us to ribbons. We had been told to seize arms from their dead. There were no dead, or very few. But these children fought well, without imagination or training but with bravery. In the end, the Germans drove us back and we were re-formed and got some weapons. But I never forgot them going forward that first time with a handful of rifles, some clubs and their courage."

German reports give a less emotional picture of Ivan Ivanovich in war. Here are three examples from German sources.

A Red Army rifle battalion attacked the outskirts of Medin at dawn in January, 1942 in a temperature of *minus* 43 degrees Fahrenheit. After heavy casualties, the attack came to a standstill on a snowfield and no further movement was possible. The survivors remained lying motionless in the snow for ten hours, without any special protection from the cold, and then renewed the attack at dusk with shouts of "Hurrah!"

A Russian task force which had broken through the German line in wooded country avoided all German attempts to destroy it for twelve days and made seven attempts to break out. On the thirteenth day, the task force, consisting by then of sixty men, was surrounded and annihilated. It had, without any supplies, and without facilities for keeping a fire going, fed itself on the bark of trees, fir shoots and snow.

A reconnaissance pilot of the Soviet Air Force shot down at Yukknov in the spring of 1942, landed by parachute in the street. He immediately opened up a vigorous tommy-gun fire on German soldiers and forced them to attack in a regular manner, employing mortars. After wounding six Germans, he shot himself through the head with one of his last bullets to avoid capture.

Courage and endurance such as this is the reverse side of the picture of the bumbling, mechanically inept Soviet soldier. He is brave. He can keep going under climatic conditions which bring most other soldiers to a standstill. He has been taught to regard an enemy soldier as a personal foe and not as the representative of a warring state. And, in any new invasion of the Soviet Union, Ivan Ivanovich's natural bravery would be sharpened by memories of what happened to this village or that the last time Russia was invaded.

During the last war the Germans reported that Russian infantrymen became flustered when they encountered, for the first time, new weapons and new tactics. But they added that once the Russian soldier learned how to cope with these weapons and tactics—and they were surprised at how swiftly the Russians learned—new weapons and tactics had less effect on the Soviet soldier than the soldiers of more civilized races.

Most visitors to Russia are astounded and shocked by the strain of cruelty in the Russian character which often is first noted in the Russians' relationship with each other. Once this is recognized, it is easier to understand both the almost unbelievable excesses of the Red Army in Germany and the Balkans and the objective, mass cruelty practiced as a business by the security organs of the Soviet State.

So we can expect Ivan Ivanovich, the potential enemy, to be cruel and barbaric to prisoners or occupied populations almost as a matter of course, even though his attitude toward the latter sometimes is tinged with an almost childlike simplicity. Children, of course, can be very cruel.

The military structure which rests upon Ivan

Ivanovich is immense. The British estimate that with full mobilization the Soviet Army could put 5,000,000 men into the field one month after the start of hostilities. There probably are close to 2,225,000 men under arms at the moment.

Estimates on the strength of the Soviet Air Force differ, but in research for this book, I found no estimate of first-line strength of combat planes lower than 30,000.

Since the end of World War II the Soviet General Staff has striven to increase the percentage of modern divisions in the army as a whole. The Russian generals who met the Allies in Germany were astounded to find that all the American and British divisions, not just the forward spearhead, were completely mechanized.

So for five years the Russians have struggled with the problem of replacing horse-drawn transport with motorized transport in the infantry divisions. The transition has been slow but in Germany, our best peephole on the Soviet Army, most of the infantry divisions of the Guards and Shock Armies now have reached the stage where Army Command can make available to any one of them the motor transport required to make it fully mobile. The goal, of course, is enough motor transport to allow the division full motorized mobility.

Eventually, the infantry or rifle divisions will contain a medium tank and self-propelled gun regiment which together with self-propelled gun batteries in the rifle regiments will give the division a strength in armor of 52 medium tanks (T-34's) and 34 self-propelled guns.

The mechanized division is the second general category of division in the Soviet Army at present. It is a precept of the Russian military doctrine that infantry and armor must work together. Each mechanized regiment contains two rifle battalions and one tank battalion and both the medium tank regiment and the heavy tank regiment contain a motorized infantry battalion.

The tank division has sufficient motorized infantry for its own protection and to hold ground it captures with tanks. It contains one more medium tank battalion and only one less rifle battalion than the mechanized division, but the armor is concentrated. Otherwise the organization is similar to that of a mechanized division.

The artillery divisions of the Soviet Army have no counterpart in the United States or British forces. Their strength in men ranges from 9,000 to 12,000 men but their weapons vary with the tasks assigned to the division. A typical divisional organization might include a brigade of 122-mm howitzers, a brigade of 152-mm howitzers and a brigade of 203-mm howitzers. To this would be added one rocket-launching brigade (30-mm rockets) and one 160-mm mortar brigade.

Anti-aircraft divisions also exist. They are smaller than the artillery divisions and, at the close of the last war, their heaviest gun was the 85-mm which hardly has enough range for today's high-flying bombers.

The table of organization for all these varied types of divisions is constantly changing. So are the weapons.

The Soviet Army emerged from World War II immensely strong in tanks and self-propelled guns and it has maintained this strength. It was estimated in 1951 that if all the rifle (infantry) divisions of the peacetime army were deployed with tank and mechanized divisions cited in the rear, the average support available for one rifle division, including its own weapons, would be 200 tanks or self-propelled guns and 80 armored cars.

Naturally, the proportion would be less after mobilization since the number of new rifle divisions organized would be greater than tank and mechanized divisions.

The Russian army, seen from our side of the hill, is impressive. It is big. Its soldiers are phenomenally tough. It has good tanks (the T-34-85 and the Josef Stalin 3), and good guns. The great weakness of the Soviet Army, reflecting the weaknesses of the nation behind the army, will not become evident until the army is committed to battle and perhaps not then unless the armies and air forces of the West have reached the point where they can punish the Russian forces and turn the invasion of western Europe into a battle rather than the series of powerful leaps to the sea so many expect it to be. Then the weaknesses of mechanical maintenance, supply and staff planning will catch up with the Soviet Army.

There is one other aspect of Russian military dogma which must be studied, if any true assessment of Soviet military effectiveness is to be reached. This is Russian partisan warfare.

Partisan warfare is what the Russians call guerrilla warfare: the harassing of the enemy by irregular troops and armed peasants behind his regular forward positions. During the civil war in Russia the Communists, lacking staffs and heavy armament, employed this form of warfare against the White Russian armies and most of the early leaders of the Red Army won their spurs in this kind of fighting.

During World War II it was extensively used by the Soviet Union. Because they were anxious to erase from peoples' minds the idea that any Russians or Ukrainians had voluntarily sided with the German invader, as hundreds of thousands did, the Soviet Government gave to the partisans more credit than actually belonged to them.

Just as the Russians' exaggeration of German war damage in Russia has had the opposite effect and induced many to discount reports of such damage, so the exaggeration of the partisans' share in the victory has produced a skeptical attitude in the West.

As always, the truth is somewhere in between and it seems to be that the partisans, in certain areas, did make a valuable contribution, enough so that the use of partisans by the Russians may be expected in any new war. The difference will be that in any new war, at the outset at least, the partisans concerned will not be Russians operating against troops who have invaded their country but French, Italian and German communists harassing, among others, French, Italian and German troops who are defending their countries.

From 1942 onwards the partisan danger was recognized by the German High Command. Forces of regular troops up to 30,000 strong were required to keep the partisans down and it was soon found that the only way to really get rid of the bands was to surround them and annihilate them.

The records of one such band, captured by the Germans when its members were annihilated, show that the group was organized, by communists sent from Moscow, in December, 1941 and was supplied through air drops.

Originally, the band numbered only 30 men. It grew to about 500 in June of 1942 but suffered severe casualties in battle and through illness. As the Red Army successes increased, so did the strength of the band until it numbered about 2,000 well-equipped men. The Germans liquidated it in October, 1943. Its documents claimed that the band had killed 4,631 Germans and 248 collaborators up to January, 1943, and that in addition it had derailed and destroyed 55 trains and blown 128 bridges.

The effect of these later operations on the German supply system in a country so poor in good communications can be imagined.

One other function of the partisans is to supply military intelligence to the Soviet Army. West European security already is very weak due to the presence of communists or their sympathizers in most of the European armies. It will be weaker still if war comes and these agents are able to send information bearing directly on the Allied plans.

This is not a book on the Russian Army. So we must forego a discussion of its tactical training and operational procedure and look rather at two vital aspects of any army: morale and leadership.

Save in wartime, when the national idea of Mother Russia is acknowledged and employed, morale in the Soviet Army means the degree of communist control and indoctrination in the forces. The communist political organization is an integral part of the army, with the duties of spreading party propaganda and educating the troops along orthodox communist lines.

There are Deputy Commanders for Political Affairs with a chain of command running parallel to that of the military command in all formations down to and including the battalion. Before and during the early months of the second World War, these Deputy Commanders or, as they were called then, Political Commissars, had the power to veto the orders of the military commanders even on strictly military matters.

Naturally the confusion was appalling even for the Russian Army at that disastrous period. So these military powers were curtailed after the Finnish campaign. They were restored briefly when morale fell under the impact of the first great German victories of 1941 but were finally abolished at the time of the Battle of Stalingrad. Like so many other stories about the Russian Army, the one that political commissars still interfere in the military command is a myth. But their power remains great.

They direct and control both the Communist Party and Komsomol, or League of Communist Youth, members in the formations under their command. They oversee all education, publish all unit newspapers, issue the "correct" or party interpretation of news events, pass on in speeches the attitude of the

Political Bureau toward the world situation and, apparently as an afterthought, are ordered to direct welfare, entertainment and sport in the unit.

In addition the Deputy Commanders for Political Affairs bury the dead.

The communist party's place in army life is an important one. Members form cells in all units down to company level and each cell of more than fifteen members organizes an office from which propaganda, news and news "interpretation" are issued by the Chief of the Party Cell Office.

It is worth remembering that party members also believe they have a mission to act as unofficial leaders in the unit and try to set examples of bravery and efficiency. Their losses in World War II were tremendous and the number of decorations they won was high.

In the army, the party pays special attention to recruiting new members. Great attention also is given to the graduation of Komsomols from that organization into the party itself.

The party's political control of the army thus is extremely strong, and morale, viewed from the point of view of communist indoctrination, is very high. Western efforts to win defectors from the Soviet forces have not been numerically successful. But when it is considered that Communist Party and Komsomol cells exist down to company level, that propaganda is ceaseless and that information from the outside world almost nonexistent, the results of such efforts can be seen in proportion. It is very difficult to subvert Soviet soldiers. The surprising thing is not that we have managed to win so few defectors but that we have got so many in Germany, Austria and other places, where contact can be made.

One mystery of World War II is what happened to the Russian airborne forces. From 1931 onward scores of thousands of Russians were trained in parachute jumping, and pilots were trained in towing gliders and troop transport flying.

But when the war came, the parachute troops were used sparingly. Two brigades were dropped west of the Dnieper River in 1943 to assist a crossing by regular ground forces but the German defenders surrounded and liquidated the airborne troops. The Germans noted that the airborne soldiers, although they fought with customary Russian tenacity, were too lightly armed and that the "spread" of the parachutists was so great after the drop that concerted action on the ground was not possible.

Airborne attack is one of the minor nightmares of the western high command in Europe. At the last report, the Soviet Army had about eight corps, perhaps 32,000 men, in an airborne army. Should the Russians attack, these corps could intervene drastically in the campaign.

As the Allied strength grows, the battleground edges eastward. A year ago the first campaign of World War III in Europe would have been fought in the area just east of the Rhine and on the river itself. Today the fighting would be a good deal further to the east. But the importance of the Rhine crossings has increased with the eastward extension of the battlefield. They must be held.

It is against the principal Rhine crossings that the Russians, it is feared, would launch their airborne forces. Should they win control of areas like Cologne, Bonn, Mainz and Worms, on the Rhine, and Frankfort on the Main, the Allied job of holding the Russian onslaught in West Germany would be much more difficult.

Holding the Rhine crossings is a prime necessity for Lieutenant General Manton S. Eddy, commanding the United States Seventh Army, and General Sir John Harding, commanding the British Army of the Rhine. That is why, in the British area, the Second Infantry Division lies close to the great river and why the Second Armored Division of the Seventh Army originally was disposed so that it could counterattack any airborne attempt to seize these crossings.

I asked General Eisenhower about Russian military leadership.

"Zhukov, Rokossovsky and Koniev, perhaps two or three others, are very good on the basis of their performance in the last war," he said. "Of course, most of what we know of them is based on their performances late in the war, when the German was on the run and when the Russians enjoyed a great preponderance in men and equipment. But those three I named are around today and they have plenty of experience in handling large bodies of troops.

"My belief," Eisenhower continued, "is that the Russians are short on good staff officers, planners in the logistical, operations and intelligence fields and that they do not have as many experienced and able corps and divisional commanders as we do in the West. But, as we found out in 1942 and 1943, commanders at that level develop very fast in war."

The General's words are borne out by the evidence

of those German generals who had the best opportunity to study the Russian command.

On the higher command levels, army and army group, or "front commanders" as the Soviet Army calls them, the Germans found that the quality improved constantly between 1941 and 1945. At the start of the war the Russian command still was suffering from the effects of the great purge of 1937, which eliminated the gifted Marshal Tukachevsky and many of his best staff officers, and from the shake-up that followed the miserable early showing of the Red Army during the winter war with Finland in 1939–1940.

The Germans, too, rate Marshal Georgi Zhukov first among the Russian generals, with Marshal Konstantin Rokossovsky and Ivan Koniev on the next level. They report that during the last year of the war, leadership on the battalion and regimental level was competent and, at times, more daring than senior commanders advised. For in the closing years of the war, the Soviet High Command employed men with prudence. Attacks were seldom launched unless the Russians were certain of a superiority in men and weapons of at least six to one.

It is at the middle levels of command, divisional and corps commanders, and on the planning and supply staffs that the Germans believe the Soviet Army is weakest.

This judgment is borne out by intelligence reports on the yearly Soviet Army maneuvers in East Germany. For the Russians more than for the Americans or British, maneuvers are an opportunity to exercise divisional, corps and army staffs in the problems of supply in the field. And, despite the tall tales of how the Russian Army moves without supplies as a horde of peasant soldiers, no modern army—and the Russian Army is rushing into modernization—can move this way. It must have shells and bullets, gas and oil, extra parts and medical supplies.

The junior officer is one of the most important men in any army. At the end of the last war, the junior officer in the Soviet Army had attained a high degree of combat efficiency. He was young, tough and fearless. In many cases, especially in the better drilled armored divisions, he maintained discipline through sheer personality. Usually he was a devout follower of communism, if not a party member, and he had that passionate belief in the "Soviet power" that marks the young men and women who have matured since the late thirties in Russia.

But occupations affect others than the occupied. The junior officer in East Germany today—and I think this is true of the junior officer in the other satellites —has suffered in comparison with the fighting fit young men of 1945.

When in the spring of 1945 General Vassily Chuikov, the Soviet Commander in Chief in East Germany, prohibited drinking on and off duty by all ranks in the Russian Group of Armies he was motivated by reports on low physical and mental fitness of the junior officers.

This prohibition, which struck at what Saint Vladimir called "the great joy of the Russians," was repealed two months later for an interesting reason. Apparently, various clever fellows in the service of the "imperialist Wall Street beasts" and the "decadent British colonialists"—mostly the latter one gathers—had been using vodka and other stimulants as a payment for information.

Since the end of World War II the most noted Russian military leaders of that conflict have been in eclipse. In the west it is believed that this was the result of a policy on the part of Stalin and the Political Bureau to reduce the stature of the successful Marshals in the eyes of the Russian people. Like all dictators, Stalin must always be on the lookout for potential rivals and it is likely he espied such rivals in the broad, youthful figure of Zhukov or the handsome, popular Rokossovsky.

At any rate, the great leaders of the last days of the war were withdrawn one by one from their prominent military commands. Zhukov, who had been as affable toward Eisenhower and Field Marshal Montgomery as it is possible for a Soviet soldier with an M.V.D. "aide" at his elbow to be, was snatched away from Berlin and replaced by Sokolovsky, an intellectual, very intelligent and almost completely unknown to the Russian people.

In 1946 and 1947, the Soviet propagandists were industriously trying to make the Russians forget the generals. Column after column of military criticism, couched in terms of slavish praise that would have embarrassed King Farouk, appeared proving that Stalin had won Stalingrad, Krivoi Rog, Sebastopol and almost every other great victory won by the Soviet armies.

Zhukov reappeared at Odessa, then headquarters of the southern military district, in the autumn of 1946. When I saw him on the street he looked as husky and jolly as ever. Not until 1951, however, did he reappear in the west and, as this is written, there are some indications that he may emerge as commander in chief of the entire central front embracing the Soviet and satellite commands in Germany, Poland, Austria and Czechoslovakia.

Marshal Rokossovsky has been in Warsaw for two years as Minister of Defense for the Polish government, entrusted with the task of modernizing and raising the "political maturity" of the Polish Army. Marshals Vassilevsky and Koniev have served as Chief of the General Staff and Commander of the Ground Forces respectively.

The return of these men to prominence may mean that Stalin believes his military requirements call for their presence; in other words, that he is preparing for war. It also can mean that he is convinced that whatever position they had in the hearts of the Russian people has been lost and it is safe to bring them back.

No aspect of Russian military power has been the subject of such confused and exaggerated thinking as the Soviet Air Force. Since 1947 the American public has been treated to a succession of far-fetched claims and suspect estimates about its strength and efficiency and, particularly, about the aircraft industry which stands behind it.

To anyone who has spent any time in the Soviet Union and who understands the secrecy that surrounds such unexplosive figures as cotton production for a single year, the solemn assurances of Washington columnists that the Russians are turning out

20,000 or 50,000 or 100,000 combat planes a year are ridiculous. Not because these figures are beyond the Russian capacity, particularly in wartime, but because such figures are the deepest of secrets in the Soviet Union, where secrecy is traditional. Personally, I doubt whether more than half a dozen people in the Soviet Union know the actual production figures for combat aircraft or tanks or guns.

None of this half dozen is confiding these figures to pundits in Washington.

What do we know about the Soviet Air Force, then?

First, we know that in World War II it had a good record, but that it was definitely the weakest, quantitatively and qualitatively, of the air forces of the three great powers that won the war. The *Yak*, the *Lavotchkin* and the *Stormovik* fighters and fighter bombers were adequate, when they were well served, as they were during the first months of the war. The *Tupolev* bomber was in the same category.

But none of these aircraft, although Russian propaganda credited them with incredible feats, was significantly impressive in combat with the Luftwaffe, which had had the heart torn out of it over the English Channel in 1940 and early 1941.

When the war ended, the Soviet Air Force had swarms of ground support fighters, a few medium-range bombers and almost no long-range bombers. Tactically, it was tied to the Soviet Army—the dominant fighting service—and a cabal of ground generals is believed to have brought about the ousting of the five air force generals who wanted to build a bomber force comparable in striking power to the Eighth Air Force of the United States or Britain's R.A.F. Bomber

Command. Such purges were not unknown in other fighting services a quarter of a century ago and it demonstrates the time lag in Soviet strategic thinking.

The Russians were well behind the West in the design of piston engines at the end of the war. The Soviet Air Force benefited from the adoption of jet fighters. For the Red Army in its advance into Germany had captured some of the latest models of German jets, particularly the Messerschmidt 262, and many of the scientists and designers who had built the aircraft. Another bonanza for the Soviet Air Force was the purchase from England of the Rolls Royce Nene engine.

At the same time the atom bomb turned the minds of Russia's strategists to long-range bombing. The men dismissed in 1946 appeared to have something on their side in 1950, and a faithful reproduction of the American *B-29*'s forced down in Siberia during the war, became the backbone of the Soviet bombing fleet.

In the last six months the Russians have brought to Germany, which must be considered their most important front in Europe, the *MIGs*, their fastest and best jet fighter, and a new twin jet bomber not yet identified by American or British intelligence. The *MIG15* can fight on fairly even terms with American *Sabres;* it probably is better than the R.A.F.'s *Vampire* in the upper air although not as good as a ground support plane. From what has been seen of the twin jet bomber, it is an inferior plane to the British designed *Canberra* now being produced in the United States.

What we can expect if war starts is that the Soviet

ground forces will be supported by flocks of well-armed and armored ground support fighters. Interest in jet interceptors for the protection of the Soviet Union's cities and industrial areas from atomic bombers and in long-range bombers for the punishment of similar targets in the United States and Great Britain has not diminished the Soviet Army's insistence on continuous and effective close air support.

There does not seem to be much prospect that Allied Air Forces will reach the superiority in numbers necessary to control the air over a European battlefield for another year. If the war starts in 1952 or 1953, initially the ground forces will have to fight under conditions totally different from those in 1944 and 1945. As we shall see when we look later on at the armies training in Europe, this contingency does not seem to have impressed itself sufficiently on junior commanders.

From the point of view of the man in the street in the United States, the most worrying development is the infrequent appearance of a four jet, long-range Soviet bomber. If war comes the Russians certainly will try to blow the heart out of Detroit, Pittsburgh, New York and a half dozen other targets. To hear some of the more excitable aviation writers talk, these cities will resemble Hiroshima a month or so after the start of the war. Perhaps, but the betting is on the other side. But at any rate, the civilian at home must understand that in a war with Russia, the United States is going to take as well as give.

The reader may find me overly optimistic. If this is so, it is because the proper use of an air force in modern war demands to a tremendous degree those

qualities in which Russian fighting forces have always
been deficient: fast maintenance, efficient staff work,
huge reserves of trained technicians and mechanics.
These, as I have pointed out before, are not particularly weaknesses of the Russian war machine; they
are weaknesses of Russia. In time, they can be re-
moved. But it will take a decade at least. Then,
watch out.

Moreover, the Soviet Air Force does not enjoy, as
did the R.A.F., the Luftwaffe or the United States
Army Force in 1939, the presence of a group of farsighted, imaginative and enterprising air officers. The
banishment of the very few who wanted to build a
bomber striking point is an indication of the strength
of the ground generals. It is the fashion in some
places nowadays to laugh at the claims and predictions of men like General Carl Spaatz or Air Marshal
Harris. But where would we be today without the
foresight and courage that developed western air potential?

In air warfare, as in every field of Russian endeavor, the clammy hand of orthodoxy reaches out to
stifle enterprise and imagination. Stalin is "the father
of the concept of the support of ground forces by
superior fighter forces." So says the Army's news-
paper, *Red Star*. The exigencies of war may force
Stalin to become the father of long-range bombing.
But today the emphasis in Soviet aviation is on the
support of the numberless legions of the ground
army.

German views on the effectiveness of Russian aviation dwell on the bravery of the pilots rather than the
performance of the machine. They found the Soviet

Air Force unable to maintain prolonged operations, due to the administrative and planning weaknesses which run through all the Russian fighting forces, but the individual pilots fanatically courageous.

The Russian Navy is the heir to a long record of defeats. It has been roundly beaten by most of the big European navies and in the second World War it was driven into its ports in the Baltic and the Black seas and never, until almost the end, exercised control over these vital sea approaches to the Soviet Union.

Since the end of the conflict Russian propagandists have beat the drum about the Navy's achievements along the northern route to Murmansk over which American and British supplies traveled, but Admiral Lord Fraser, who commanded the British escorts on that perilous and costly route, told me that the Red destroyers and other escort craft were of little help.

"Save on one or two occasions," he said, "we never saw the fellows until we came into port. Then they would come rushing out making a great noise about all the submarines they had sunk and all the German cruisers their submarines had torpedoed. I don't think they were lacking in bravery. I think they were so few that they were carefully sheltered during the war and they let us take the punishment."

The chief importance of the Red Navy today lies in its submarine fleet. Like the Russian air force, the submarine fleet is subject to wild exaggerations and some estimates run as high as 500 first-line undersea craft.

The information made available to me in preparing

this book points to a present (September, 1951) strength of about 265 submarines of which about 80 are long-range craft fitted with snorkels allowing them to cruise long distances submerged.

As in aircraft production, the Russians have benefited from the capture of German designers and builders and the present building program is said to be about 15 long-range submarines a year. As these come into service, the smaller submarines, some of them dating back to the middle 1930's, are broken up.

Even 80 long-range submarines is a real threat especially if the Soviet Army can seize the coasts of Norway, the Low Countries and France and the bases that lie there. Operating from such bases modern submarines, adequately maintained and directed, could raise hob with trans-Atlantic traffic. But— *adequately maintained and directed.* Here again we encounter the great question. Can the Russians keep their weapons, jet planes, huge tanks and long-range submarines, in operation?

The Soviet Army emerges as the most experienced, the most proficient and the most enterprising of the three services. If war comes, it will bear the main burden of the Russian war effort. Already it has attained in Germany singularly advantageous positions for the launching of an attack on western Europe.

General Vassily Chuikov, commanding the German front, has at his disposal six armies, approximately 400,000 men.

During the spring, summer and early autumn, the period in which operations would be most likely to begin, two of these armies move forward to positions near the frontier of East Germany.

The Third Shock (Attack) Army is located in the area Letzlinger-Heide opposite the forward divisions of the British Army of the Rhine in Lower Saxony. The Eighth Guards Army takes position in the Eisenach-Ohrdruff area of Thuringia, a location which is *west* of the principal United States training area at Graffenwoehr in eastern Bavaria.

Behind these two armies, each of which has four divisions, including two armored divisions, are disposed the First, Second, Third and Fourth Guards Mechanized Armies.

The infantry divisions of all these armies have been modernized. The armored divisions have been given the T-34-85, the best Russian medium tank. By the autumn of 1951 all the divisions will be up to strength, for the first time since 1945, and a rigorous system of discipline introduced by General Chuikov has raised the efficiency of the whole army group. For, poor though East Germany is, it is a paradise to the youngsters from the farm and the mine in Russia and it is believed that the Soviet Army suffered more than the western armies from that slackness and laziness which is the occupational disease of occupation armies.

During the last two training and maneuver periods, which in Germany usually begin in late May and last until the middle of November, the group of armies has concentrated on problems connected with the crossings of rivers. There also has been considerable emphasis on the tactics of envelopment. Chuikov, like most other senior officers in the Soviet Army gravely aware of its deficiencies, has hammered away at meticulous operational planning in the field.

The training and maneuvering of the Russian armies is observed by many thousand pairs of German eyes owned in the majority by folk who wish the Soviets nothing but evil and who know a good deal about war.

The picture that emerges from their reports is of a big, heavily armored force that is being driven hard 365 days a year and that is getting the best equipment Moscow can give it.

The Soviet Air Force in East Germany is being built up to a strength of 500 jet fighters, most of them *MIG15*'s, and 400 bombers, a large percent of which will be the twin jet bomber mentioned above.

Finally a large headquarters is being constructed in the Wunsdorf area south of Berlin. It is reported to be large enough to house 35,000 troops and the installation includes underground war rooms and communications centers.

The conclusion which one must reach is that if the Soviet Union strikes, she is best prepared in Germany to strike hard. But as we shall see in the succeeding chapter she is not preparing to strike alone. The Atlantic bloc is not the only power bloc in this tragic world.

4. The Role of the Satellites

The inclusion of the satellite states—Bulgaria, Rumania, Hungary, Czechoslovakia, Poland, Albania and East Germany—into the new Russian empire is a frightening reinforcement to the Soviet Union in its quest for world domination.

Nearly 88,000,000 people have been brought under the rule of Moscow. The industrial system of the ancient states of Poland and Czechoslovakia is now producing for the benefit of the Kremlin. Millions of tough, hardy soldiers have been added to the enormous manpower already at the disposal of the Russian General Staff. Finally, the type of industrial and military reinforcement most urgently needed by the Soviet Union—skilled mechanics, scientific technicians, industrial managers—is available in these countries.

Since the start of the cold war there has been a strong tendency in the United States to believe that there exists in each of these countries an important revolutionary potential and that the governments imposed upon these states, by the Russians, rule only because they are backed by the Soviet Union. Let war come, the wiseacres say, and these nations will rise and throw off the Russian yoke.

Such daydreams are encouraged, understandably, by the large number of political refugees who have reached the United States from these countries. It is not remarkable that these people sincerely exaggerate the amount of resistance to Soviet rule in their homelands and it is right and just that they carry on the fight from America against the hideous apparatus of tyranny that has gripped the satellite states.

But it is extremely dangerous to the well-being of the United States to accept blindly their estimates of the strength of the resistance to Russia in these countries without examining more objectively the conditions in eastern Europe, under which Russia rules.

The next war, when it comes, will be fought and won by the Army, Air Force and Navy of the United States, in that order. It would be tragic folly today, therefore, to accept without reservation these promissory notes of future resistance and, as a result, to make inadequate allocation of men and materials for the eventual liberation of these countries.

No sane person will deny that there has been and still is great opposition to Russia and communism throughout the satellite states. Nor that there still exists in some of these states, notably Bulgaria, a fierce tradition of national resistance to any occupying power. Nor that the nationalist concept in Poland and Hungary is so strong that it will be some decades before the average Pole or Hungarian is drilled to place the interests of world communism, which are of course the interests of Soviet Russia, ahead of the interests of Poland or Hungary.

To these circumstances we must add the incredible brutality, ignorance and clumsiness of the Russians in dealing with their "allies" in the east, the impoverishing diversion of the industrial and agricultural products of these states to the Soviet Union and the steady fall in the standard of living throughout East Europe.

This is a lot. Does it add up to an explosive situation? Does it mean that in the event of war we can count on millions of effective allies snapping at Russian communications, assassinating Russian political and military liaison officers, and mounting popular rebellions against communist rule?

A great many people, wise, good and earnest, would have us think so. I must file a respectful demurrer.

Let us examine first the apparatus of communist control. Primarily this is the secret police. Those who have never been in a police state are luckily unaware of how all-pervasive is the power of the secret police or of how strongly it affects the life of every individual in the state. When we consider the stories of resistance in this satellite or that, we must remember that any act of resistance, even so small a thing as telling a joke about a local communist leader, can be followed by cruel and arbitrary punishment not only of the "criminal" involved but of his or her family.

Understand, moreover, that those punished have no recourse and that those who might wish to go to their assistance dare not even mention this normal human desire. And remember that anyone—the corner grocer, the village doctor, the local agricultural agent—may be an informer for the secret police.

Above the secret police stands the party. Our loathing of communism has made us underestimate its appeal to the young and the underprivileged. And the opportunities it offers, particularly in the period at the end of a long war when regimes are falling, to the daring and the reckless.

Communism in eastern Europe does not rest, as the communists boast, on a firm foundation of popular support. It does rest on the loyalty of a tough, tricky group of former "have-nots" who have become the "haves" under communism. Are they Marxist intellectuals? Of course not, save for a very few. They are men and women who have learned that blind obedience to Moscow rewards them in a manner they never dreamed of in their sordid lives in the back streets of eastern Europe or their dull lives in the civil service, the army or the university.

Possessed of all the propaganda weapons of the state, they, at the bidding of the Russians, have trained these weapons upon the youth. Why? For one thing, youth has no past. The adolescent of seventeen, born in the uneasy Europe that listened to the ranting voice of Hitler, bred in the blind futility of war, has no memory, as his elders have, of better, quieter days when the people of East Europe enjoyed a degree of liberty that would seem unbelievable to the average man today.

Youth is enthusiastic. It has no standard by which it can measure communism. It is seduced by promises of a bright future and by assurances of good jobs for the faithful. The old units of environmental training —the family, the church, the school—have been either smashed or so perverted that youth has no other place to look for the answers it always seeks than the party.

There is one other factor which must never be

forgotten in our analysis of the hold which communism has on the peoples of East Europe. This is the absolute ban on information from the free world. Great work has been done by the Voice of America and the stations of Radio Free Europe. But good though it is, this work is a drop of clear water in a bucket of communist mud. It is not only the incessant thumping of the propaganda drums that we must fight in the satellites; it is the lack of any outside information by which that propaganda can be judged.

We are aware that standards of living are falling throughout the satellite states. Is the Rumanian farmer or the Czech industrial worker aware that the standard of living of an American farmer or a British industrial worker is far better? Of course not.

There is, of course, passive resistance, just as there is in the Soviet Union, resistance to government decrees and policies, usually economic, which in the United States would be expressed in strikes. There are scattered instances of assassination, sabotage and industrial slowdowns. But there is no armed underground of importance. To believe that there is and that it will burst into action the moment war comes is dangerous.

It is a safe prediction, however, that if war comes, the United States government will be deluged by reports of armed resistance in this country or that and with appeals for immediate, expensive aid to the various resistance movements.

The postwar histories of the satellite states have been marred by the trials of innocent men labeled traitors and saboteurs. Some of these, especially in the immediate postwar period, undoubtedly were men who stood for the principles of western democracy and who tried and failed to halt the march to power of the communist parties. But we should remember that a great many others tried and sentenced were communists who had taken the wrong turning on the party line or had incited the dislike of the Russians or of party members more powerful than they. It is unwise to attribute to the washing of party linen at show trials the characteristics of revolt.

One other point. The peoples of most of the satellite states have been the poor relations of western Europe for generations. In peace they believed themselves exploited by the West, although that exploitation was a shadow of what is being done now by the Russians. In war they were the hangers-on, hoping to gobble a province or a seaport as their reward for alliance. Today they have no choice. But—and it is a very big but—they are part of a formidable power bloc which to them, because they have no standard of comparison, appears immensely strong. It must be that a considerable percentage of the population of the satellite states, not only the communists but others as well, consider the Russian conquest of western Europe inevitable and see themselves as the Soviets' trusted lieutenants in the occupation and looting of the rich states to the west.

This, of course, is nothing new for Balkan adventurers and opportunists. They snapped at similar bait when it was offered by Hitler's Germany before the invasion of Russia in 1941 and for the same reasons. Let us not be bemused by German and other claims that the Axis powers and their toadies were fighting a "holy war" when they invaded the Soviet Union in 1941. They were out for power and loot, all they could get.

One more point is important to any assessment of the satellites' loyalty to Moscow. There existed, as I have said, in certain of the satellite countries a degree of liberty of the individual far greater than anything that exists today. But there was also corruption, fascism, police brutality, insane nationalism and greed. Communism in eastern Europe, we must understand, has not replaced democracy in the western style but a fumbling attempt toward that democracy which encompassed racial hatred, political intolerance and economic ruthlessness. To Americans bred in freedom, the present system in Rumania appears terrible. It is possible that it does not appear so terrible to the Rumanian peasant.

Adding and subtracting the circumstances that affect political attitudes in the satellites today, we reach the conclusion that although there is passive resistance to communist rule, we would be foolish to believe that this will be instantly transformed into armed rebellion in time of war. We must understand that considerable sections of the various populations are getting enough out of the present regimes to give those regimes some loyalty and that, just as in Hitler's Germany, the men at the top are committed to the continuation of these regimes.

The communist leaders of Poland or Hungary or Bulgaria are not going to surrender their power without a fight. For surrender means suicide or death before a firing squad. Without any western demand for unconditional surrender, they have reached the point where "no surrender" is their only watchword in war or peace.

⁄The first, and to the Russians, most important result of the conquest of the satellite states is the extension of the Russian safety zone to the west. From the purely military standpoint a frontier on the Elbe is better than one on the Vistula. Despite all the official propaganda on the growth of communism in the Peoples Republics, this probably is the most satisfying thing about the Soviet Union's domination of East Europe to the experts in power politics who rule Russia.

⁄ But there is much else. Polish coal, Hungarian wheat, Czechoslovak steel. Beyond these concrete products pumped into the lifeblood of the eastern empire there is the human contribution of well-educated, skillful technicians to work on the great new industrial enterprises of the Soviet Union, to reinforce the Russian scientific workers and to add their knowledge and techniques to that of the Soviet masters.

As I have pointed out, the Russian industrial inferiority to the United States or to the United States and Great Britain combined is very great. But it is less great, although still terribly important, when the production of the satellite states is added to that of the Soviet Union. Were Russia to grab the industrial centers of West Europe, something it certainly will try to do in time of war, and add them to what it now has in the Soviet Union and the satellites, then the western superiority would be drastically cut.

To do that, of course, the Russians must have the

assistance in any war of the military potential of the satellites.

The late Adolf Hitler, whose works have been of great assistance to the Russians, wrote in *Mein Kampf* that "any alliance whose purpose is not the intention to wage war is senseless and useless." I think we can take it for granted that the Russians are not embracing their comrades in the satellites without knowledge of their military potential.

This is very great. On the broadest basis, the satellite system includes peoples like the Poles, East Germans and Bulgars whose gallantry in war is proverbial. Given time—and the Russians have had six years and more—the military masses can be marshalled to the Kremlin's will.

The annexation of the military forces of the satellite states to those of the Soviet Union has followed a clearly discernible pattern. The objective, according to General Eisenhower's staff, is readiness for offensive action by 1952.

The first step has been the recasting, in all propaganda in the country concerned, of the army's role in the society. The army is pictured, as it is in Russia, as an ally of the people. Naturally, this takes some doing in some of the satellites where, for centuries, the army has been the government's arm of oppression. The propaganda strives to implant the idea that the Rumanian or the Polish or the Hungarian army could become a collection of palladins like the Soviet Army were it only to cast out the reactionaries and spies now in high places.

Once this propaganda campaign has been launched, the communist government of the country proceeds to reorganize the military structure, the general staff, the command, the supply organization and the field units on the Russian pattern. This calls for the assistance of a Soviet Military Mission and since the satellite armies suffer from the military's customary resistance to change, even in its own interest, the process is a long one.

The change includes not only the structural changes mentioned in the preceding paragraph but changes in military doctrine. If the Russian requirement for air superiority in a certain offensive situation is 6 to 1, then that requirement becomes Polish or Czechoslovak or Bulgarian tactical doctrine. Soviet military terminology is introduced and Soviet staff routine adopted.

The third step is the replacement of weapons by Soviet weapons, tanks, guns, mortars, machine guns and rifles.

Finally those officers and noncommissioned officers who had served in or with western armies—their number was very high in the Polish and Czechoslovak armies—are largely eliminated or degraded and the divisional cadres are filled up with young men from the various communist youth organizations or with prisoners from World War II who have received thorough political indoctrination during their stay in the Soviet Union.

These steps have not taken place simultaneously. The process is furthest along in Bulgaria and Rumania, early additions to the Soviet system, and lags most in Poland and Czechoslovakia. The triumph of communist tyranny came relatively late in both these countries, the armies had strong ties with western armies, notably the British, and, particularly in Poland, the nation had a strong national antagonism toward the Russians and an equally strong national identification with the army.

Analysis of the military preparations of the satellite armies indicates that the Russians hope to have completed their transformation from national armies to subsidiary communist armies that can be used operationally on the offensive with the Soviet Army by the summer of 1952.

The process of conversion to a Soviet-type army has been completed in Bulgaria and Rumania. The Bulgarian Army is now about 200,000 strong comprising about fourteen divisions, two of which are mechanized. The Rumanian Army is reported to number 205,000 men with about the same proportion of mechanized troops as the Bulgarian Army.

In Hungary the army is smaller but, on the whole, more modern. General I. V. Tsvetayev, who was the military commandant of Moscow during part of the war, is the Inspector General of the Hungarian Army and he has produced a compact army of just over 100,000 men including two mechanized divisions, one armored division and four rifle (infantry) divisions.

The Czechoslovakian Army is still in the process of reorganization on the Soviet pattern although this is nearing completion. Thus far it has reached only a driblet of Russian weapons and it has been weakened by the repeated denunciation of senior officers as "spies and saboteurs," and subsequent purges. On the information now available it appears that the Russians plan eventually on a Czechoslovak army of fifteen divisions, three of them mechanized and one armored.

Poland, home of some of Europe's most notable warriors, has given the Russians plenty of trouble. Not even the advent of Marshal Rokossovsky has been able to quell the fierce pride of all ranks of the Polish Army in that army's heroes and great traditions. Since most of the heroes fought against Russia and most of the traditions were born in Polish triumphs over the Russians, the political reorientation of the Polish Army has been difficult.

Despite some fumbling, the Russians appear to be more interested and emphatic about the Polish Army than the armies of the other satellites. Their plans for it are ambitious.

By the end of the spring of 1952, it is hoped that sixteen Polish divisions will be ready, four of them mechanized with a high percentage of tanks and twelve of them rifle divisions reorganized on the Russian pattern with the same standard of equipment.

In the other satellites, the armies are receiving second-rate equipment, weapons that have been replaced in the Russian armies by newer, more efficient types. In Poland, the new divisions are getting equipment which is just as good as that going to the bulk of the Soviet Army although not as good as that reaching the Russian Group of Armies in East Germany.

The last of the states to receive the dubious honor of a Russian satellite is East Germany, the German Democratic Republic. It is the last but by no means the least. For its 18,000,000 people include some of the best military material in Europe, material the

Russians have been fashioning into a new German Army since the autumn of 1948, long before the western powers had even contemplated the rearmament of western Germany.

The *Bereitschaften* or readiness squads of the Peoples Police are the cadre for an East German Army. There are about 54,000 men in this force. (The number often has been exaggerated by confusing the *Bereitschaften* with the overall force of the Peoples Police which includes traffic cops, railroads police and detectives.)

These 54,000 men are drawn mostly from the provinces of Brandenburg and Mecklenburg, which contributed so heavily to the great German armies of the first and second world wars. A high percentage of them are former soldiers of Hitler's Wehrmacht who received their political indoctrination while prisoners of war in Russia. They are officered largely by professional soldiers who turned their coats as prisoners in Russia or who graduated into the East German Army from the police forces of the various states and cities of the German Democratic Republic.

At the moment the organization of the *Bereitschaften* is a curious parallel to that of Germany's Versailles Army of a generation ago.

That army of 100,000 was packed with generals serving as majors, captains as sergeants. It represented the residue of brains and efficiency of the old Imperial army. Because of the partition of Germany, the Russians have not been able to cast their net quite as far, but the standard of experience and ability in the *Bereitschaften* is very high.

British intelligence estimates are that the East

Germans, using the present *Bereitschaften* as cadres, could form an army of 400,000 men in the German Democratic Republic. My own impression is that the Russians, aware of Polish and Czech fear of the Germans, which is no less strong than that in Norway or France, will not expand the *Bereitschaften* to this number except in case of war.

But they are capable now of raising an army of a quarter million men based on the *Bereitschaften*. This is equal to what the western powers consider giving the Federal Republic of West Germany, and taking into account the military tradition of the East Germans and the high quality of the officers and non-commissioned officers now in the *Bereitschaften*, it would be a formidable additon to Russian strength.

The readiness units of the Peoples Police have been organized into twenty-four composite formations, approximately 1,800 strong, each of which is similar to a mechanized regiment in the Soviet Army. Each of these formations is made up of a command group, four combat units or battalions, three of infantry and one of artillery. There are also seven supporting companies and an administrative unit.

The Russians keep a hand on the controls. There is a Russian senior officer and three subordinates in the command group of each composite formation. In addition 158 senior officers of the *Bereitschaften* have recently returned from a year's training with the Soviet Army in Russia. These men hold key commands.

After some delay the *Bereitschaften*, like the armies of the Peoples Democracies in East Europe, is receiving ample supplies of equipment. Most of it is of

Russian manufacture but some has been produced by the revived light armaments industry in the German Democratic Republic.

Heavy and light field guns, howitzers and antitank and anti-aircraft guns have been supplied. The number of tanks thus far reaching the *Bereitschaften* units is small, but they are T-34-85's, the best of the Soviet medium tanks. In common with other satellite armies and, indeed, with the Soviet Army, there is a shortage of trucks although light armored cars are reaching the *Bereitschaften* in large quantities.

√ The Germans have surprised the Russians by their high standards in maintenance of vehicles and weapons.

"Compared with the Russian Army's vehicles, those of the *Bereitschaften* are clean, in good running order and constantly checked," ran one report. "It is not unusual for a local Soviet commander to borrow mechanics from the nearest *Bereitschaften* unit to instruct his own men on the maintenance of their vehicles. Of course, much of the heavy overhaul work done for the Soviet Group of Armies is carried out by German auxiliaries."

The *Bereitschaften* personnel is now divided as follows:

(1) Twenty-four composite formations distributed throughout East Germany. The table of organization for each of these units calls for 371 officers and non-commissioned officers and 1,432 men.

(2) Five specialist units, three of which are engineer units. These are attached to

the main headquarters, whose commander is Inspector General (of Police) K. H. Hoffmann.
(3) Three field training centers.
(4) Nine schools including one large one
for Political Indoctrination and Cul-
ture.
(5) Six specialist schools.
(6) Various miscellaneous units including a
supply dump and hospitals.

There has been some very lively writing about the
"new Luftwaffe" which the Russians are supposed to
be creating. All that has been done is to organize a
Main Administration for Air Police. This has about
sixty officials, most of them former Luftwaffe officers,
but this Administration thus far has done nothing
but draw up plans for a Police Air Force somewhere
in the distant future. It has no planes and no airfields.

There is also a Sea Police organization with a
strength of about 4,400 men. This force operates a
number of small, fast, armed craft in the Baltic. Its
duties are confined to police duties and to training in
mine sweeping.

The *Bereitschaften* units, although the men are
well fed and well paid, have been plagued by desertion, or, to use the new word coined by the United
States Army, "defection." Many of the soldiers when
the units were first organized in the autumn of 1948
had joined, in prison camps in Russia, as a means of
getting back to Germany. When they reached East
Germany they deserted.

But the stream of deserters did not stop. Hundreds

of men desert every year despite the rewards of service and the continuous political indoctrination.

The proximity of the frontier and the ease with which a soldier, on leave, can reach the haven of West Berlin raise the question of whether, given a similar opportunity for desertion, the soldiers of the other satellites might not act in the same manner. In Poland and Czechoslovakia, we know, many members of the officer corps probably would take an opportunity to desert, but there are no indications that the rank and file is infected with a desire to "go west."

The desertions by members of the *Bereitschaften* raise another problem for the Russians. As a race, the Russians are not trusting. For centuries informers and spies have had a major place in Russian society. No amount of servile talk on the part of the Germans, especially old officers of the Wehrmacht, convinces the Soviet secret police and high command in Germany that the *Bereitschaften* are as loyal as its members assert. This suspicion is reinforced by the high number of desertions and aggravated by the Russian national memory of what happened in the Soviet Union when the Germans came in 1941.

In short, the German Communists in the Socialist Unity (Communist) party and the senior officers of the readiness units of the Peoples Police suffer from the same attitude on the part of the Russians that the West Germans encounter in their dealings with the French, British and, to a much lesser extent, the Americans. It is that after 1939–1945 no one is eager to trust the Germans. West European distrust of Germany is well understood. We should understand that in their efforts to incorporate East Germany into their satellite system, the Russians have encountered both in their own people and in the communist governments of eastern Europe a deep-seated fear and suspicion of Germany.

The irreconcilability of East Germany with the other satellites is one of the major problems facing the Russians in their task of welding the satellites into a going military concern. There are others, of course, but before we accept the verdict of the wishful thinkers that the whole program is "impossible" let us examine the boundaries of east European rearmament as the Russians have set them.

Despite a great many reports to the contrary the Russians are not at the moment (January, 1952) sending new jet fighter or bomber types to the satellite air forces. These forces are second-rate; there is nothing in the Rumanian or Bulgarian or Czech air force to match the American and British jets going to the Italian, French and Belgian air forces.

East European rearmament as the Russians conceive it is rearmament for the ground troops only. For ground troops can be controlled to some extent and a determined pilot in a fast plane who wants to get away can do it.

Save in East Germany where West Berlin always beckons, it seems probable that the Russians will be able to weld the satellite armies to the main Soviet forces, that they will be able to raise the standard of armament of these forces to something approximating the Soviet level, and that the reorganization of these armies along Russian lines will be successfully completed.

At the beginning of this chapter I mentioned that the reinforcement of the satellites is a terrifying factor in the world situation. Let us see what the military reinforcement is in terms of what the western powers are trying to do.

By the spring of 1952 there will be a Polish army of sixteen divisions. Soviet-type divisions are somewhat smaller than those of the West—about 12,000 men is a good estimate of the Polish divisional strength—but these sixteen divisions, in all about 192,000 men, represent in combat units a force as large as the entire French Army in Europe.

It is often suggested that the Russians in the satellite states have assumed an impossible task in attempting to co-ordinate the military efforts of disparate states. The Poles, you are told, hate the Czechs and the Hungarians hate the Rumanians. All true, or at least true in 1945.

But in war it is folly to underestimate the enemy. We in the West are striving to drive the Germans, Italians, French and Norwegians in one team. If we can accomplish this without the complete standardization of weapons, training and staff organization, which the Soviet Army has already completed in eastern Europe, why cannot the Russians do the same?

We in the West are a long way from completing that kind of standardization. We are not, aside from the single, salient personality of Eisenhower, in possession of a unifying individual or force like Russian communism which for the weal of Russia and the woe of the West has broken national aspirations and hammered the satellites into co-operation and co-ordination.

So in the event of war we will be fighting not Russia alone but the armed forces of her satellites, a reinforcement of between 65 and 75 divisions. This represents a force larger than that now envisaged for the defense of western Europe. It is made up of tough soldiers, men accustomed to privation and a low standard of living. Its weapons are good, if not as good as those of the Soviet army.

We have seen in these chapters just what we are up against in the military force of Russia and its satellites. What do we have in the West? What are our calculations based upon? How strong are the old and famous states that make up the West European alliance? How will we fight the Russians if they come?

5. The International Army

"What's all this stuff add up to," a perplexed Congressman asked at SHAPE, last summer, "NATO, the Council of Europe, the Schuman Plan? What are we going to get out of it? What's it all mean, anyway?"

Wiser people than this legislator, and there cannot be more than 145,000,000 of them in the United States, have asked the same questions. It would be nice if definite, black-and-white answers were available now. They are not, nor will they be for some time, for Europe is in the midst of economic, military and structural changes greater than any ever before attempted in time of peace. What we can do is chart the main direction which the military reconstruction of Europe is taking.

The first objective of the North Atlantic Treaty Organization and its affiliated commands is to deter war, specifically to deter any Soviet attack in Europe and, since Europe is where the war would be won or lost, to make Russian aggression impossible.

We are certain that if war comes it will be in the form of a Russian attack.

"Democracies are always on the defensive at the start of a war," General Eisenhower told me during one of our conversations. "That's where the Russians, or any totalitarian government, always have the edge. They can build up striking forces, they can move troops behind a curtain of censorship. We can't surprise them in the sense of strategic surprise."

What General Eisenhower and his staff are trying to do is to construct in western Europe a basis of defense so strong that if the Russians do attack they can be held short of the objectives, such as the Ruhr, which they must win to fight on. This is, as I have indicated, the second Allied aim. The first is to prevent war by deterring the Russians.

The optimum condition now envisaged is one in which the Russians are deterred from attacking and western Europe, through the Council of Europe, the Schuman Plan and the North Atlantic Treaty Organization, integrates itself politically, economically and militarily to a point where the Russians can never attack.

In the light of a thousand years of European strife this condition strikes some as a Utopian daydream. But it also impresses many Europeans, hardheaded men like France's Jean Monnet and Germany's Konrad Adenauer, as the only solution. When men like this talk of the future United Europe, they do not sound like men talking of the unobtainable. But they emphasize that all the projects now afoot must progress hand in hand. The great goal is not reachable if one is omitted. Without the Schuman Plan or common defense or drastic surrenders of political sovereignty little can be accomplished. Above all, in the interim, the West must be strong enough to deter Soviet attack and, of course, to smash it if it comes.

Eventually we can look forward to the creation of a United Europe strong enough to stand alone. Men like General Eisenhower believe that once the armed forces of the continent and Great Britain are filled out to the extent now planned and—this is most important—the regular divisions are backed by trained reserves who can be mobilized, then American troops can be gradually withdrawn. But that day is far off. As this is written the United States is the greatest European power on the land and sea and in the air.

Europe can well say, "Nobody knows the trouble we've seen" since the end of World War II. From the military standpoint, western Europe was defenseless from 1945 to 1950 and consequently subjected to heavy Russian political pressure. It is only now beginning to attain something approaching adequate defense. Those who criticize France or Britain or Norway for not doing more should compare what those countries are doing today with what they were, or were not, doing three years ago.

American help to Europe began in the economic and ended in the military field. The United States found that Marshall Aid, although it improved the economic position of most of the recipient countries, did not avert the danger of Soviet attack. It has not, as a matter of fact, subdued communism in some of the most important recipient nations as the elections of June 1951 in France demonstrated.

The answer to this is clear. The government of the United States, fearful of being attacked for underwriting socialism abroad, saw that most of the aid went to the individual corporations. The result was that the great industrialists got new plants, raw materials and higher production, with fewer markets, and the worker, who in theory was supposed to benefit through higher wages, got very little. The mistake was in the estimate of the kind of men who run the great enterprises of western Europe. Their attitude toward the worker is archaic and their approach to labor relations makes that of the least enlightened American corporations seem like a combination of St. Francis and the Fabian Society. To believe that the benefits given them by American aid would reach the workers was childish.

This affects the military position in one important sense. The E.C.A. aid did not remove communism, and as long as communism flourishes in western Europe we can expect partisan activity against the lines of communications and treason at certain levels of the armed forces in time of war, and unstable governments in peace.

The military re-entry of the United States into western Europe on a large scale was forced upon it by the Russians. Of the many mistakes which the Political Bureau has made since 1945, one of the greatest was the Berlin blockade of 1948–1949. It is important to the present because it demonstrates the ABC of how to deal with the Soviet Union.

When the Allies were weak in June, 1948, it was impossible to negotiate profitably to raise the blockade. When in April, 1949 they were strong, as a result of the air lift—a great political weapon—it was possible to negotiate and the Russians backed down. What we have done since is to transfer the lesson learned in Berlin to larger fields, to Korea and to all of Western Europe.

The sharp increase in the military strength of the United States in western Europe has produced another situation which directly affects the whole military position of the west and Europe's psychological preparation for defense.

This is the apprehension which that increase has aroused in the minds of millions of people who cannot be considered communists by any stretch of the imagination. Nor can they claim to have better information about Soviet plans than we, although some of them, notably the British, approach their information in a calmer frame of mind. The fact remains that a considerable proportion of the people of western Europe do not like rearmament, ours or theirs, and we will be extremely foolish if we eschew sweet reason for commands in convincing them of the wisdom of our plans.

This is one of the many situations in the whole problem where General Eisenhower proved himself invaluable. He is a reasonable man and a reasoning one. In the winter of 1950 he toured the capitals of West Europe, selling just three things: the time was urgent, the countries must rearm and, if they did, there was a good chance that Soviet invasion might be avoided.

In various keys, he has been selling this ever since. It is a commentary on how slowly west European rearmament has moved, and how fast the Soviet Union has progressed during the same period, that in September, 1951 Eisenhower had to warn the newly elected executive board of the North Atlantic Treaty Organization that it must maintain a sense of "urgency" that would not permit any cut in the defense plans of the West.

"The threat is great and the time is short," he said, "and the future of Western civilization is at stake."

Eisenhower assailed the idea, held by many West European politicians, that a number of formed divisions are enough. "It's reserves that count," he says, "reserves, well-trained, experienced reserves. The day is past when a butcher or a baker could grab a rifle and go out and take his place in his company and march off to war. Today he has to have a lot of training, he must be freshened up on his training every year if he's a reservist. War's too complex nowadays, the minute man is gone."

The General's vehemence on this subject betrays his recognition of the attraction that slowing down on rearmament exerts for many politicians. Here we return to two basic factors affecting European defense: the fear of war that millions read into rearmament; and the governments' reluctance to subordinate the hard-won economic gains of the past few years to the needs of rearmament.

The first is understandable and American officials abroad have shown too little imagination in trying to understand it. The European fears war not because he is afraid to fight when war comes, but because he knows what war is like. To him war is not simply a matter of seeing the soldiers off to the front and accepting limited rationing: it is bombing, occupation, fighting in his own back yard or street, poverty and famine, and until we recognize this point of view we will be hampered in our efforts to rearm Europe.

The European would be stupid indeed if he were not afraid of starting another war. Consequently the chest thumpers in Washington disturb him; one of the keys to the success of the American commanders in Germany in dealing with the Germans is that they have never indulged in this sort of histrionics. Europe wants security, not war.

Under these circumstances the first steps toward winning that security were suspect and disliked. No one seemed to mind when the North Atlantic Treaty Organization was established, but the protests came thick and hot when troops reinforced the existing occupation forces in Germany, when raw materials were allocated for armaments and when conscription began to reach into the homes of the continent.

But all these objections to rearmament were dwarfed by the political storm which arose over the question of a contribution by the Federal Republic of Germany to the defense of Europe. This is a vital issue of European politics; it is also a vital issue of European defense, for without the Germans the burden on the French, the British and the Americans will be far greater.

As long ago as the autumn of 1949 when Field Marshal Viscount Montgomery and his staff at the headquarters of European Defense at Fontainebleau were trying to make something out of nothing, the empty-handed professionals were discussing ways and means of getting troops. Germany loomed large in their calculations; and there was no overwhelming dissent by the French officers attached to the headquarters because they, like everyone else at that time, envisaged the addition of German soldiers in small units to existing Allied formations.

A year later the Pentagon in Washington was hot on the trail. With political shortsightedness notable even there, its staff planners envisaged German divisions leaping to arms at Uncle Sam's say-so and filling the ranks of the defenders of the West. Apparently they overlooked not only the fact that the Germans are not popular in Europe, but also the possibility that the Germans, as a result of their experiences between 1939 and 1945, might not be equally enthusiastic about rearmament.

The American statement of September, 1950 that the Germans were going to be rearmed, period, was a blunder. It had the worst possible effect on public opinion in Europe, especially in France; it aroused strong resentment in Germany; and it probably set back actual negotiations on the subject of German rearmament by at least six months. As this is written, more than a year later, United States policy in Germany and United States prestige in Europe still suffer from that blunder.

Take one example. Rearmament of Germany, in any form, was to be accompanied by the abrogation of the Occupation Statute in Germany. As soon as the German government realized that the Pentagon was panting to arm the German people it began to demand far more sovereignty than the Allies were prepared to transfer to it. This delayed the writing of the treaties granting Germany sovereignty and this in turn delayed rearmament.

The effect upon the Germans was sensational. For five years the western powers, particularly the United States, had told them that war and armaments must be forgotten, that Germany had sinned grievously in following its leaders into rearmament, that henceforth the people must devote their abilities, which are many, to peace and forget their martial past. Not unnaturally the Germans quoted our own propaganda back at us and the students in half a dozen universities signed pledges not to serve in any new German army.

The uproar gradually disappeared but it has left scars, notably upon the influence of the United States in Germany.

A great many Germans also took the attitude that any steps towards rearming themselves would provoke a Russian attack. They understood Russia's fear of Germany and they understood the weakness of the Allied forces in Germany during the period when German rearmament would be organized. There were seven divisions or their equivalent in United States, British and French zones of occupation in September, 1950, and the French and British divisions were well under strength.

Dr. Kurt Schumacher, leader of the Social Democrats, the most powerful opposition party in the Federal Republic, immediately took the line that before Germany could consider rearmament it must be protected from Soviet attack and that such protection could only be given by at least thirty Allied divisions stationed along the eastern frontiers of the Republic.

Beyond these political and national reactions lay an important psychological condition. The German people as a whole, having suffered so terribly in the last war, wanted nothing to do with rearmament, which they considered was only a prelude to a new war in which they would suffer even more terribly. No one in authority, German or American, took the trouble during the first tumultuous months of the great debate in Germany to tell the people that rearmament was being discussed because it seemed the only way by which Germany, in partnership with the rest of the free world, could avoid becoming another Korea.

The prestige and influence of the United States in the rest of Europe also took a terrific drubbing as a result of the Pentagon's ill-considered action. The communists, of course, had been telling the working classes of the continent for five years that America was really another fascist state, that it favored the Germans over the French or the Dutch or the British and that its military leaders were aching to rearm the Germans for a new war of aggression.

These were not secret activities by the communists. Anyone in Europe could read their newspapers and listen to their speeches. But apparently they had not penetrated the Pentagon. Or perhaps they had and were brushed off with the usual, "Well, what do we care about what they say?"

Nothing, of course. But we must be terribly careful to see that what we *do* is done in such a manner that it does not help the communists.

We must accept, I think, that the bullheaded approach of the Pentagon contributed to anti-American feeling in England and France, that it strengthened the communist position, so badly damaged by the unprovoked aggression by the North Koreans, and contributed materially to the confusion and uncertainty that surrounds German rearmament in Europe.

The rearmament of Germany, in any form, involves certain grave risks. These spring not only from the martial exploits of the Germans in the past—after all, it is eighty years since Germany won a war—but from her geographical and historical position. There is the risk that a strong Germany, perhaps the strongest partner in a united Europe, might lead that Europe against the Soviet Union in a war of revenge—for Germany. There is the risk that a strong Germany, considering itself the balance between Soviet and American strength, might choose to ally herself with Russia. These are distant prospects, long chances. But history is studded with long chances that developed into terrible facts.

It is shortsighted to believe that the policy we, as a people, wish the Germans to follow will inevitably be followed. Or that the behavior of a government or a people ten years in the future can be confidently predicted on the basis of present actions.

These risks must be weighed against the urgent danger of Soviet aggression in Europe. This is the basis for the rearmament of Germany, or as the State Department, which likes to call a spade a garden implement, would have it, a German defense contribution.

The risks we run in Germany are future risks. The danger of Soviet attack is with us today. Viewing the then puny efforts of the French rearmament, the lack of interest of the British in defending Europe, and the sluggish reaction of other European governments to the necessity for arms and men as a counterbalance to Soviet strength, it is not surprising that to the planners in the Pentagon, German rearmament seemed the only way out. The objective could be defended; the manner wherein the objective was presented could not.

After four years in Germany, I do not discount the risks in rearming the Germans. But if it is to be done,

then the method now taking shape, a contribution
to a European army, is the safest way. And the risks
are compensated for in my mind by the hideous dangers that face western Europe unless it rearms to
deter Soviet invasion. Such rearmament to be effective must contain German contribution. I do not
think this is the way many of us would like things to
be. But unfortunately it is the way things are.

We are prone to forget that Russia, no less than
Germany in the past, is a militarist nation and that
military traditions have been drilled into the Russian
populace for three decades. Germany is not the only
nation that reveres the army or the only nation which
considers the army and military might a proper and
just way of settling international disputes. We have
been bemused by the spectacle of international communism into forgetting that this basically political
weapon is used effectively only because, in most
cases, it has been backed by a huge army and air
force.

We made an initial blunder on the method of pre-
senting the rearmament of Germany to the world.
All things considered, we were fortunate that the
blunder was not greater. The postwar school of war
literature, of which Messrs. Mailer and Jones are the
leading lights, has continually cast the generals in
the wrong role. My own experience with generals,
possibly as great as these authors', is that they are not
the planning, guileful fascists of their imagination.
There may be a few with stars on their shoulders who
burn to emulate Hitler or Mussolini, but possibly
there are a few bookkeepers and even novelists with
the same ambition. As a whole, the generals I have

known were honest, courageous, hard-working men. They were not politically experienced, with one or two notable exceptions, and the blunder over Germany was a result of their immaturity.

Fortunately for the United States, Eisenhower was on hand to regain the ground they had lost.

For it was Eisenhower, advised by John J. McCloy, the United States High Commissioner in Germany, who finally found the middle road between Europe's frantic opposition to the re-creation of a German national army and the pressing need for a German defense contribution. Others, especially René Pleven, then the French Prime Minister, had put up the signposts pointing toward this road. But only Eisenhower could have led Europe down it.

This road leads to the creation of a European army in which French, German, Dutch, Belgian, Italian and other contingents will serve, wearing the same uniform and seeking a common objective—the preservation of peace.

Almost as soon as he took over command at SHAPE, Eisenhower was faced with the difficult task of choosing between two very different concepts of German rearmament. One was called the Petersberg Plan. It had emerged from a series of conferences between United States, British and French general officers and German military advisors to the Federal Government, led by former generals Hans Speidel and Adolf Heusinger, held at Petersberg, seat of the Allied High Commission, at Koenigswinter on the east bank of the Rhine across from Bonn.

The Petersberg Plan was right down the Pentagon

alley. It talked of the re-creation of a German national army of at least twelve full divisions and the establishment of a tactical air force to support these divisions in the field. Worse still, from the European point of view, it contemplated that these divisions would serve as an army under their own generals with their own staff. This meant not only the re-creation of a German military force, which was needed and helpful, but the re-creation of the German General Staff whose malign influence in the past terrified the rest of Europe and which, if it were to emerge from the Allied-German planning, would terrify Europe anew.

For over two years the idea of a European army had been kicking around in Paris. Under it, Germany would make a contribution to European defense but German units would be limited to about 6,000 men; there would be no German general staff; and the ceiling on German command positions would have been remarkably low. This plan, for which the French politicians if not the generals professed great enthusiasm, erred as much on the side of caution as the Petersberg Plan did on the side of audacity.

Eisenhower took up the idea and reached the conclusion that the only way in which Germany could be rearmed without outraging the other states of western Europe was by a contribution to a European army. The French, at his urging, called a European Defense Forces Conference which first met in February of 1951 in Paris.

To this conference came French, German, Italian, Belgian and Luxembourg representatives. In October, 1951, the Dutch, overcoming both isolationism and their hearty hatred of the Germans, joined. One by one the technical problems arising out of the organization in peace of an international army—Marlborough, Wellington and Eisenhower had all found it difficult enough even in time of war—have been solved and the project is squarely upon the road.

Under this plan the Germans will be given operational forces—divisions of about 13,000 men at the start, although the strength may rise to 15,000 in time. It is expected that eventually there will be twelve German divisions with six more in reserve, a front line force of at least 160,000 men, and an overall military establishment of more than a quarter of a million.

According to the original plans the German contribution will not exceed at any time more than one fifth of the total Allied land formations under SHAPE. And while the German contribution will be all the army that Germany is permitted, other nations like France, Belgium and the Netherlands will be allowed to maintain troops for the protection of their overseas possessions.

Moreover, the German divisions will not have a German armament industry to supply them; certain weapons will be concentrated in corps and army formations; and much of the administration and logistical functions of the European Army will be out of German hands. The object is to prevent the Germans from pulling their twelve divisions out of the European Army and acting independently.

The concept is new and enterprising. It seems to solve the basic question of whether Germany can be safely rearmed. It is a concept that should be realized;

indeed, in view of Europe's weakness, it must be realized. As this is written the first steps are being taken toward realization. One note of caution remains. The Germans themselves can upset the whole project by insisting on too much. To return to a well-known theme: Europe is afraid of the Russians but it is also afraid of the Germans. It was not the Russians who bombed Rotterdam or executed harmless Italian peasants or burned French villages. It was the Germans.

Occasionally wandering around France one will see a street sign reading something like this: RUE GEORGES LETOUR, FUSILLÉ PAR LES ALLEMANDS—and the date. The lesson is clear; it was not the S.S. or the S.A. or the army's security police who shot Georges but the Germans, the whole nation. This is what the Germans have to overcome. The burden of proof rests on them and on no one else. If they push too hard, if they demand too much, then the whole business will fall apart.

The enthusiasm generated in Paris for the European Army as the method by which Germany could be rearmed without endangering France's military position was very strong in the autumn of 1951. Once the French had Eisenhower's backing and German acquiescence to the scheme, they saw clear sailing ahead and were inclined to discount the military disadvantages of their idea.

Let us examine more closely the military aspects of the European Army as it is envisaged by the French, forgetting for the time being that it represents a great step forward in the political unity of Europe and judging it only as an army that would have to fight and defeat, with American and British help, the Russians.

The French consider that the divisions, or as they call them *groupements*, of each nationality would depend for supplies and support in the field on international formations. This means that the special troops—amphibious tank regiments, heavy artillery, ammunition supply companies, and bridging engineers—would be international. Normally, of course, they are corps and army troops. Under the French concept, if a German division or *groupement* were seeking to cross a river, a French heavy artillery regiment would support it, the engineers who would put the bridge across would be Italian, the ammunition would be brought to the bridgehead by Danes, and the tanks that swam the river and secured the lodgement on the other side would be manned by Dutchmen.

This is the sort of tactical situation that we have to consider when we translate the concept of a European army down to the terms of the men who must fight and die in support of that concept.

The command headquarters of corps or army, under the French concept, would be international in the sense that they would be staffed by officers from the European Army nations.

All this would bring German troops to the defense of Europe. But could Europe be defended under those conditions? Will the other European powers including France be willing to cut the size of their divisions to the 13,000 allotted to the Germans? The French say yes—now.

Language is one difficulty. If this were an Esperanto Army all would be plain sailing. The French contend that liaison officers, bilingual or even trilingual, will be able to transmit orders. But what a poor substitute liaison officers are for man-to-man consultation between the commander of a French division and a Norwegian tank destroyer battalion. And is there time for this sort of consultation in modern war? And are experienced officers with the required languages available to form this corps of language liaison officers?

Even if these officers are available and liaison is rapid, will there be standardization of military terms? During World War II there was plenty of difficulty between American and British troops because a military term well understood by the Americans meant something entirely different to the British. And national habits of thought and mind count, too. The British are prone to say, "It's rather warm here," when as a matter of fact they are having the hell shot out of them. The United States Army would report it "had" a town or a terrain feature when as a matter of fact it was only close to it and was about to attack.

As the plan stands now there is another difficulty. The Germans want equality and the French say they will have it. The French planners say that the Germans will be appointed to senior commands and that the Federal Government will have the same right to recruit soldiers and retain them under its own control as other governments. But the French think the German government should have a minimum of troops under its own control and that Germans will be "eligible" for higher command under the European Defense Commissioner, who will be the administrator for the scheme and also the umpire of the various national disputes that are bound to arise.

Will the Germans accept the plan without assurance that this Commissioner, who probably will be French, will give them equality of command and will not be prejudiced against the appointment of German officers to important commands?

Finally, where do the American and British divisions fit into the plan? The United States Army is one of the most strongly nationalist in the world. The British opinion of continental soldiers, especially the French, is low. Will they, on the field of battle, which is where it counts, accept French or German leadership resulting from political considerations?

The formation of a European army does not end the troubles that plague Eisenhower in his arduous task of molding a common European defense. Even when the army is on its feet and ready to fight, he faces certain other difficulties.

One of these is the general doubt in Europe, especially in Germany, over the ability of the French to lead Europe's military renaissance. It is no good saying that the Germans will have to take it and like it. In time there will be other courses open to them. And it is useless for Americans to maintain that, since France is the sheet anchor of United States hopes for a successful defense of Europe, we have overcome all the doubts of France that exist elsewhere.

The Germans, to take one instance, do not believe in French military leadership. They feel that the military thinking of the French high command is dated and obtuse and that the kind and duration of the training given French soldiers is unsuitable for the war they may have to fight.

Another difficulty lies in the approach of the other nations to the British contribution. The British at the moment are the leading ally of the United States in Europe. In men, weapons, equipment and planes, they put more into the defense of the continent in the vital year of 1951 than anyone else. But their suspicion of the French, as great as that of the Germans, is matched by the suspicion of the French, the Belgians and some of the others that in the event of war the British will, as one French general put it, "Fight with one eye on the ports of embarkation for Britain."

Personally, I think this is nonsense. The French will never forgive the British for not surrendering in 1940; it made their own capitulation seem so much worse. But the French still feel that Dunkirk was a desertion and that the same thing might happen again. Whether they are entitled to feel this way or not is beside the question. The point is that they do feel this way and this sentiment must be taken into account. Later on we will see how the military thinking of both the British and French is affected by the tragic events of May and June, 1940.

National rivalries old as the Oath of Strasbourg enter into other aspects of the military picture. Do we defend Germany on the Elbe or the Oder? Do we try to hold the neck of the Danish peninsula or do we withdraw to a glacis around Hamburg? Is Norway worth the divisions necessary to hold it? Is the atomic bomb to be used tactically in areas which we hope will welcome the western powers as liberators from Russian conquest?

None of these questions can be answered in simple military terms. Every one of them has political as well as military aspects. Moreover they are affected by changing economic conditions in the country concerned.

The United States made a fundamental mistake, now retrieved by Eisenhower, in believing that the nations of western Europe were as ready to rearm as was the United States because Washington accepted European fear of the Soviet Union as indicating readiness to rearm. This error was compounded by the belief that the peoples of western Europe were in a position to sacrifice for rearmament, a belief accompanied by the almost ridiculous comparison with sacrifices in the United States.

How can Americans expect French industrial workers to be impressed by the American's sacrifice of a refrigerator when to the Frenchman sacrifice means less money to buy bread because of higher taxes, less work at the factory because of the shift to rearmament, and, according to what the communists tell him, less security from war.

The great policies laid down by the United States since 1948 in the main have been good. But they have been poorly presented to Europe, mainly because so little was understood of what the average European had endured in the past or what he was going through today. Our prayer should be: "Oh, Lord, deliver us from Public Relations Officers."

6. "The Indispensable Man"

"There is the indispensable man," said Arthur Krock after a long conversation with General Eisenhower in Paris early in 1951. He was expressing what hundreds of others also felt: that at that time, when Europe was faced with the prospect of rearmament against Soviet aggression, no one else could do the job.

We know from preceding chapters what the job is. The military objective is to get the men, the planes, the ships and the weapons and then to devise the strategic plans which will insure that, if the worst comes, the Soviet onslaught can be defeated. The political objective, perhaps even more complex and difficult, is to convince the members of the North Atlantic Treaty Organization that they must, at considerable sacrifice to their own economies, make available to Supreme Headquarters men, equipment, planes and ships.

This, of course, is putting the job in the simplest terms. But it is, I believe, the way Eisenhower approaches his task. One of the most remarkable characteristics of this remarkable man is his ability to draw from a mass of evidence in the form of memoranda, schedules and intelligence reports a simple approach to the main problem. His mind is capable of weighing up scores of different facts, each of them vital, and producing a simple equation for solution.

In 1944 this simplicity of approach on the part of Eisenhower was one of the decisive factors in the defeat of the Germans. He was plagued by many brilliant men each offering some panacea for quick victory after the Allied armies had broken out of the Normandy beachhead.

Patton wanted this, Montgomery wanted that and Prime Minister Churchill wanted something else. But Eisenhower saw the war whole. He intended to fight the German Army as far from its main base, Germany, as possible, thus giving the greatly superior Allied air forces the fullest opportunity to impede German communications. This plan would also insure that in battles fought on the perimeter of Germany the full weight of Allied armed strength, operating on relatively shorter lines of communication, would be brought to bear against a German army always short of fuel or food or ammunition and dependent on communications under constant attack.

As a result of the losses suffered by the German armies outside the Reich and of the fearful hammering Germany was taking from the air and from the armies of the Soviet Union on the eastern front, the opposition the Allies encountered once they had struck across the Rhine was far less than had been expected.

Eisenhower's strategic thinking during the tempestuous days of late August, September and October of 1944 also demonstrated not only his ability to reason and handle subordinate generals like Montgomery and Patton but also his inflexibility of purpose in the face of so persuasive an orator as Winston Churchill.

In those days Dwight D. Eisenhower, despite conclusions to the contrary, approached his problems, military and political, with a mind largely conditioned by his military training and experience. My personal experience is that his mind has broadened greatly in the intervening years. The years at Columbia afforded him a chance to study and reflect upon aspects of American and international problems with which he had had only a nodding acquaintance in the past. Lifted out of the somewhat narrow confines of military life, he read a great deal and met a great many men whose importance was only dimly felt by Lieutenant Colonel or even Lieutenant General Eisenhower. The result today is that he is more rounded, more aware of the complexity of problems at home and abroad.

To take one instance, he is aware, as most military men are not, of the tremendous importance of national morale. In production "we have quality and efficiency," he once remarked. "We have to strengthen quantity and continuity. You cannot be strong unless you have economic strength. But morale is terribly important. And morale is going up. The greatest change I see in Europe is the steady rise in morale. And morale means confidence and willingness to work hard and sacrifice now to save the West.

"If we get into the position of two ideologies fighting for men's minds, we will win. Our moral, intellectual and economic concepts appeal more to men than any others. We will win. . . .

"Belief, faith is important," Eisenhower says. "Democracy isn't sophisticated. People have to be educated to make it work, yes, but they also have to have faith and belief as well as education."

Eisenhower is a confident man, although by nature he is not nearly as optimistic as some assume. But he believes the job in Europe can be done and he is quite willing to "use up my credit, if we can make it [rearmament] work."

"Sometimes," he said one day, "I get angry when anything I do is criticized as politics. Of course, lots of things in my job here touch on politics. But what I am trying to do is more important than politics. It is to prepare Europe to save itself."

According to the General, Europe's great shortage in the sphere of morale is leadership, which is "more important than dollars in Europe.

"Let's get the young men persuaded that it is important for them to go out and get interested in persuading Europe to stand together. Let's get them to understand that they have to forget about national boundaries and about watching other nations. Make them think on European terms rather than on French or German or Dutch terms."

Eisenhower, as is customary, was pacing the floor. He picked up a mashie and swung at an imaginary ball, put the club back in the corner and resumed his restless promenade. He picked up a paper, glanced at it, and dropped it on the desk. He poured a glass of water and drank it thirstily.

"Above all, we have to give the people a chance everywhere. If there is one thing I believe in, it's the dignity of the individual. We ought to expect some changes in Europe, give the individual a chance. . . .

"Those Russians. That's a totalitarian state. Everyone knows that but they don't think of what it means.

It means that given freedom, freedom to let the individual develop, they can never stop us."

At another time when he was still at Columbia he mused:

"They come and tell me the Russians have this and the Russians have that. But the Russian problem is always presented to me as though the Russians were a hundred per cent. Don't believe it.

"They have their difficulties same as everyone else. When someone says they have a thousand tanks, I always wonder if that means a thousand tanks all in good shape with all the gas and all the shells and all the mechanics they need. In war it's a good idea to think that the other fellow has everything he needs. That's the way we used to plan operations. But don't let's get worried about it. After all, we're pretty strong, too."

Discussing the shape of things today and the shape of things to come in Europe, Eisenhower strikes a realistic note.

"What we're trying to do," he said recently at his headquarters, "is to develop a mechanism that can preserve peace, that can make it possible for free countries to develop themselves in their social and political objectives for the betterment of all the people living in those countries.

"There is in Europe and the United States and in the free world generally sufficient force, sufficient power and a sufficient array of resources to take care of ourselves and make sure that we are not attacked as long as we are peaceable, don't become aggressive, and as long as we are animated by some basic desire for security toward a common purpose.

"If we will unify ourselves in a common understanding, this thing can be done—" he glanced at the
map of Europe on the wall—"if our hearts are in this
thing, it can be done."

General Eisenhower's insistence that there is no
aggressive purpose to the concept of NATO and
SHAPE has banished many of the fears that were felt
when these first came into being. Again and again,
in cabinet rooms, in headquarters and in hurried press
conferences at airfields, he has said, as he told me
in September:

"I assure you, if there was any possible aggressive
idea, if I were to be used to extend any nation's influence or its prestige, I would not be here now."

What will be the result of Eisenhower's efforts?
He believes that if the free world is granted the time
to gather its strength there will come a time when the
Soviet Union will be ready to weigh "any proposal
for general disarmament," and that once the West is
strong, Russia might be willing to try peaceful co-
existence rather than talk about it.

How strong must the west be to reach this state?

"When we can defend Europe. Then we can talk
reasonably and possibly profitably with the Russians.
You know, none of this is easy. It takes time, it
takes money. It means sacrifices on the part of a lot
of people. But it's a lot better than fighting an ex-
hausting global war. Don't make any mistake about
that."

Eisenhower recognizes the possibility that the
Soviet Union will reject all western approaches toward disarmament.

"Then we've got to maintain what we have. That's cheaper, of course, than getting the materiel, which is what we're doing now, keeping it in good shape and the troops and reserves well trained. You've got to have trained, effective reserves. Then we will balance them in military strength and be far stronger ideologically and in economics. We'll win."

In Eisenhower's opinion, not until early in 1954 will it be possible to contemplate the withdrawal of any United States forces from the continent. By then, he hopes that Europe will have a sound economy and will be able to maintain its collective and individual defense programs without inflation. That means reserves, and "democracies are defended by reserves."

"They are never defended by troops actually in uniform. They cannot be, because since we do not provoke wars, there is no D-Day for us. It is determined by the enemy."

Neither Eisenhower nor any other United States military leader with whom this correspondent talked in the preparation of this book believed that there would ever be a day when all American forces could be withdrawn from Europe. Naval and air bases, and ground troops to protect them, will be necessary for years to come; and both Eisenhower and his Chief of Staff General Alfred M. Gruenther believe that although Europe's basic security must come from within, the United States must continue to help out with air and naval forces.

But under no circumstances do they believe that the number of United States divisions in Europe can be reduced before 1954 at the earliest. Even then it will be a reduction as Eisenhower predicts, at the rate of "a division at a time—no mass withdrawal."

How does Eisenhower see the military problem of how the Russians could be stopped if they attack? Like other military men, Eisenhower admits that Soviet attacks would hit other areas beside his European command, but like all realists he understands that Russian success between the North Cape and the Mediterranean would hurt the western world most.

His first job from the standpoint of actual military preparations in Europe was to broaden the base of Allied defense. This meant moving further to the east the first check line on which the Soviet spearheads could be met and held. A year ago that line was on the Rhine. Today it is being pushed east to run south from the base of the Danish peninsula through Kassel to Fulda, Würzburg, Nürnberg and Regensburg in southern Germany; and as each new division or air group joins the Allied side the possibilities of meeting and checking the Russians along this line increases.

"So we're pushing the base of our defense further east," Eisenhower commented. "We've left the Rhine behind as a frontier. Of course, we have good anchors to the north and south, Jutland and Switzerland. We can hit them hard."

I asked about the pincer tactics envisaged by many European military men. These call for a planned withdrawal in the center, followed by heavy attacks from the north and south by Allied forces.

"It's something to think about," he admitted; "it's what we did in 'the bulge' [the Ardennes battle in December 1944–January 1945] but you have to have the strength. If the German strength is there, that plus the French of course ought to be enough to hold the perimeter so they couldn't get too far west. But I must have the strength. Any planning always comes down to that—'if we have the strength.'"

How much strength? By the end of 1951, SHAPE was counting on ten French, six American and four British divisions, as well as the equivalent of three more divisions supplied by the Belgians, Dutch, Danes and Norwegians, and a Canadian infantry brigade. By the start of the Soviet maneuver period in April of 1952, always the critical military period in Europe, it is hoped that the national contingents of the other nations will be equivalent to five divisions.

At first glance this is a formidable force. Twenty-five western-size divisions with all their ancillary corps and army troops represent about forty-five Soviet-size divisions. The flaw, which we will inspect at greater length later, is that in the case of France the divisions will be well below normal strength. Although the French Defense Minister Georges Bidault pledges the mobilization of the balance of these divisions within forty-eight hours, it leaves a feeling of uneasiness, even though SHAPE relies greatly on reserve strength.

If the European army concept is translated into a workable military force, then the West can expect the addition by the summer of 1953 of twelve German divisions, although if French plans are accepted, these divisions will be considerably smaller than regular United States, British or French divisions.

This, plus German reserve strength, is a formidable reinforcement. The allied armies in western Europe will be reaching that point where the Soviet Union, Eisenhower profoundly believes, will be forced to recast its present policies and try to seek an armistice in the cold war. Such an armistice, if the West is wise and wary, could mean the end of the threat of a shooting war for some years to come.

Of course, confidence in such an outcome does not rest solely on German reinforcement. It rests also upon the improved European morale which both soldiers and politicians believe will flow from the possession of strength. It rests, to a considerable degree, upon the fact that by 1953, the allied air forces on the continent will begin to receive the fruits of the planning and experimentation started in the last half of the 1940's. Britain's *Valiant* jet bomber and *P-1067* jet fighter should be reaching the R.A.F. squadrons in appreciable numbers by then. Pilotless planes and other weapons made in the United States should be transmuted from headlines to service.

Finally there is the prospect that by 1953 atomic weapons will be available for tactical use. If they are, then they will redress the Soviet superiority in manpower. And there are some indications already that, even without atomic weapons in tactical use, that superiority is not as overwhelming as it seemed a year or two ago.

There has been a steady improvement in the performance of orthodox weapons, although precious few of them have reached the United States army in Germany. There is considerable evidence that Soviet equipment in Korea coupled with almost unlimited manpower has not been good enough to win. The mass attacks launched by the Chinese have been halted with progressively higher casualties.

All this, my British friends assert, is forcing the

Russians to re-examine some of their tactical doc-
trines. They are beginning to realize that the tactics
of mass break-throughs at three or four carefully selected points on an enemy line, tactics which were
very effective against the German army of 1944 and
1945, are not so effective against American or British
troops.

For the American and British troops now in Germany are infinitely better armed save in heavy tanks
than the German troops encountered by the Soviet
Army in 1944 and 1945. In addition the two air forces
are larger, although not as large as the Soviet Air
Force, and of a much higher quality than the fading
Luftwaffe of the last two years of World War II.

If the Russians attack in Europe, they must face
the hard central fact that tactics which were successful enough against the brave but poorly equipped
Germans of the closing months of the last war will
not be effective against better equipped and equally
brave American and British troops. Even the initial
Soviet superiority in the air will be overcome.

The question is whether the Soviet High Command
is elastic enough to change its tactics. After all, they
can say, and probably do say, that the men fighting
in Korea are Chinese and North Koreans and not the
Guards divisions of the Soviet Army and that in the
event of war in the west the Russian soldiers will
sweep all before them.

I would wager, however, that there are some staff
majors and colonels in Moscow who are bothering
their chiefs with analyses of what has happened in
Korea and suggestions for changes in Soviet tactical
doctrine. But given the reactionary attitude of any

high command or general staff to changes in the tactics that won the last war, I also would wager that Colonel Ivanovich and Major Stenkov are being told to go away and not bother the Marshals.

The prospect of having 25 divisions for the defense of Europe by the spring of 1952 is far from satisfactory from the standpoint of most Allied senior officers. They want more—soldiers always do—and their estimates of what they must have run to 45, 55 and even 80 divisions.

But it seems to me that too many of them, particularly the French, are thinking of defense in terms of linear defense like the trenches that stretched from Switzerland to the sea in 1914–1918 and the Maginot line of 1939–1940. Younger commanders feel confident that a good deal can be done with something less, although they do not abate their cries for more.

"Let's look at what we've got to face," a young British general said recently. "We've got an army on the other side that's big and even ponderous. Its tactical teaching calls for advances by great leaps, each leap followed by a pause to build up. Chuikov hasn't written me his plans, but I think of it as something like this: one leap to get well into our territory; another to drive us out of our bases east of the Rhine; and then another leap, a hell of a big one, to get across the Rhine."

I asked why there would be pauses between the leaps. This general and others, Americans as well as British, believe that these delays will be forced upon the Soviet command by maintenance and supply troubles.

"You see, this time it will be a mechanized army—

the whole damned thing, not just the tanks and a few crack infantry outfits. Well, mechanization means fuel and spare parts and maintenance. You can't feed a tank or a lorry on the thatch from a house and you can't put a self-propelled gun in the pink by rubbing its hocks. We're a hell of a way ahead of them in our own supply and maintenance arrangements and your people are a good way in front of us. Yet we have to halt occasionally. So will the old Russky. Then we'll give him a knock.

"This time when he leaps there isn't going to be any bloody fool of a Hitler shouting 'The front stays where it is' and ordering people not to give up any ground. He's not going to put great masses of us in the bag. We're more mobile than he is, and when he leaps he's going to land on air. Then we're going to catch him off-balance and hit him. Provided, that is, that those bloody fellows in the air give us some support.

"Of course we need more troops. Got to have them—more of them than we have now at any rate. And 'The Ike' is right when he says we need reserves. But if we can get twenty-five or thirty good, full divisions in here, get 'em trained and equipment somewhere near standard, we'll give the Russky a bellyful. As your chaps say, 'We'll counterpunch them silly.' "

The tactical direction of the men now in the field in Europe is the affair of the local commanders. General Eisenhower busies himself with strategy.

"I don't get more than five or six decisions to make a day," he said ruefully, "but they're all beauts. Feel better, though, now that we've got the headquarters set up outside of Paris. I'm a country boy."

Eisenhower got into the country a lot during the autumn of 1951 when the British, French and United States ground and air forces in Germany staged separate maneuvers. These were occasions he welcomed, not only because they gave him a chance to get out from behind a desk but because he could transfer some of his own confidence in the future to the men in the field.

Fifty times a day he would be out of his car or his jeep to speak to this unit or that. His visits were well prepared.

"Make sure that sergeant knows all the answers about his tank," I heard an American major tell a young lieutenant.

"He's been with it three years," the lieutenant answered; "if he doesn't know them now, he never will."

Even with all this preparation, these chance meetings did a great deal. For Eisenhower has a facility for instilling his own interest, his own confidence in others.

His message basically is this: work hard, learn your job and then eventually "you can go home to your girls and I can go fishing."

"These are the fellows it all depends on," he said one afternoon at the end of a three-day tour. "If they'll work together, co-operate together, then we've laid the foundation. It's more important that these people co-operate in maneuvers than proving their efficiency. That'll come, in fact a lot of these troops are in damned good shape now. The British are always well trained. What we need is continuous working together. Unity's the word."

At times, Eisenhower seems to underrate the difficulty of gaining such co-operation on the governmental level. This springs from the success he has had in the past in pulling co-operation out of Anglo-American headquarters in wartime. He feels, as do many Americans, that the rivalries and jealousies between European powers are petty compared to the danger that faces Europe, and he is encouraged, of course, by the fundamental agreement he finds in other military men.

I do not think the Eisenhower of 1945 would have grasped so quickly the fundamental differences in national economies which directly affect abilities to rearm.

"Look at Norway," he will say, "they've got full employment or mighty near it. If you raised another Norwegian unit, even a small one, it would take men out of productive employment. That's what we can't do. We have to keep the economies stable just as we have to maintain good public morale. Of course, I get worried. The franc and the pound. We just have to keep working together, forgetting ourselves, and we'll do the job."

Eisenhower has been fortunate in his Chief of Staff. General Gruenther is what the army calls "a brain," with more justification than in some cases where the epithet is applied. An incisive mind, an encyclopedic memory and a gift of brilliant exposition are the most apparent parts of his mental equipment.

There was a great deal of criticism when Eisenhower named Field Marshal Viscount Montgomery as his Deputy Commander. A great deal of this criticism, most of it in the United States, results from the rather curious belief that a successful general also must have some of the attributes of a successful politician. It is, of course, gratifying when a man in Eisenhower's position has political maturity, tolerance and insight into the nonmilitary mind. But these are not essential to the successful commander in the field and not even his enemies—and Montgomery has plenty on both sides of the Atlantic—can gainsay his success as a soldier. A general's job, in war, is to win battles. This Montgomery did.

During the years since the war there has been a tendency to underestimate Montgomery. He is a finished soldier. He knows the problems of major command. And, despite his austere exterior, he has retained a genuine knowledge of what makes the soldier tick. He does not praise because he enjoys praise, but because he thinks a man or a unit has earned it.

Not long ago, he remarked that although he had been "somewhat critical" of the French Army in the past—a nugget of British understatement—he had found in watching the French forces during their autumn maneuvers a "tremendous improvement." And "approbation from Sir Hubert Stanley is praise indeed."

The fourth man at the top of SHAPE is General Lauris Norstad, Eisenhower's air commander and commander in chief of the United States Air Force in Europe, another remarkable man. I first met Norstad at a dinner at General Spaatz's villa outside Algiers early in 1943. He was then a Brigadier General, thirty-six years old, vibrant with energy, intelligence and ambition.

In some ways Norstad is very like Eisenhower. He

has the same interest, and almost as much experience in what the commander in chief calls "grand strategy": the co-ordination of economic, political and military requirements, methods and objectives into a complete whole.

He also will have, should war start in the next two years, one of the most difficult jobs in Europe, for he will have to fight three battles at once: the battle for air superiority—with insufficient planes in the theatre; the battle to break through and bomb the concentration areas and immediate communications of the Soviet Group of Armies; and the battle to give allied ground forces something approaching adequate air support for their operations.

Like Eisenhower, he will have a variety of allied forces at his command, British, French, Norwegian and others. But his main reliance must be placed on the United States Air Force in Europe and the Royal Air Force on the continent and at bases in Britain.

There is a good deal in Norstad's make-up to antagonize the common or garden variety of ground general. He is young, he lacks some of Eisenhower's tolerance for the other man's point of view and, in the tradition of Mitchell and Spaatz, he is somewhat oversold on air power. But his fine brain, his energy and his consuming desire to get things done probably outweigh these factors.

The SHAPE command is the top command level in Europe. Under it are three other commands: the Northern Command, embracing Norway, Denmark and the vital North Sea area, under Admiral Sir Patrick Brind of the Royal Navy; the Mediterranean Command, stretching from Gibraltar eastward to Turkey, under Admiral Robert B. Carney, United States Navy; and the Central Command, embracing all western Europe under General Alphonse Juin of the French Army.

From the standpoint of whether Europe stands or falls, the latter is the most important. Both the United States and Britain have put the most into it in the form of men and equipment both for ground and air forces. Its importance can be measured by enumeration of the great military prizes it includes: The Ruhr, the Saar, Lorraine, each a great industrial area; Antwerp, Marseilles, Le Havre and the smaller ports of the French coast; the airfields of Normandy, Belgium and the Netherlands.

If these fall to enemy hands, no war will be easy or quick. But the front line is Germany where the United States is putting forth its greatest effort to deter Soviet attack. Let us consider it not as a country but as a salient point in western defense, which it is today, and as a battleground, which it may be tomorrow.

7. The Seventh Army

The "big picture" in the defense of Europe is best seen at SHAPE. The "little picture," in which the defense of Europe is interpreted in terms of blocking a road or defending a ridge, comes alive only in Germany, and then only if you leave the prosperous cities of western Germany like Düsseldorf and Munich and move eastward to the flat, misty plains in the north or the knobby hills and shallow valleys in the center and south.

If war comes, this is where the first blow will fall.

The difference between the atmosphere along the Königsallee in Düsseldorf and that of the villages along the frontier is startling. Yet a four-hour drive from the cafés, with their sleek, plump women stuffing themselves with cream cakes and the slim, very polite young men, brings you to quiet villages where "they" are only an hour's march away and the eccentric silhouettes of tanks move lumpily over the sodden earth.

The defense of this front line rests mainly on the United States, British and French armies with attached formations from other nations. The largest, most experienced and best trained of these armies is the American Seventh Army commanded by Lieutenant General Manton S. Eddy.

The Seventh Army with its parent organization, the European Command located at Heidelberg, is the basis of American strength in Europe. Unlike the British Army of the Rhine or the French Army of Occupation, the Seventh must fight any opening battle with what it has in hand; it cannot expect quick reinforcement. The British and French forces in Germany may be considered within the pattern of the overall defense effort of those countries. The American forces form a self-contained unit, thousands of miles from their bases in the United States.

The terrain which the Seventh Army would defend and on which it would have to meet any Russian attack is difficult. It is rough, broken by stubby hills and heavy forests. Its eastern perimeter is a mountain wall that runs northwestward along the border of Czechoslovakia, writhes westward at Hof where the frontier of East Germany begins and then turns northwestward again to meet the border of Lower Saxony, in the British zone, at Eichenberg.

This is a big responsibility. During the last half of 1951, French infantry units began to move into the northern area around Kassel and Wetzlar, but the overall responsibility for defense remained American.

The mountain wall on the east and the secrecy with which the Soviet Army in East Germany can envelop its operational planning favor an attacker moving into the area of responsibility of the Seventh Army. Along a frontier this long there can be no question, with the limited forces under Eddy's command, of continuous linear defense. What the Seventh Army has to do is watch the main gaps in the mountain wall through which any large force must move and take its chances with subsidiary forces moving through smaller gaps.

Of these avenues of approach the most important
is the Fulda Gap. This is true not because the gap
is very large but because its eastern end is close to
Eisenach, one of the principal tank depots of the
Soviet Group of Armies, and Eisenach is on a road
network leading eastward to Erfurt, Weimar and
Leipzig. Fulda, at the western end of the gap, is in
the United States zone only 50 miles from Frankfort,
one of the principal American bases, and 70 miles to
the Rhine, a river barrier which is one of the chief
geographical objectives in any move westward by the
Soviet armies.

Further south is the Plauen (Plavno) Gap from
which forces could move against Nürnberg and
Munich, two bulwarks of the United States military
position in Bavaria. There are, of course, other roads
through the mountains. But none of these fulfill the
conditions of width and easy access, both to military
objectives in the United States zone and to supply
bases in the Soviet build-up area, that mark these two
gaps.

The great rivers of Germany, the Rhine and the
Elbe, run north and south. In the area between them,
the first battleground of a new conflict, the most important river in the United States area of defense is
the Main which flows westward to meet the Rhine
near Wiesbaden through Bamberg, Würzburg and
Aschaffenburg. It is not much of a barrier; it can be
forded and it would not be a major impediment to
a Russian army with its ability to build bridges and
rafts quickly, but as the soldiers say, "It beats the hell
out of no river at all."

The Main, heavily held by defensive forces able to

deliver strong counterstrokes at any defender, is one means of channeling a Soviet attack.

Another is the effective use of demolition along the main road and rail approaches from the Soviet zone into the United States area of responsibility. Extensive demolition and mining are tactics which the United States did not have to use often in World War II, but the army learned a great deal about it from the Germans who in Italy and France often, through the intelligent use of demolitions, forced the Allied armies to fight on the terrain chosen by the Germans as easiest to defend.

In the opening phase of any new war the Seventh Army would have to rely on engineers to blow roads, tunnels and hillsides so that the Russian advance would be directed into the areas where American men, guns and tanks would fight in a favorable position. The Russians could leave the roads and the railroads and move through the mountains. This would have been difficult, but not too difficult, for the Russian Army of 1945. It will be much more difficult for the new, heavily mechanized army of 1951. One of the penalties of modern equipment is that it ties an army to the roads and this is particularly disadvantageous to an attacking army.

In the autumn maneuvers of the Seventh Army in 1951, the picture unfolded by the defending divisions was one of a stubborn retreat to a line running north and south just east of Frankfort covering the crossings of the Rhine. From this line, as always happens in maneuvers, the defensive forces launched a successful attack on the "aggressor" army.

Maneuvers are not designed to portray reality but

to afford commanders and troops experience in meeting certain sorts of attack or defense under different conditions. The realistic part of this maneuver lay in the fact that the Russians would almost certainly drive through the United States zone toward the Rhine crossings. At Eisenach, on the frontier of the Soviet zone, they are closer to the great river barrier than anywhere else along the western border of the German Democratic Republic.

Even when the Seventh Army is fully reinforced and has a strength of four infantry divisions and the equivalent of two armored divisions, it will be attacked, in the event of war, by superior Soviet ground forces and by a greatly superior Soviet air force. It will have to give up ground; and it will have to choose a point at which it will stand and an area from which it can counterattack the most dangerous enemy thrusts.

The line of the Main is the area from which an attack could be launched; the point at which the army turns and fights is something which must be selected on the ground at the time. But of course, it cannot be too close to the Rhine lest a sudden Russian leap across the river force the withdrawal of these American troops along the Main.

While we are looking at the probable shape of things to come, this is a good time to remember the advantage which the possession of a large, well-trained airborne force would give an aggressor. If the crossings of the Rhine, like the big Frankenthal bridge south of Worms which was an airborne objective in last autumn's maneuvers, could be seized and held until the Soviet ground troops linked up with the parachutists and glider-borne troops holding the bridgehead, then the whole American—and Allied— campaign in Germany would be thrown off balance.

These conjectures which "might" happen "if" are complicated by the fact that the Seventh Army would not be the only army attacked and that the Allied air forces, whose support or lack of it in this period would be terribly important, perhaps even decisive, will have other calls besides those issued from American headquarters.

We must expect three main attacks into West Germany at the very least: one in the British zone across the north German plain; one in the center, between the Army of the Rhine and the Seventh Army, pointed at Kassel and the autobahn running south toward Frankfort and the Rhine; and a major effort in the American zone with the main thrust aimed through the Fulda Gap plus smaller drives through Plauen and across the Czechoslovakian border further to the southeast.

All these attacks will be preceded by intensive bombing, covered by a numerically superior fighter air force and pushed with all the stolid courage of which the Russian soldier is capable. I am not trying to emulate Dickens' fat boy and make your flesh creep. These are the facts we must accept, face and defeat.

The bright side of the picture lies in the fact that nowhere in Germany, indeed nowhere in Europe, is the defense picture better than in the United States zone.

Two years ago the United States ground forces in Germany comprised the First Infantry Division and

the Constabulary, in all about 41,000 men. At the
time when the Chinese had thrown their weight into
Korea and when it seemed as though the Soviet Union
might try to make another Korea out of Germany,
America was virtually defenseless in one of the key
areas of the world. This is no longer true.

Today the Seventh Army is composed of the First,
Fourth, 28th and 43rd Infantry divisions, the Second
Armored division and the Constabulary, a combat
force, counting divisional and corps troops, of about
150,000 men.

Men and weapons are not enough. Training and
morale count tremendously. Here General Eddy and
his divisional commanders have done a magnificent
job, one too little appreciated by Americans.

When Eddy took over command of the ground
forces in Germany—they were not reorganized into
the Seventh Army until some time later—he was faced
with the task of shaking an occupation army out of
its customary routine and putting it into a state of
alert.

In view of the life of the United States Army in
Germany between 1945 and 1949 this was a sizable
task: movies and bingo, dances and Parent Teachers'
Association meetings, leaves in Garmisch and spring
trips to see the tulips in Holland, bridge parties and
bowling alleys. It was all very nice, very comfortable
and about the worst and most unrealistic preparation
imaginable for service in a situation which might ex-
plode into a Third World War at any moment.

The troops were smart enough. General Clarence R.
Heubner, a strict disciplinarian, had seen to that. But
they, like their officers, were immersed in the pleasant

round of garrison life, plus the attractions of German girls and plenty of beer, both easily obtainable with the adequate pay of the G.I. in Germany. There were maneuvers, very important to earnest young officers and worrying to farsighted older officers, but not great distractions to the amenities of occupation life. The army, in its own words, "never had it so good."

This was the routine and this the atmosphere Eddy had to change. Yet he could not change it too drastically because, as he said, "If you get an army all fired up, you can't keep it fired up. You have to have them in good shape mentally and physically but too much alertness is as bad as too little. The edge wears off and the whole thing flops in your face."

His first major step was to put combat troops on the alert in the field or in barracks roughly one third of the time. The existing field-training system was tightened and amplified. Above all, continuous drills which sent battalions and regiments out into the field from barracks at the sound of a siren impressed upon everyone the idea that someday this might not be a drill, and that the unit and the men that were well trained today would have a better chance of living and winning tomorrow if war came.

Great emphasis was laid on training at the squad, platoon and company level.

"Look here," Eddy says, "the old Germans built themselves a damn fine army. But this isn't a big country, the maneuver areas aren't big. They just didn't have the room to throw corps and armies around. But they licked it by hammering home the essentials down on the level of the small units. Then when they brought

them together into the big units, divisions or corps,
everyone knew his job and the big unit worked well.
Of course there was friction, bound to be. But I think
emphasis on small unit training is one way we can
lick restricted maneuver areas. The other is making
these fellows—the private, the non-com and the officer—know they've got a job to do and that they
ought to be right proud of that job."

Under Eddy, strenuously backed by General
Thomas C. Handy, commander in chief of the European Command, the state of training and alertness of
the two original Seventh Army units—the First Division and the Constabulary—reached a state not seen
among American forces in Europe since the end of
the war. Patrolling of the frontier areas by the Constabulary was combined with training, and the training cycle for the year was interspersed with frequent
unit field exercises, smaller than the annual big maneuvers, which got troops out into the open country
much more often.

Regiments just in from such training would halt in
the midst of cleaning equipment at the sound of a
siren, grab weapons and vehicles and hit the road to
take up defensive positions five or six miles away,
move from position to position twice and three times a
night, and finally return to barracks forty-eight hours
later, profanely sure that there "ain't never no rest in
this army."

All this upset a lot of the customs hallowed by five
years of occupation routine. I saw a mild-mannered
major from the Adjutant General's department ex-
plode when, after a long drive from Nürnberg to
preside over a court martial, he saw the other mem-

bers of the court, the witnesses and the guards—in fact everyone but the prisoner and himself—take off for the hills as the siren sounded.

"Well, major," said the regimental commander, "if you can guarantee the Russians won't upset your court-martial schedule, I won't upset it."

Morale went up instead of down, as a minority had predicted, largely because for thousands of youngsters this, rather than the interminable round of barracks life interspersed with drinking and wenching bouts, was "the army." Not that the Seventh Army soldier lost his taste for beer or women. He just couldn't devote as much time to them any more.

There were other harassments. The rapid expansion of the army in the United States robbed the Seventh Army of many of its best noncommissioned officers. Senior officers, especially early in 1951, noted that with the Navy and Air Forces accepting volunteers, the men sent to the army by conscription were below the educational and intelligence standards of the other services.

Almost since the start of the expansion of the Seventh Army from two divisions to six there have been promises of new equipment and materiel. Some has arrived, most of it has accompanied the three infantry divisions and one armored division that have arrived as reinforcement, but there remains a serious deficiency in medium tanks able to fight the Soviet T-34-85 on equal terms.

The majority of the vehicles in the First Division and the Constabulary have been rebuilt at workshops, and their users claim they are "as good as new." Perhaps this is true for peacetime conditions, but would

it be true in war? Communications equipment, especially field radios, is inadequate.

One thing that strikes anyone familiar with the
army in Germany is the serious wastage of men on
nonessential duties. Listening to the American Forces
Network one afternoon, I learned that the program of
jazz music to which I had listened was sponsored by
the Information and Education Division of the Fourth
Infantry Division

Now the I. and E. has done good work in Europe
with its efforts to tell the soldier why he is where he is
and what he is fighting for. But does it have to assign
men to work out a program of dance music?

The autumn maneuvers of 1951 revealed some of
the strengths and a great many of the weaknesses of
the Seventh Army. Involving over 150,000 men, including a French corps and a field regiment of British
artillery, Exercise Combine was the largest maneuver
to be held in the United States zone since the end of
the war.

"Our greatest weakness," Eddy admitted, "was the
failure to use passive resistance to air attack. By passive resistance the army means camouflage, dispersal
of men and equipment, digging in whenever and
wherever the soldier halts and march discipline when
he is moving."

There were some shocking displays of ignorance of
what air power can do in war. Once along the main
autobahn, the great superhighway running south from
Frankfort toward Munich, which would be a main
artery of supply in war, five gasoline trucks were
bunched while their drivers sat by the road for a com-
radely smoke. Artillery took up positions with nothing

between the guns and the sky but a piece of netting naked of the burlap strips that are supposed to simulate trees and bushes. Tanks stood off the road visible for miles, since only a few branches hid their outline. Tanks, trucks and men gathered at crossroads sometimes for as long as a half hour to chew over a problem.

There is some explanation for the lack of camouflage. The United States civil authorities in the American zone warned the army before the maneuvers that the greatest care must be taken not to destroy crops, trees and plants in the countryside. The troops were told that they must not tear up plants or rip limbs off trees to use for camouflage of tanks and vehicles. This order was rescinded midway through the maneuvers but, like many orders issued in the midst of war games, it did not filter down to the troops.

This sensitivity to complaints by the Germans, who up to that time had not lifted a hand to help themselves in rearmament, does not of course explain the failure to disperse troops and vehicles on the roads.

This is terribly important. For in the first battles of any war fought in Europe in the next two years, the allied armies will fight without air superiority. Under those conditions, passive defense is a necessity. One difficulty, of course, is that there are very few officers or soldiers in the Seventh Army who have ever fought without air superiority. Consequently, there is an almost total lack of understanding of what enemy superiority in the air means to ground forces fighting against it. Neither the troops nor the officers seemed to understand that loitering at a crossroads would, under those conditions, bring on heavy air attack, or that guns and tanks poorly camouflaged and bunched would be singled out for repeated bombing and strafing.

Maneuvers, evidently, do not change much. Kipling, writing about maneuvers in India seventy years ago, noted that troops did things they would never have attempted in war. So it went in Exercise Combine. Tanks moved diagonally across an enemy front. Infantry marched or rode blithely through woods, which in war would have been full of snipers, without throwing out advance parties.

Despite the repeated warnings, there was a tendency to take partisan activity lightly. The day before the maneuvers ended, a group of aggressor partisans showed up at a gasoline and oil depot far behind the front line of the Seventh Army and destroyed it. This made a few believers out of scoffers, but my impression is that generally there is very little understanding of the confusion, delay and damage that partisans can cause in the rear areas of an army fighting in the field.

The Seventh Army like the United States Army as a whole is being rapidly expanded. One result is that reserve officers coming back to service have been promoted rapidly, perhaps too rapidly, and the lower echelon of officers—second and first lieutenants and captains—is inexperienced. The men who came overseas with the new divisions in these jobs are now majors and lieutenant colonels in many cases. Headquarters of the Seventh Army understands this weakness and believes that the rigorous program of unit training now outlined for the incoming divisions—two of which, the 28th and 43rd, are National Guard divisions—will overcome this inexperience.

Most of the difficulties mentioned thus far are inseparable from any force just shaking down, one that includes a very high percentage of men who have never been in combat. One weakness, however, that of automatically assigning to a machine a job a man might do better and quicker, seems to me to result directly from a national trait, our blind faith in machines.

There was a salient example of this in Exercise Combine. A regimental command post separated by only a few miles from another regimental C.P. of the same division, sent an important message by wire to the second C.P. Since it was important, the message had to be coded at one end and decoded at the other. The whole operation took more than five hours and when the information did arrive at its destination, it was out of date. A messenger in a jeep could have taken the message in clear and delivered it in fifteen minutes.

This is another aspect of a general psychological approach which was very evident during the closing months of World War II when, once a German road block was encountered, there was a tendency to call on guns, tanks, and air support to eliminate it; in other words to rely perhaps too heavily on machines. The result was delay, which of course was what the Germans sought, and it seemed to me then, and does now, that we delayed to save half a dozen lives on one day, only to lose two dozen on another because of the delay.

The United States Army, moreover, is just as susceptible as the Russian Army to inordinate worship of the tactics that won "the last time." During both the American and British maneuvers in the autumn of

1951 there was a tendency for armored commanders
of the Seventh Army to dash across country, flanks
exposed and a general attitude of "hell for leather"
enveloping the command.

Now this was all very well under General George
Patton. The Patton flanks were sealed very effectively
by unlimited air power. He was, during most of his
sensational career, pursuing a defeated enemy desperately anxious to disengage and reach strongholds
further east. Patton had more men, more guns, more
tanks and more supplies than the enemy.

In the opening phases of the war the United States
will have to fight if the Russians attack, the conditions
will be exactly reversed. It will be the enemy who
has the superiority in planes, tanks, guns and men.
Under such conditions "Patton tactics," as the young
men who ride the tanks call them, will not be as effective as they were in 1944 and 1945. It will be a period
when the evasion or deflection of enemy blows, con-
cealment and sharp counterattacks necessarily will
be the best tactics.

The Seventh Army has one problem which does not
affect the other Allied forces in Germany: the care of
dependents in the event of attack. The importance of
this problem has been exaggerated but it still is great.

In the event of Soviet attack, Seventh Army and
European Command together will have to care for
well over 100,000 dependents and civilian employees
of the United States government in Germany.

In addition, the moment the blow falls, hundreds of
thousands of Germans, deeply aware from their own
experience of Russian savagery in war, will take to
the roads and move westward. Anyone who experi-

enced the campaigns in Belgium and France in 1940, as I did, realizes the tremendous burden which refugees of any kind impose upon an army fighting in the field. Roads are clogged and efforts to keep refugee traffic on certain ones are frustrated by enemy machine gunning of those roads, which forces the refugees onto the highways being used by the army. Transport, medical facilities and food have to be assigned to refugees. In addition, the refugees are not all what they seem. Thousands of those who poured westward from eastern France and eastern Belgium in 1940 were German agents and saboteurs. The Russians are not novices at war and presumably they will play the same trick.

The evacuation of dependents—wives, children and other relatives of fighting men—and civilian employees and their families from the United States zone will be a tremendous job, involving at least 20,000 soldiers who could be put to better use. Early in 1951, it was estimated that it would take twenty-one hours to evacuate American dependents and civilian employees from one city, Munich. The time has been lowered progressively as better arrangements have been completed.

But European Command in the autumn of 1951 decided not to bar travel to Germany of the families of the new divisions reinforcing the Seventh Army. The number of dependents is rising, and the question of how quickly they can be evacuated in the event of war remains one of the most worrying facing the American command.

Some authorities believe that losses will be as high as thirty per cent due to enemy bombing and machine gunning. Others feel that there will be enough time before the blow falls to get dependents out of Germany.

This idea is favored in the British Army of the Rhine which is not as heavily encumbered with dependents as the Seventh Army. The British, looking at the situation from the military viewpoint, believe that there will be "some days' " warning before any Soviet attack. Consequently, although they have units in advanced positions, they do not spend as much time on border patrolling as do the Americans, preferring to train units in roles to which they will be assigned should war come.

One factor which must be accepted is that in the event of a Soviet invasion, the enemy will have copious information about the location of various allied units, depots and airfields. No one can screen 50,000,000 Germans and, as a result of the undoubted presence in West Germany of thousands of spies for the Soviet Union, the first day of attack would see enemy bomb strikes on the major installations and troop concentration areas in the United States zone. The counter-espionage agencies of the American authorities in Germany have done their best, but we have been employing Germans in our zone almost since the start of the occupation and it would be a bold C.I.C. agent who would say that the German employees of the United States Army in Germany are "clean."

Of course, this cuts the other way, too. From the outset, the Soviet armies of occupation have been more dependent on German help than have the allied armies. Although these Germans, too, have been screened by Russian counterespionage agencies, there is a good deal of reason to doubt the efficiency of this screening. Moreover, the Russian military establishment in Germany has been larger than those of the allies and has needed the help of indigenous industry a great deal more. Soviet tanks and guns are repaired and Soviet trucks rebuilt in German factories.

Finally, although the western powers are not loved in western Germany, they are not hated the way the Russians are in the east. Such hatred inspires many to espionage. A lot of the information they send through is of doubtful authenticity, but some is very valuable indeed. Much of what we know about the Soviet Army as a whole is based on German reports about the Russian forces in East Germany.

Obviously, the United States Seventh Army faces many problems and has many weaknesses to overcome. But there are two salient points in its favor: already it is a greatly improved army in numbers, training, some equipment and morale over that which guarded the front line of the western world in early 1951; and a rigorous training program and steady reinforcement provide the basis for optimism for the future. The enlisted men are of very high caliber, physically and mentally. I doubt if any army in history has ever had so many men in its ranks with high-school and college degrees. The officers are improving on the lower echelons and are very good at the top.

What the Seventh Army needs is within the power of the people of the United States to give. It is shocking to realize that soldiers representing the foremost industrial power of all time would have to go to battle tomorrow less well armed than their enemies. Think that one over the next time you worry whether there will be enough television sets next year. The Seventh Army needs modern arms and equipment now. The Russians are not going to be frightened by tall stories in the headlines about wonder-working, new equipment. Certainly, they are not going to be deterred. The only time such weapons will cause them to blink an eye will be when the weapons are here in Germany, ready to be used against them.

The Seventh Army has been fortunate in its commander. Matt Eddy is the kind of soldier and general evidently missed by Messrs. Mailer and Jones.

He is a wise, cool tactician who commanded the Ninth Infantry Division and the XII Corps during World War II. In a command which contained a high percentage of glory hunters, he was economical and wary until he saw the moment for attack. Then he hit very hard.

I never saw him flustered. One day he returned to headquarters of the Ninth Division looking as though he'd been rolled in the mud. There was blood on his shoulder.

"Oh, one of our battalions poked its neck out a little too far," he told his anxious staff, "so, of course, the Germans tried to step on it. But they remembered what they'd been taught and took a bite out of the enemy's foot. Nothing to get excited about. Picked up a couple of wounded and brought them back in the jeep. That's all. Long as we remember our training and don't get excited, we're going to be all right. Soldiers like these, they learn good and fast."

Eddy is a big, bulky man of sixty, still agile enough to go through a night infiltration course incognito.

"Put your ass down, soldier," a sergeant said to Eddy

as they scrambled over the muddy earth with lines of tracer bullets above them. "It is down, sergeant," said the General.

Eddy is a disciplinarian but without bite. Riding together in a jeep last spring, he was exasperated by the behavior of an M.P. in the preceding jeep who waved Germans to the side of the road with imperious gestures. Eddy is not mealy-mouthed, but he swears naturally and not for effect as some other generals do. When, at the end of our trip, he climbed out of the jeep and headed for the M.P., I prepared to hear a classical chewing out.

Not at all. Eddy took the M.P. by the arm.

"Soldier," he said, "these people along here aren't trying to hold us up. But it's mighty hard work getting an ox or a horse to move over fast. You just try it. And you want to remember that we want to have these folks as allies. Doesn't do any good to holler at them and talk tough. They got a bellyful of that from their own army. Just take it easy, soldier, just take it easy."

Eddy has an almost instinctive success with soldiers. A lot of generals try to be fatherly and talk about "my boys." I never heard the phrase pass Eddy's lips, but he talks to soldiers in a direct, homespun manner that achieves its purpose of putting the words across. And he is no different when he talks to other generals or to anyone else.

One day not long ago, he was wandering around the maneuver area at Graffenwoehr.

"Sergeant, you think a recoiless rifle that size is going to do you any good?" he asked.

The sergeant, warmed by such informality, said

that he thought it would do him as much good as a pea shooter in battle.

"That's about it," said Eddy. "Thanks, sergeant." And he wandered off.

One day this winter I climbed a hill and stood on the top facing east. It was clear and the thin sun touched the chocolate fields and the deep green woods. To the right an American tank waddled through a farm village and a company of infantry stumbled through the fields around the village. There was a rattle of rifle fire from some of the defenders on the hill. The wind brought us the labored breathing of the tank in the village.

"Lie down, you guys," said the sergeant commanding the platoon holding the crest of the hill. "Don't let them see you."

He was about twenty-four, very serious.

"You see," he explained, "these guys are supposed to be Russians coming from down that road, that's where they'll probably come anyhow, so it's good practice, see? So we let them come, the first bunch, and then blow that bridge and then hit them when we catch them around that draw."

This is where it all ends. This is the ultimate expression of what the west is doing. The long deliberations in quiet offices in Washington, London and Paris. The statesmen solemnly scratching signatures to pacts and treaties. The generals planning on the big maps and noting production figures and tables of organization. The man at the machine in Detroit or Pittsburgh. The awkward squads marching and countermarching in some dusty prairie camp. It all comes down to this: a line of men on the crest of a hill, waiting to fight as men have waited on hilltops since first they went to war; a line of hills with a gap through which the enemy may come; quiet farming villages, as were Gettysburg and La Haye Sainte.

If we are strong enough these Americans in the cold on the hilltop may not have to fight. If we are strong enough. In the Seventh Army, the United States has made a good beginning toward strength in Europe. Its men and its officers can do a great deal. But the balance of the job is up to the people of the United States. And to our allies. For the defense of Europe is not solely an American responsibility or even an American and continental responsibility. Let us look at the British.

8. Britain Will Fight!

Not long ago an old friend, a distinguished commentator on foreign affairs, asked me if I thought that, in the event of war, the British would fight. The question startled me. Everyone knows there has been a decay of British economic, political and military power since 1945. This has increased our own burden as the leader of the West. Indeed, had Britain emerged from World War II as strong as it was at the end of the First World War, it is doubtful whether there would have been a cold war.

The question is almost natural in the topsy-turvy world of today. In this strange world, our former allies in Russia are our most implacable foes. This has forced many people to conclude that our foes of the last war can be counted as trusted allies, a conclusion that under certain conditions can be extremely dangerous. Granted the distaste with which most Americans viewed the Labor Governments of 1945–1951, it is understandable that some people viewing the decline of British power would ask whether the British, our unquestioned allies of a decade ago, will fight.

The answer, of course, is yes.

They will not only fight, if war comes, they will fight harder and more skillfully than any other nation ranged on our side. But they will fight as allies, not as vassals.

A great deal of the anti-Americanism in Britain,

which is as strong among the Tories, although better concealed, as it is in the Labor Party, springs from the conviction that the United States has not appreciated sufficiently what Britain did in the last war, the conditions under which its people have lived since 1945 and the rearmament effort it is making today. When the comments on Britain of our less inhibited Congressmen or the attacks on her in some newspapers are cabled back to London, it is not surprising that the British feel they are being discounted as an ally, that their right to speak on their own behalf in defense matters has been disregarded and their condition depressed to that of a very junior partner.

The British character is so much a part of rearmament, moral and physical, that it is surprising more attention has not been paid to the manner in which, in the past, it has come to the rescue of the United Kingdom. People have been counting the British out since 1797. In 1939, when first I came to London, a lot of correspondents and writers on international affairs were writing articles and books, very interesting ones, too, proving that Britain was finished.

Their subject matter would sound familiar today: the failure of the British economy to keep up with the rest of the world, the amateur soldiers of England compared to the massed legions of totalitarianism across the Rhine, the casual acceptance of danger by the British as the summer of 1939 wore on toward war. So it is today.

Of 1940, we remember Dunkirk and the Battle of Britain. We have forgotten the great renaissance of national energy that provided the sinews of war, the unknown people who worked day in and day out until they collapsed beside their machines, the stubborn courage that endured the first great air attacks of the war. These as much as the leadership of Churchill or the gallantry of the young men of the R.A.F. were of the quality of Britain in adversity; these too should be remembered.

Since the high noon of victory in 1945, the state of Britain has been poor. The British have taken economic disaster as they take all disaster, with a certain grim humor that reflects Arthur Murphy's remark of two hundred years ago: "The people of England are never so happy as when you tell them they are ruined." But they do not like their present economic straits and they are making and will make frantic efforts to improve their lot. In this we must help. For these are the people, perhaps the only people, on whom we can count.

It reflects a certain ignorance of the world to express surprise that the British are not happy over rearmament. Why on earth should they be?

Just as they seemed to be making some headway in restoring their economy, rearmament became necessary and the economy received another jolt. Just as the social benefits which the people wanted were becoming a fact, some of these benefits had to be curtailed. Just as they had hoped that the shadow of war had been lifted, again it crept across the channel to lay its somber fingers on the great cities and smiling countryside.

This unhappiness over rearmament, like anti-Americanism, is not the property of the Labor Party alone. I have heard as scathing criticism of United

States policy in the dining rooms of the West End as ever I heard in the pubs of the East End. The difference is that the Conservatives, by and large, were quicker to awaken to the menace of the Soviet Union. A strange exchange of alertness; for fifteen years ago, the Laborites generally were quicker in their appreciation of the danger of Hitler and German rearmament than the mass of the Conservative party, with the salient exceptions of Churchill, Eden and Duff Cooper. Of course, Labor did very little about it.

"Whether we like it or not, we have to be part of the rearmament effort," a Tory leader said during the Foreign Ministers conference of May, 1950. "When they announced they had the atomic bomb, it ended the last vestiges of our isolation. We have to keep them as far from England as possible, we have to be prepared to keep troops in Europe for indefinite periods, something we never did before. But we don't like it; why should we?"

The recurrent phrase "we don't like it" perhaps has led to the belief in the United States that the British ability to fight, if war comes, is in doubt. It is not, it never was. But if an American considers the position of Britain in a new world war, he will understand why no Englishman "likes" rearmament.

Primarily, it is because rearmament in the minds of most Englishmen, and in the minds of most Europeans, too, always has been a preliminary to war. The politicians and the generals have used the phrase "We must be strong to keep the peace," so often; then a year or two later have led their people to war. No one really believes it any more.

War for Britain, another war, means ruin. What the bombs of the Germans began, the bombs of the Russians will finish.

"Where will we be after another four or five years of austerity, another four or five years spending and fighting and working like mad?" the British ask. So you ask, what they will do if the balloon goes up?

"Naturally, we'll fight and we'll give the Russians a damned good hiding," they say in Mayfair or the county clubs in the country. And in the farming villages and the smoking dirty factory towns of the north they say:

"Those Russians, hurt the workingman all over the world, they have. Making a mockery out of socialism, that's what they've done. If it comes, we'll have to fight and we'll fight just like we always do and get no credit for it from you Americans when it's over."

There is, you see, a curious blend of military optimism and economic pessimism. A queer people, but a great one.

Although the British government has agreed to the main rearmament measures proposed by the United States as the best means of deterring the Soviet Union from war, it never has been as apprehensive about the imminence of war as the United States government. This does not spring, as some think, from any fondness for the Soviet Union on the part of officials of the Labor Party—there were few more outspoken anti-Communists than Ernest Bevin—but from the appraisal of the British intelligence services.

These services enjoy and deserve a world-wide reputation. We know when they have been wrong; errors such as the Fuchs case or the Pontecorvo escape are well publicized. Less is said about their triumphs, which are many and varied.

When early in 1950 the drive toward rearmament was getting under way in Europe, I lunched with a high official of British intelligence in London. Here is the way he saw the Soviet Union and the chances of war, then.

"Frankly, I think your fellows are too much impressed by the size and strength of the Soviet Army. Of course, it's big, the biggest in the world and you chaps almost worship bigness. But, you know, war isn't fought by armies. It's fought by peoples and nations and we don't think the Russian nation is as strong as the size of the army indicates.

"For one thing, you discount the effects of the war on the Soviet Union. That's natural enough. You've never been occupied or destroyed. We weren't occupied here, but we were knocked about a bit. And we know from our own experience, with a hundred times the technical skill and available manufactured materials at hand than the Russians had, that it's a long difficult job.

"Think of their casualties. They were terrible. What did Stalin estimate in 1945, about seven million, wasn't it? Well, you don't recover from such losses in a hurry. Certainly you don't recover fast enough to challenge the United States and this country in war six or seven years later. Of course, the political challenge is there, it always has been since the revolution. They tucked it away in the closet in 1941 when they needed help, but we were enemies then just as we are enemies now."

The official was not complacent.

"They're making the world hell," he continued. "I get so tired of people saying that what the Russians are doing is the result of western misunderstanding. We understand them only too well.

"We get reports from all over the world, from Australia to Iceland. In every single place their objective is the same: to destroy the influence of the West in the economy and the politics of the country. You can say that this does not mean war. To me it is just as much a preparation for war as the construction of tanks and aircraft. The war is coming, all right, but my own guess is that it won't be along until about 1955.

"These governments like Stalin's, or Hitler's for that matter, are all wound up inside. They have to keep moving. Since 1945, this Russian government has kept moving by political means. But although we will never stamp out communism in France or Italy or India, we are making it impossible for communism to get power without the use of force.

"Now those chaps in the Kremlin have to win power, more and more power. They live on it. And someday, somewhere they are going to find that they have to use force to get power in a really important country, say Italy or Germany. When they do that, it will be war. But not for some time. And not until they believe they are forced to use military instead of political means. In the meantime, they'll do everything they can to make people all over the world believe they stand for peace. Theirs is a sort of black mass of politics, a complete perversion of everything men have believed in for centuries. We will have to stamp it out just as we stamped out Hitlerism."

This is the broad, undetailed analysis of a chilling world situation. Its virtues are those of the British people in their approach to the problem of meeting the Russian danger, a lack of hysteria, a consciousness of the political danger and a more analytic view of the Soviet Union's strengths and weakness than is customary among the more violent politicos of Washington.

Now it is easy to construe such virtues as faults; complacency and blindness have been charged against the British. This raises the question of whether, after five years of war and seven of austere self-denial, the heart of the British nation remains sound. If it were not, then all our fears over anti-Americanism, sentiment against rearmament and political blindness would be justified.

The last fifteen years have taxed the British people's resources of endurance and courage as they have never been taxed before, not even under the hammer blows of Napoleon and the appalling losses of the Somme and Passchendaele in World War I.

The war fell heavily on all. The peace, six years of socialist rule and recurrent economic crises imposed staggering burdens on the middle class. And although it has been the custom of intellectuals in Bloomsbury to sneer at the middle class, it was the sons and daughters of this class who fought the Empire's battles in the two world wars and it was the fathers and mothers who kept alive, in the midst of bombs and fire, the standards for which men fought and died.

The leveling process of socialism took away, or tried to take away, all that generations of constant

endeavor had brought this class. The value of investments and pensions melted. The homes so zealously
guarded became down-at-heel and grimy. The financial task of sending the boys to public schools became
too great for all but the rich. The class hung on,
fighting grimly at the polls, but it has received a
grievous blow.

If it goes, something British goes with it. This is
not the Britain of night clubs, young guards officers
and titled gentry. This is the Britain of small homes,
unbending courtesy and tiny snobberies. It is also the
Britain that sent its youth to die in the air over England in 1940, that saw uncomplaining its savings go
for the great national effort of that year, that stood
when the earth was shaking and was embarrassed
by its own courage.

It may be, as the socialists say, that the great
improvement in the lot of the industrial masses will
compensate Britain for the ebbing vitality of this
class. The people who work the great mills and industrial plants of the north and the Midlands undoubtedly are better fed and more prosperous than
their fathers of a generation ago. But has this improvement been accompanied by the growth of responsibility to the country or, as many fear, has the
class war bitten so deeply into the fabric of British
society that it will never again be possible to unite
the British people in a great national effort?

We would be foolish not to consider such questions. But we are equally foolish not to accept as well
the strengths of Britain in this time of trouble.

Honesty in public life, reverence for the law, love
of political liberty, all these have survived war and

austerity. The British people were slow to recognize the danger of Hitler. But when they did recognize it, what a formidable antagonist they became. Similarly they have been slow to accept the Soviet danger. This, I believe, results partly from the fact that the Soviet-British alliance of 1941–1945 was much more deeply felt in Britain than in the United States. The attack on Russia gave Britons a breathing spell and they were grateful for the Soviet resistance to the Germans. Similarly, having been bombed themselves, they had a better understanding of what the Russians were going through than did the Americans.

Yet if slow to accept the Soviet danger, I believe the British people have accepted it now. There is a strong streak of fatalism in the character of the islanders. They are accustomed at stated times to fight in the defense of what they believe in, although the custom has never become popular. They will go to war without abundant ballyhoo, there will be little flag waving and no one is going to shout joyfully about a crusade.

But, as is their custom, they will fight until they have won or there is no one left.

Britain ended World War II with powerful armies in Germany, Italy, India, Burma and Malaya. Thousands of ships flying the White Ensign of the Royal Navy were at sea from Scapa Flow to Tokyo Bay. Heavy, medium and light bombers and swarms of fighters rose from a thousand airfields scattered across the world. The nation behind this great military effort was more fully mobilized than any other American ally. In addition, there was the Indian Army, the largest volunteer army on the Allied side, with its 2,000,000 men.

In the new battle to fight economic decay all this power was swept away. "Far called," the carriers and cruisers returned to England to be broken up or to be put into storage. The great bombers rusted on the airfields and the armies flowed back toward England and the dubious delights of peace. If the United States started from scratch on its rearmament program, Britain began five yards behind the line.

What have the British contributed to the material rearmament of the West? Much more than we know, for the British have not publicized their rearmament as the French have theirs.

By the end of 1952, the British Army is to be raised to a strength of ten regular and twelve Territorial (National Guard) divisions, or about 375,000 combat soldiers. Eisenhower will have available by the middle of 1952 five British regular divisions in Europe and will be able to tap three more regular divisions in Britain and the twelve Territorial divisions, should they be needed on the continent.

This is an impressive force especially when the quality of the troops is considered. Also, it should be remembered that the units sent to Germany, unlike those in some of the continental armies, are up to strength. When the British put a battalion into an operation, it is a battalion, not two companies and the skeleton of a third.

When rearmament began, the British Army of the Rhine in Germany was at about the same strength as the United States Seventh Army; i.e., two divisions.

Attached to it were a Belgian army corps with a strength equivalent to one weak division, a Danish brigade and a Norwegian brigade.

The two original divisions were the Second Infantry Division and the Seventh Armored Division. The latter had a long and glorious record in World War II. It fought the Germans and Italians back and forth across the sandy wastes of Libya, then pursued the broken Afrika Korps after Alamein and was one of the finest armored divisions of the Allied Expeditionary Force in Europe. Rejoicing in the nickname of "the Desert Rats," the Seventh Armored has maintained a high state of training and morale throughout its service in Germany.

The first sizable British reinforcement was the 11th Armored Division. This was followed by the Sixth Armored Division.

By the end of 1951, Britain had four regular divisions in Germany to defend some of the most inviting terrain in Europe. The territorial responsibility of the British Army of the Rhine runs from the base of the Danish peninsula south to the northern boundary of the United States zone. Aside from the hills around Minden, the territory is largely flat, rolling countryside. Through the center of it, past the cities of Hanover and Brunswick and making directly for the Ruhr, runs the autobahn from Berlin.

The nature of the ground precludes any chance of channeling a possible Soviet attack. The Russians could invade almost anywhere along the frontier without encountering a terrain feature on which the British could base a defense until, in the center, they encountered the hills around Minden. These are ap-

proximately one hundred miles west of the border of
the Soviet zone.

But, as I have pointed out in an earlier chapter,
the geographical character of any Russian attack in
Germany is almost predetermined by the location of
the main objects of that attack, the Ruhr and the
Rhine crossings.

In mapping their defensive tactics, the British
have to count on the probability that any Russian
attack would move westward across the flat country
north of the line Bielefeld-Hanover-Brunswick with
the left flank extended to cover the main autobahn
into the Ruhr and the right flank moving rapidly
across the north German plain, dropping off army
corps to take the great ports of Bremen and Hamburg.

Gathering momentum, the right flank would turn
southwestward as it neared the Dutch border and
prepare for its first sizable geographical barrier, the
mouths of the Rhine.

The whole operation in this area of British responsibility would be accompanied in all probability by
more direct penetrations through the United States
sector aimed at the Rhine crossings there. Seen
against the map of Europe, such an operation is not
unlike, although its proportions are greater, the
famous plan of Graf Von Schlieffen which the Germans used at the outbreak of the 1914–1918 war.
In the projected Soviet plan, as in the Schlieffen plan,
all depends on keeping the right flank strong so that
once the upper Rhine is crossed the Soviet divisions
pushing southward will have enough strength to push
swiftly to the envelopment of the Ruhr. It would be

a big plan, a bold one. But the Russians, like Americans, like to "think big."

The British plans to meet a Soviet attack necessarily are shrouded in secrecy. However, certain principles of an active defense against an enemy with superiority in everything except courage, ingenuity and generalship have emerged from recent British maneuvers.

First and basic is the reaction against any type of linear defense. "Even if we had all the soldiers in the world," one British staff officer said, "we wouldn't try it. Think what happened to the French in 1940."

British dispositions will be arranged, then, so that the main mass of maneuver will be husbanded beyond the immediate area of battle with only light armored forces and some motorized infantry plus the R.A.F. planes to harass the oncoming Soviet columns.

One of the difficulties of such a tactical plan, however, is that the British responsibility includes not only the defense of Germany against any drive to the west, but the protection of the Danish peninsula. Unless Danish military strength increases rapidly, this is an inevitable responsibility and it will mean the diversion of a considerable force from the five British divisions of the Army of the Rhine.

In the event of war, the Allied high command will be faced with the difficulty, facing all such commands, of deciding what can and what cannot be held. The Allies cannot be strong everywhere.

The British Army, now systematically rebuilding for the defense of Europe, is the first peacetime British army to include a very high percentage of

National Service (conscripted) soldiers. The "old armies" that held and died in 1914 and 1940 were very largely regular armies plus a sprinkling of reservists. This is a different type of force.

In some infantry units the National Service soldiers make up as high as 65% of the enlisted men. The percentage is somewhat lower in the armored divisions and the officers hope that the introduction of better pay and greater amenities—this was done in 1950—will eventually produce an army in which only about 45% of the men in the infantry divisions and 35% in the armored divisions are conscripts.

Whatever the eventual percentage, it is pleasant to write that the morale of the British National Service man is good. He does not like leaving home for two years service in the army any more than does the French or Belgian conscript. But once he is in, he does not sulk.

Pondering this difference between the British and the continental conscript, some American officers have come to the conclusion that the regimental system of the British Army is the cause for the greater interest of the British recruit.

"I used to chuckle over such things as distinctive cap badges and regimental customs and traditions," one distinguished American soldier said, "until I realized that it all has a definitely good effect on the young fellow joining the service.

"He's not just a recruit in an army, you see. He becomes part of a tradition that goes back hundreds of years. He has a new home. I heard a young officer on their maneuvers tell a bunch of youngsters they mustn't let the Green Howards down. And they didn't. They had moved from one family circle at home to another out here.

"So I've come to the conclusion it's a damned good thing. And it's not just the kids coming in; look at the things that regiments like the Gloucesters do in war after war, century after century. Some of that sort of tradition won't hurt anybody."

The state of training of the British divisions is very high, much higher than that of any of the continental powers. Indeed, were it not for the pinchpenny policies of the War Office in London, it would be as high as that of the veteran American divisions in Germany. But the War Office and the Treasury have combined to keep the Army of the Rhine short of equipment and consequently there has not been as much field training as the officers desire.

Morale was once defined as the state in which the private believes that his squad is the best in the platoon, his platoon the best in the company, his company the best in the regiment, so on up to the point where there is an absolute belief in the ability of *his* army to knock the spots out of any other army in the world.

If the definition is true, and I think it is, then the morale of the British Army is high. During the autumn maneuvers it was evident again that although the British private admires some articles of American equipment and is by turns envious and amused on the subject of American amenities for troops in the field, he refuses to believe that there is any other army or nation that can touch his.

This occasionally irritates Congressmen who expect slavering gratitude and adulation, but it is a very suitable sentiment in allies.

When rearmament in Britain got underway, the British Army was weapon and equipment poor with one important exception. It had the Centurion tank, a magnificently machined fifty tonner. As this is written, the Centurion Mark III with its 20-pounder gun, low silhouette, heavy armor and stabilizer is the best tank in the Allied forces in Germany.

The British also have stepped up the fire power of their infantry battalions and have introduced the 17-pounder antitank gun, a notable weapon of the closing years of World War II to infantry battalions.

With rearmament the Rover, the British version of the jeep, is coming into service, there is a flow of new trucks and cannon, and the outlook generally is far better than in the continental forces. One reason is that maintenance is good although the British to a greater degree than the Americans rely on German help in the maintenance of their motorized equipment.

During the autumn maneuvers of 1951, the Army of the Rhine appeared well trained, enthusiastic and alert. In general, its soldiers seemed to be more aware than those of other armies that what they were doing might become real.

March discipline on the roads was excellent, camouflage very good. When the British infantryman was told to dig in, he really dug. I asked a sergeant how this had been accomplished.

"Well, we have a lot of old-timers who remember what it was like in France and the desert before the R.A.F. got the upper 'and, as you might say," he replied. "So we tell these lads about that—bloody convincing the sergeant major is—and when they get out 'ere, they really dig. There's a whole squad along that fence there but you didn't see them, I'll bet, until you stopped the car."

On maneuvers, as in life, the British tend to take things more casually than do Americans. There is less of the "die for dear old Rutgers" atmosphere around unit headquarters, but no one seemed any the less efficient for that. On the other hand, British units seemed easier to surprise on the maneuvers and less capable of swift movement. One American armored unit complained that they seemed "to take forever" to get started, but admitted that once underway the British "kept at it all day and all night if necessary."

Staff work in the maneuvers, in which the problem was to check and then counterattack an invading force, was very good and the troop movements, although somewhat slower than those of the Seventh Army, were competently managed. The British remain cautious in the opening phases of any operation and for those watching their army in the field for the first time, it is difficult to reconcile this caution with those sudden flare-ups of aggressive combativeness that marks the Briton in battle.

Physically, the British soldier is not as impressive as the American. He usually is shorter and moves more slowly. But he has a great deal of endurance, plus a phlegmatic mind that enables him to concentrate on the job on hand without undue speculation about what may happen an hour in the future.

A good deal of space has been devoted to the British Army, principally because it is one of the forces on our side that has been consistently underestimated since rearmament began. This underestimation results from our own pride, natural enough, in the brilliant achievements of American troops in the second World War; and from six years of criticism of British military leaders by American writers.

It seems to me that in the present period of grave danger, some effort must be made to put the record right. Someone should point out that although Montgomery was an irascible, self-centered man—none of our generals suffered from these bad qualities, of course!—he was also a consistently successful general. The point should also be made that Field Marshal Alexander had a record of brilliant success from 1940 to 1945 in commands ranging from divisional commander to theatre commander and that dozens of younger British commanders fought with distinction all over the world.

The worst result of the criticism of the British generals has been the tendency of the average reader in the United States to identify this supposed ineptitude in the higher ranks with inefficiency and lack of determination in the rank and file of the British Army.

Nothing could be further from the truth. And some of the writers of the critical essays know it. Why they have not corrected this impression is beyond me, especially as they are well aware of the tremendous importance to the future of the United States of a resolute British ally.

One British service, fortunately, has escaped the spitballs. This is the Royal Air Force. Today, the Royal Air Force again is making a heavy contribution to European defense; tomorrow, if the new fighter and bomber types now going into production live up to expectation, that contribution may be very great indeed.

It is pleasant to find that so many of the young men of the R.A.F. in 1940 have survived the war, and the peace, to emerge a decade later as tactical commanders of the R.A.F. The present fighter force in Germany of 15 squadrons—it will be a good deal larger by the middle of 1952—is not as big as the R.A.F. would like it to be. But its men are as good as any fliers in Europe.

The fighter squadrons scattered over northern Germany now are organized into the Second Tactical Air Force, R.A.F. They are flying *Vampire V*'s and *Meteors*, the latter as photo reconnaissance planes.

Neither of these aircraft is as good as the *Sabres* which the U.S.A.F. are flying in Korea, but not, up to the autumn of 1951, in Germany. Nor are they as good as the *P1067* made by Hawker which the R.A.F. believes will prove to be the best fighter in the world.

Group Captain "Johnny" Johnson, who ended World War II as the highest scoring ace in the R.A.F., had something to say about his aircraft.

"The 'Vamp' is a fine plane for the job now, that is ground support. It's maneuverable, carries plenty of stuff and fast enough for that sort of work.

"But of course, if the balloon goes up, we'll have to have something a great deal better to deal with the best Russian fighters. We think that will be the Hawker. It sounds wonderful in tests. But we need it here. The sooner the better."

Thus an experienced and well-known airman states

flatly one of the most troublesome problems facing the British and American ground and air commanders in Germany: Is the air force mission, in the event of war, the destruction of the enemy air force or is it the protection of the ground forces?

This one is a good problem to chew over. Later, in a final summation of our strengths and weaknesses in the defense of Europe, it can be treated at length.

No experienced airman on the flying side, American or British, showed much enthusiasm over ground support. That, they thought, could come later. What they want to do, and expect to be ordered to do, is go up and claw the enemy fighters and bombers out of the skies. And because we would be fighting, in the opening phase of any conflict at least, without superiority in numbers, although we are pretty certain to have qualitative superiority in pilots and, perhaps, aircraft, the question is as vital as any facing the Allied High Command today.

9. France—Problem Child of the Atlantic Alliance

France is the problem child of the Atlantic alliance. The whole western world relies heavily on the fortitude, skill and endurance of the French Army, which is to be the largest NATO army. And, since an army represents the people from whom it is drawn, we are also relying on the French. If, in the event of attack, France goes, the rest of Europe goes with it. If France will not make the effort necessary to raise a force strong enough to help make Europe militarily independent, then Europe will not become militarily independent. So much depends on this wayward daughter of the nations.

Why is France a problem? The soldier says because her divisions are undermanned and poorly trained. The politician says because she has no stable government and no prospect of one unless it is a highly dangerous dictatorship of the right under General Charles de Gaulle. The economist says because wages are too low, the custom walls too high or, since economists disagree as often as politicians, because the wages are too high and the customs barriers too low. Each answer is part of the truth, yet the reason for France's difficulties is less easily definable. It goes deeper; its roots are not in statistical charts but in men and women, the French.

A young French diplomat in Bonn was talking of

his experiences in the war when he was a junior officer in General Leclerc's armored division.

"In my company almost everyone had escaped
from France during the German occupation. There
was nothing, really nothing we would not do for
France. There was dedication.

"All through our forces one found little groups
like that. We were not trained soldiers, no. But we
became good soldiers when we were trained because
we believed. Most of us were De Gaullists then. Some
of us believed in De Gaulle, all of us in France. But,
my dear friend, we were so few, so very few. And
when we returned, those that were left, we found
that all the old people—the people who had led
France before, led it to disaster—were back doing the
same things, with almost the same power.

"In France, too, there were many who fought the
Germans. But when we returned we found that many
of these fought the Germans for France and Russia.
Not for France alone, a better France."

Had there been more like him, the future of France
would be brighter today.

For he and his friends believed in France. And it is
a crisis of belief that confronts France today. The
mental and physical energies of France have been
wasted by war and occupation, but so have those of
many other countries. It is foolish to think that
France and the French can never again be capable of
great deeds and glorious accomplishments. But such
deeds and accomplishments will not be done until
the French again believe in the need for great
national and individual effort.

The present psychological malaise of France has

many aspects. One which affects the young men in the army very strongly is cynicism over the results of the war.

Those who left France to fight say that they returned to find that the people who had stayed at home, many of whom had prudently kept a foot in each camp, emerged from the war better off than those who risked their lives for France either in the resistance or in the army of liberation. Anger at those who remain at home is common among all fighting men, but in France the war, from the very outset, had some of the aspects of a civil war. From 1939 onward there was a deep division among the French over the need to fight the Germans, just as today there is a division over the need to fight the Russians.

Another most disturbing factor is the belief among the French poor that United States aid since the war has benefited the rich and the middle class at the expense of the poor. People like this are not impressed by an increase in over-all industrial production no matter how much such figures enchant economists in Washington. They want that increase translated into better pay and greater opportunities.

Americans in Europe have learned by now not to expect fulsome praise for what United States aid has done for Europe since the war. Their disgust at the lack of gratitude they sometimes encounter in France leads them to forget that the French working class resentment over its limited share in the benefits of such help has a factual basis.

Of course, the chief beneficiaries of American help, the industrialists of France and Germany, do not appear madly grateful either. One French textile mag-

nate provided a good example last year. He was
asked if he would sell some land near Paris to
SHAPE, which wanted to build a headquarters on it.
The Frenchman had received millions of francs
through E.C.A. aid in the form of modern equipment
and raw materials. But he did not want to sell the
land to SHAPE. He explained that the headquarters
might disturb the brood mares at his nearby stud
farm.

It is easy to find in France other symptoms of
illness which can shake an American's faith in the
revival of the country. Neutralism, for instance, is
dead as a political issue in France at present, but
neutralism as a state of mind is very much alive.

Neutralism, of course, is a great deal more than the
belief that France can stay out of the great world
conflict now going on. It also is apathy toward political currents outside France, a withdrawal of interest
from everything that does not directly and immediately affect France and the French. And it contains
a high percentage of wishful thinking.

"Life is so damned good here for those that have,"
an American said, "that they are just turning their
faces from anything that seems to threaten it."

That same evening I walked along the Champs
Elysées with a French friend. We sat for a while at a
café watching the crowds walking in the cool evening.

"It's a pleasant life," he said. "Why should we
want to become involved in all your American com-
motion? We don't want anyone's land. We don't want
to conquer anything. France had all it wanted of
that a hundred years ago. We wish only to live peace-
fully. If the Russians want communism, let them have

it. If the Poles want it, the same thing. The communists never can take over in France, the French people basically are too sensible. So let France alone to live and enjoy itself."

Or hear a French diplomat, a man of sixty, experienced and skeptical.

"Why should France not be neutral? Some country must preserve its sanity. The Russians have frightened you Americans so badly you are rushing into a totalitarianism which is just as distasteful to thinking Frenchmen as communism. You say that the Russians can attack Europe. Possibly, but I don't believe they will. If they do, will ten or fifteen or twenty French divisions make any difference?"

Anti-Americanism usually works the same side of the street. The Americans are boors, money grabbers —this in France—and fascists. This sort of thing, put about by the intellectuals of the left, is irritating but not dangerous.

What is dangerous is the anti-Americanism which in France, and to a certain degree in Britain, springs from the belief that the United States is hell bent on war, a war that will be fought over the dead bodies and dead cities of Europe.

Much of the confidence which Europeans have in Eisenhower springs from the belief that Eisenhower has his feet on the ground and that he does not contemplate rushing into war. In fact, it was only when the French people realized that Eisenhower would be in control that French politicians felt they could openly suggest German rearmament.

The good that Eisenhower does in this respect is periodically undone by some loud-mouthed politician, and the whole continent begins to shiver at the thought of an atomic war unleashed by madmen in Washington.

Finally, and perhaps most disturbing, there is the apathy that accompanies all these attitudes. Sometimes one hears the ghosts of 1938 and 1939 in Paris when Frenchmen say of the Russians, as they did of the Germans, "Don't worry, it won't happen. After all, they are reasonable people. They respect France and the French tradition."

These are the attitudes that run through French life from top to bottom. But although they are the attitudes of the people, each attitude an aspect of that extraordinary psychological malaise which has gripped France since the war, those at the top have much to answer for.

With a few shining exceptions—men like Jean Monnet—it seems to me that the great industrialists of France are the most predatory, reactionary and unrealistic in the world. Their behavior is worse because it is seen against the background of a country whose sons have contributed so much to man's emancipation.

These are the men who did business with Hitler, who said slyly in June of 1940, "Rather Hitler than Blum." These are the men who will try to do business with Stalin.

How many of them are interested in the rearmament of Europe? Very few. Let the Americans and the British make the armaments, the trucks and the equipment, and at the same time cut their own production of peacetime goods and lower their competitive positions in foreign markets.

It is no good telling the French industrial worker he must sacrifice to help the rearmament program. French industry has left him precious little to sacrifice. But there is plenty of fat to be cut off the French middle class and the rich if the French government really intends to contribute to rearmament on the scale promised.

Indecision at the top naturally has affected the French masses. Thus far no government has told the French people that if France is to live up to its commitments under the North Atlantic Treaty Organization, then France has got to endure some measure of austerity. And in this case, by France I mean the great French middle class that supports the governments of the center and would, if asked to relinquish too much, support a government of the extreme right. In this class there is a crisis both of belief and leadership.

Until the French proletariat is convinced that its economic betters are making some sacrifice for France, then, the working masses will not support rearmament with enthusiasm. Until a French government gets their support, communism will continue to win listeners with its slick story that rearmament is an American invention for making the rich richer and the poor poorer.

Many of the French take refuge in the past, particularly the last fifteen years. Truly it is a sad story. But haven't the French worked it to death as an excuse?

Certainly defeat and occupation pull the guts out of a country. But France is not poor either in resources or manpower. France has had bad governments—all nations have at times—but why suffer them forever? It is a fair land and could be a strong one.

In North Africa in 1942 I remember writing that no Frenchman seemed to believe in anything any longer. There are still too many such people in France.

Yet the people of France, the industrial workers and the peasants, can work as long and as hard as any in Europe. French engineers, French businessmen, are alert and enterprising. There is a solid stubbornness beneath the cynicism, if something or someone can evoke it. It has not been done. France, in this hour of peril, seems a great ship drifting idly across summer seas toward the rocks, the crew idle and the officers quarreling.

When the apathy and the lack of imagination at the industrial and political top in France is understood, it is surprising how much has been done. Most of what has been done at that level must be attributed to Eisenhower.

For it has been his job to find the weapons in France and the other NATO countries, to wheedle and exhort and command. To the French leaders he gave some of the faith they need. Not all of it, not enough. The faith that will revive France must come from within. But Eisenhower did what he could and although France is not doing as much as it could, it is doing a great deal better than anyone expected.

The French Army is the principal allied weapon on the continent of Europe. The defense of Europe rests primarily upon the French, the Americans, the British and, if they can be rearmed in a manner that will not do Europe more harm than good, the Germans.

France has promised General Eisenhower fifteen divisions by the summer of 1952. According to Defense Minister Georges Bidault, France would have ten divisions "along the Rhine" by early in that year.

If war were to start this year, the French believe they could have twenty divisions under arms thirty days after the proclamation of a European emergency. It is hoped that such an emergency would be recognized and proclaimed by the North Atlantic Treaty Organization at least ten days before the Russians moved.

When French politicians or generals talk of divisions, they do not mean in every case fully manned divisions like the United States First Division or the British Seventh Armored. There are regular divisions in the French Army in Germany, but the bulk of the French divisions now organized would have to be brought to full strength with reservists when an emergency is proclaimed. Even some of the five regular divisions in Germany were well below operational strength in 1951.

There are also French divisions composed almost entirely of reservists which are classed as semi-active. These divisions would take much longer to mobilize in the event of war. But the French system for using reservists is ingenious. Armored units in those divisions which are not up to strength are fully manned by regular soldiers. The infantry and artillery units are at about three-quarter strength and again the men are mostly regulars. However, the service units, those of supply and maintenance and the medical corps, are maintained at skeleton strength. Once a state of emergency is proclaimed these are brought up to full strength by the addition of reservists.

So the system uses reservists in positions where the transfer from civilian to military life is least arduous. It is not a difficult transition from driving a truck in Paris to driving a supply truck in the army, although the latter occupation may be less hazardous. The reservists, by and large, go to those jobs where a long period of acclimatization is not necessary.

During the summer of 1951 the French held their first major postwar test of the reserve system. They found that five reserve divisions were filled up with reservists in a very short period.

The Second Division, based on Nancy, was mobilized without any warning on a September night. Within thirty-six hours every unit of the division had been assembled, equipped and was ready for action. The division moved eastward, and on the third night it was in the maneuver area near Speyer in Germany. That night it did an assault crossing of the Rhine.

It was an impressive demonstration of the speed and effectiveness of French mobilization plans. One of the ferries that carried troops across the Rhine was constructed by an engineer platoon commanded by a railway official. There was not a single regular noncommissioned officer in the platoon. In a single night the platoon ferried an entire company of tanks across the river without mishap.

The French system of mobilizing and maintaining reserve divisions seems to be much better than the British system for bringing the Territorial Army divi-

sions to action. In the first place the French have
taken a great deal of care to see that the transition
from civilian to military life is accomplished as easily
as possible and that the reservist's military job is
something like his job in civilian life. This is made
easier by the presence in the divisions of a backbone
of regulars.

The difficulty, of course, is that there must be fully
manned regular divisions in Germany to take the first
shock of any assault. This commitment, plus that of
Indo-China—a valid, although perhaps overworked,
French excuse—limits the number of regulars available for service in the reserve divisions. Ultimately
the French would have to fall back on the mobilization of divisions composed almost completely of
reservists. However, the system, as it now stands,
seems to promise a number of divisions of fairly high
quality for use in the first thirty days of the emergency.

The British system differs in that the Territorial
Army divisions are made up almost entirely of civilians. For instance, the London Armored Division is
made up of men from that city who would move in
a few days from their civilian jobs to the guns of
tanks and the wheels of armored cars. Many of them
have received yearly training in camps, but would
they be well enough trained to meet the Soviet Army?
I think not, especially since they would not be armed
with Centurion tanks but with the Comets and Crom-
wells which the regular armored divisions no longer
use.

Furthermore, as a distinguished British military
critic has pointed out, modern war demands the

highest peak of physical and mental fitness. Even if
a reservist has been a stevedore on the docks, it takes
him some time to become accustomed to the irregular
hours and meals of an army on the move or in action.

The advantage the British enjoy over the French
is experience. They have a much larger number of
reservists who fought in the last war and who will
accustom themselves to military life much quicker
than young Frenchmen with a year or so of training
since 1945.

A decisive factor in the French military situation,
if we turn our backs for the moment on the all-impor-
tant morale factor, is equipment.

The five divisions in Germany, as late as November, 1951, were equipped largely with American weapons and trucks, some of which dated back to the last
year of World War II. Maintenance has not been
good.

"We could fight with them," General Augustin
Guillaume, the former French commander in chief in
Germany, said, "but we would be at a grave disad-
vantage in any combined operation with the American and British armies because of our old equipment.
It could not move as fast or as far as yours and consequently it would be very, very difficult to co-ordinate
our tactics.

"Standardization of tactics is an ideal we all pur-
sue," he said with a dark smile, "but it is impossible
unless there is standardization of weapons. And
frankly, I do not care whose weapons they are. I will
take a British rifle, an American tank and an Italian
cannon just so long as they are good and everyone

has the same weapons. Then we can proceed to standardize our equipment and after that our tactics. That is a long time away. Is it not what we used to say in Moscow, 'pie in the sky?' "

The five divisions in Germany are the divisions which the French consider at a state of readiness. Behind them are five other divisions which can be mobilized "at once," that is, within three days. These are the divisions which are at about 65% of their strength but which can be classed as organized divisions. These five presumably are the other half of the ten divisions which M. Bidault promised to have along the Rhine by early in 1952.

The French say they have arms for these five divisions. But the arms and equipment would be up to eight years old and it would have suffered, as all equipment suffers, from storage and poor maintenance.

So the present prospect is that the French have five divisions in Germany and eastern France up to, or very close to, full strength. They have five more reserve divisions which they say they could mobilize at once and for which they have arms. The interpretations of "at once" vary. The French put it at within three days, but there are some skeptics at SHAPE who think ten days would be more like it.

But ten divisions is not what Europe needs or what the French have promised. There are another five divisions to be found before the summer of 1952 is out to bring the number to the fifteen promised SHAPE. And that number is not the maximum; the French have talked largely about thirty divisions by 1954. But considering the present attitude of the French

people toward the effort to rearm, the lack of weapons
for fifteen extra divisions, and the absence of the kind
of officers and noncommissioned officers who would
train these divisions, this estimate is just nonsense.
Given arms and equipment from the United States
and the end of the war in Indo-China, which would
release enough regular officers and noncommissioned
men to provide the cadres for ten divisions, it will be,
I believe, just possible for the French to raise ten
divisions, in addition to the fifteen now promised, by
the end of 1954.

The French Army is the heir to a glorious tradition.
One cannot see its columns moving through the
countryside of Champagne in the early spring without hearing the golden trumpets that blew for Auster-
litz or the deep shouts of the Guard as it made that
last assault on the stubborn red squares at Waterloo.

But to be realistic, one must also remember that
this army, acclaimed as the finest standing army in
the world, wavered and broke under the German
thrust in 1940 and collapsed into a catastrophe which
revealed not only bad morale from top to bottom but
a singular inability on the part of the high command
to understand that the military world had changed
since 1918.

Complete defeat and occupation have scarred the
French people and their army. But there are heart-
ening signs of recovery in the army. Indeed there is
more awareness of the external dangers that beset
France among the young officers than one encounters
in Paris or the French provinces, and there is very
little of the appalling attitude of "there's nothing

we can do" that pervades large sections of the civilian population.

Driving along the cobbled roads of northern Germany during the British maneuvers I met two companies of French infantry who were about to put in an attack on the British left flank. They were milling about in the center of the village with that lack of appreciation of what air attack can do found only in those who have never been bombed or strafed.

A colonel, a round, energetic person of about forty, was laying out the plan of attack. Gathered around him were his young officers, and I thought that nowhere in that maneuver area, which then held over 125,000 men, could one find a finer set of men. Their thin faces were intelligent and eager, they rattled questions in all the accents of France and they dashed back to their vehicles to get the attack underway, the personification of vigorous, professional competence.

Later I talked to one of these young officers.

"The men are all right. Most of them are conscripted and they do not like the increase in the term of conscription which has delayed their return to their homes. But their food is better than it ever was in the old army and now that we are getting vehicles and weapons they are more interested in what we have to do."

I asked him how they liked being in Germany. He grinned.

"For a Frenchman no country is like his own. Fortunately we have the opportunity to give them leave in France very often. And we are normally stationed in a pleasanter part of Germany than this."

What did he, an officer in an infantry company, think the French army needed?

"Weapons, of course, but more than that, experienced soldiers. I myself saw some fighting in 1944 and 1945. But we have almost no experienced non-commissioned officers. They are in Indo-China.

"Many of our soldiers are very interested in learning about weapons," he continued. "They come of a generation that envied the American Army its vehicles and its tanks. But when they have learned the mechanical part, we have so few to teach them how the weapons should be used in the field. Certainly if that war in Indo-China was over we would have the means to make a very fine army much sooner."

He went off with his men and I saw them sift through the trees toward another British position. Later I talked to a nineteen-year-old soldier from the Pas de Calais. He was polite but restrained until I told him I knew the country around Arras, his home, a dreary part of France.

"Certainly, I do not like being away from home," he said. "But one can see that this is the right thing to do. But me, I think also we should be watching our communists at home. There are many in the north, you know, in the coal mines. I think sometimes of what would happen to my people there if war came with Russia and I was fighting in Germany."

He found it comforting, he said, to discover so many troops from other nations involved in the maneuvers.

"There are Dutchmen down the road and this afternoon we attacked some British. They know more than we do, but I think we did well. Our officers? They are good, but I do not know much about the generals. Generals have a bad name in France, you know."

Here he touched on one of the most disturbing aspects of French morale. The soldiers and young officers have very little confidence in the generals. This may be because the French officer corps inherited a legacy of defeat from 1940. I remember no such attitude in 1939; instead there was warm regard for the genius of Gamelin. But recently I have heard French soldiers reveal a complete lack of confidence and respect in their high command.

One measure that has increased the interest of the French soldier in the job to be done in Germany is the movement of some units into the United States zone's northern sector around Kassel. The French military revival in Germany began much later than the British and American, and until a year ago most of it was snugly accommodated in the far southwest of Germany without responsibility or incentive.

General Guillaume, an energetic soldier who spent enough time in Moscow to realize the gravity of the Russian danger, routed the French army out of its casernes and instituted a rigorous system of field training. The results are beginning to show now. But it will be some time before the French standard of training approaches either the British or the American. Thorough training, of course, depends on ample supplies of equipment and the French do not have them. Until they do and until the equipment is modern, their standard will lag behind the other armies in Germany.

In the end, of course, it is not the French Army

that is the primary concern but the moral health of
France. One argument for a respectable French army
is that it will increase French national prestige and
pride. We have heard this so often from politicians
and generals that we believe it. But the state of
French morale today raises the question of whether
the re-establishment of French military power will
in fact raise national morale.

The basic weakness of French morale is not solely
the result of communist strength in France. Two
years of careful work have weeded out most of the
known communists in the army. But communists are
not the only rebels against discipline in a nation as
individualistic as France.

I asked a French staff colonel at SHAPE how the
young men now coming in to the French Army compared with those during the first World War and the
years between the wars. He said that unquestionably
they were better physically and mentally than those
fed into the old army.

"But they are not military material," he said. "These
young men are not interested in becoming officers or
even in our great traditions. They come in and do
their duty. They are quick to learn and more reliable
than the old soldiers. But there is no spirit, no *élan*."

I asked him why this should be.

"Perhaps, my friend, because we French are over-
propagandized. Let us put it that way, rather than, as
some of your people say, overcivilized.

"These young men were brought up in war. They
heard propaganda from the Germans, propaganda
from Vichy, propaganda from de Gaulle, propaganda
from the B.B.C., propaganda from the Americans.

"When the war was over, they got another dose, this time from the Communists. Then more propaganda from various governments and from various foreign countries all interested in swinging France to their sides. You cannot be surprised if they are confused and uncertain. They have made a mental retreat. To them France is not the whole country, as it was to my generation, but one little corner—a farm, a shop, a house. That is all they can be sure of."

Are they encouraged by the older people?

"It is hard to say. Some, of course. But there are many of my generation who say, 'Enough, France has had enough, leave us to ourselves.'"

There certainly is a tendency among many French to leave the job to the United States. Why not, they say, you have the atom bomb, you have the people and many divisions. We will do what we can, but we cannot do much. France has done enough.

Yet it is a curious aspect of French character that these same people fly into a rage whenever the subject of rearming the Germans is raised.

"Sometimes I think they don't want to be defended," an exasperated Brigadier General at SHAPE said. "They take so long doing anything themselves and yet they get scared when we talk about using some German divisions."

The French difficulty, of course, is that very few Frenchmen are convinced that the Soviet Union is a greater threat to France than Germany. The only people who can prove this to the French are the Germans themselves. It will take a great deal more restraint than the Germans have shown in the past if they are to prove to the French their willingness to be good Europeans, once they get arms in their hands.

The fear of the Germans was the motivating force behind the two great political conceptions which postwar France has contributed to the Atlantic community: the Schuman Plan and the European Army Plan. In each case France was moving, selfishly if you will, toward a united Europe in which the common industrial resources and the common military resources are pooled.

The European Army's military feasibility is still in doubt but the dimensions of the initial force are impressive: 559,000 men in 43 divisions of 12,000 to 13,000 men each. But that army is still on paper and not in the field.

Until the European Army is a fact, the French Army remains the chief source of western land power on the continent. If we are to be relatively secure in the critical summer of 1952, we need the French Army then, not a European army two years later.

France, as we see, is doing a lot. It is not doing as much as it could do. Nor has the morale of the French people responded as favorably to the re-establishment of the French military power as our generals and statesmen expected.

The question of whether France will fight is one that must be asked. It may be considered insulting, superfluous or cynical by various Americans; nevertheless, in view of the reliance placed on France and the geographical position of France, the question and its answer are of the utmost importance to the people of the United States.

Despite the moral ills that beset France, I am convinced that the spirit of France is reviving. But there is a long distance to go before complete recovery is reached, the sort of recovery necessary to fight a long, costly and fierce war. The malaise is psychological, not physical. Therefore although the United States can assist recovery with material aid, ultimately recovery must come from within the French people themselves.

That recovery will not come as the result of having an army to cheer about. It will not flourish under a dictatorship of the left or the right. It will come only when the French recover their faith in the lives they lead. And when I speak of the French I do not mean the harpies of the Crillon Bar or the international crowd at Cannes, but the millions of French workers who live on the dreary borders of poverty, yet who are the basis of the French nation.

Nowhere else in Europe, not even in the crowded Ruhr, does the life of the industrial worker seem as harsh, as empty as in the industrial areas of France. Until those who guide France's economy are ready to insure that the French worker receives a greater share of France's economic wealth, and until French industrialists and union leaders understand that it is upon the worker that the psychological health of France rests, then the chances of true French moral recovery are dim.

The little, wiry man with the inevitable cigarette who is the French worker is terribly important to Europe. Unless he can see ahead a better life in terms of material comfort for himself and mental opportunities for his children, the revival of France is bound to drag. Given that future, releasing all the energies and aspirations that lie latent in France, what an ally he will be!

Unboubtedly, the French Army as we know it to-day would fight if the Soviet Union attacked. But until those conditions in France which encourage approaches to communism, the extreme right or neu-tralism are eliminated, then the ability of France to . play its rightful share in the defense of that civiliza-tion to which it has contributed so much will remain in doubt.

10. The Calculated Risk of Rearming Germany

The Germans are a peculiar people in peculiar circumstances. Utterly defeated in 1945, they find themselves five years later courted by the very powers that had defeated them and asked to resume those warlike trappings that those same powers had ordered them to forget. In our present circumstances, however, the somersaults of history, although amusing, are not vital. What is vital is that Germany, or to be specific, the Federal Republic of Germany, is an indispensable part of the defense of Europe.

West Germany will not make the largest contribution to that defense. It will not have the dominant voice in the planning of that defense, in the foreseeable future at least. It is not going to make the arms and equipment for that defense under present plans. But all the final plans for the defense of Europe, as they are now drawn, include the wholehearted cooperation of the West Germans.

Under these circumstances it is not surprising that the Germans, a people noted for their political uncertainty, should be bewildered. We are rearming the Germans to defend Europe against the Russians, either passively or actively; yet the Germans think, or by now have become convinced, that in 1941–1945 they were defending Europe against the Russians who were then allied with the Americans, British and French who now are urging the Germans to rearm.

188

It would take cooler political brains than those in West Germany to accommodate such a reversal of policies.

The Germans have not won a war in over eighty years. Even if we discount all the damage that Hitler did to German military planning between 1941 and 1944—after that, what Hitler did could not affect the war's ultimate outcome—objective examination of the German record shows that the German high command in Russia, France and Italy made mistake after mistake.

If you had the opportunity to discuss the Korean war with German generals, as I have had, you would find that much of their strategic and tactical thinking is geared to their golden years of 1940 and 1941; they still have very little conception of what sea power can do to restore a bad situation on land—none of them foresaw the Inchon landing—and in many other respects they are out of touch with modern three-dimensional warfare.

Study the history of World War II as it was written on the battlefields, not in the memoirs of German and Allied generals. You will find almost incredible mistakes in tactics by German commanders and staffs. Alam El Halfa, that forgotten but terribly important battle in the desert in the summer of 1942, is an example. There was also shocking failure to recognize the potentialities of new equipment—the slow development of radar in Germany is an example—and breakdowns of supply in the field, due as much to sheer inefficiency as to allied bombing.

Why then are we in such frantic hurry to get the Germans on our side?

To start with, there are a lot of them. There are 50,000,000 Germans in the Federal Republic, a population 9,000,000 greater than that of France. It would be possible, under the most favorable conditions, to raise forty German divisions. They are a virile and fecund people.

Next, they are, or always have been in the past, good soldiers. They are brave. They are thorough. They are aggressive. They take discipline. And discipline, much as liberals may dislike the idea, is the foundation stone of armies.

They also have a military tradition. There are at the moment thousands of former German officers and noncommissioned officers who have fought the Russians in the field. There are hundreds of ex-staff officers who planned the great campaigns of 1940, 1941 and 1942. On the surface this is the most accomplished martial race in Europe.

I say "on the surface" because we always must beware of repeating the mistake made by the West in 1940 when it was too easily assumed that the French were the most accomplished soldiers in the world. It may be that the terrible losses of two world wars have sapped Germany's martial might. My own view is that Germany lost its ability to play the role of a great power on the battlefields of Verdun and Chemin des Dames, at Sebastopol and Stalingrad. This does not mean, however, that the Germans cannot perform the great, and for them, redeeming service of forming the most important and useful reinforcement the Atlantic powers can hope to gain in Europe.

Another word of caution. The Germans of the new

German Army will not be the stubborn, ingenious, wary veterans of Smolensk or Alamein or St. Lô. The overwhelming majority will be the young men who have grown up since the war. A few will have World War II records. But it would be no more advisable to build a new German army out of the remnants of the Wehrmacht than it would be to seek the new United States divisions from among the veterans of Normandy. War is a young man's game. Only the professionals, and precious few of them, are much good in a second war. Colonel Thomason of the Marines wrote that a man has one war and one wound in his life.

To the United States, the Germans are important not only because they are the great reinforcement for the defense of Europe. They are important because, in view of the current state of Europe, it is only by using the Germans that a balance can be struck between the Soviet Union and the West that will allow, in time, the withdrawal of the bulk of United States ground forces from the continent.

It is reasoned at SHAPE that both a deterrent to and a defense against Russian aggression can be constructed, given French, Italian and German rearmament, with the addition of smaller but effective forces from Norway, Belgium, the Netherlands, Denmark, Greece and Turkey, plus the qualitative air superiority of the Royal Air Force and those United States Air Force units which, until our hour strikes, always will be stationed abroad.

Of course the SHAPE planners do not expect Europe to "go it alone" if the Russians jump. Their aim is a defense sufficiently strong to hold the Russians in check until American atomic power (expressed through air power) and American land power (expressed through immediate reserves, airborne and shipborne) can be brought to bear.

SHAPE reasons further that the rearmament of Germany and the other western European countries will so shift the military balance in favor of the West that not only will the Soviet Union be deterred from attacking the West by military means but it also will seek to end that prolonged political crisis of intimidation, political penetration and propaganda in West Europe which we call the cold war.

There are two conditions which modify this happy picture.

Ever since the rearmament of Germany came up for open discussion at the headquarters of Field Marshal Viscount Montgomery in the autumn of 1949, various pundits have agreed that it was necessary and then added the statement, "Of course, we are taking a risk."

They mean, of course, we take a risk in arming so belligerent, martial and militarily accomplished a people as the Germans.

We also take another risk, perhaps more dangerous. Seventy million Germans administered a staggering, almost a lethal, body blow to the Russians in 1941 and 1942. The Germans in the field, the Germans in the high command and one German, Hitler, made mistakes in those years, but the military accomplishment of the Germans was tremendous. The Russians held them in the early stages with less help from the West than we believe, and eventually drove them back. But as the Duke of Wellington said at Waterloo, another great defensive battle, it was a damned close run thing.

Does anyone suggest that the Russians are not frightened by the rearmament of the Germans, that it may not move them, from purely military considerations alone, to strike before that rearmament can be completed?

There was also another side to the German war in Russia which, combined with the narrow margin by which Russia escaped defeat, might hasten a Soviet attack to halt German rearmament. The destruction wreaked by the German armies in the Soviet Union, when they retreated, was on a scale greater than anything done by bombs or shells in the West. Since it is impossible to believe that the Russians themselves would have destroyed the steel works at Stalino or the workers' tenements at Minsk or a thousand scattered villages, as they advanced, we must accept the Russian story that these were destroyed by the Germans.

I might add that this is not hearsay. I saw Stalino, Voroshilovgrad, Zaporozhe, Minsk, Makeevka, and innumerable villages along the dusty roads leading to them in 1946 and 1947. The destruction was more complete than anything I had seen in the West. This staggering destruction was done by the Germans in retreat. They left a scar that twenty years will not heal.

Put the two together—the narrow margin by which the Soviet Union escaped military defeat in 1941 and 1942, at tremendous cost, and the damage wrought by the retreating Germans in 1943 and 1944—and you get the real risk. It is that the Russians will be so frightened by their own propagandists that they will accept unquestioningly orders from above to attack the West and prevent another German invasion.

The average Russian has been taught for six years to hate the Americans. The lesson has taken hold, although there are ways of breaking it down. But no one had to teach him to hate the Germans.

No one who went through the last war can be complacent over the rearmament of the Germans. No one can overlook the great risks that this rearmament will either re-create a military monster in Europe, with which we cannot deal, or incite the Russians to a preventive war. In the isolation of the mind, I have tried to reach a point of view. It is that, accepting all dangers, we must find some way to rearm Germany and bind her to the West. If we fail to do this we will fail Europe and fail ourselves.

But rearmament in Germany has raised some grave problems in the Federal Republic. The Allies propose but the Germans dispose.

One problem is that rearmament cannot be disconnected from many other problems which face the German people. As we have seen, the Pentagon made the grave mistake of treating German rearmament as a purely military matter, separated from those other problems which beset the new republic.

In the autumn of 1950 the western powers, especially the United States, made it all too clear that they wanted German rearmament and were determined to have it. This when the West also was trying to win German acceptance of the Schuman Plan and the whole idea of an integrated Europe. So much emphasis was placed on the importance of German rearmament that the Germans thought they were in clover. We told them how much we wanted the horse and then asked them what the price was. It was bad horse trading which is the same as saying it was bad politics. The proper way to buy a horse cheaply is to give the impression you can get along nicely without it.

At the same time, the United States, Britain and France were about to embark on a delicate and important system of negotiations designed to bind the Federal Republic to the western world. These negotiations would have gone much faster and more smoothly had we not first told the Germans that we wanted them in the western community not only because they were a democratic state but because they could raise fifteen or twenty divisions.

But the negotiations between the western occupation powers and the Germans were complicated by two other considerations having an important effect on the average German. One is neutrality and the other is unity.

Whether or not Germany can be reunified, there was and is a strong feeling in Germany that divided or united it can be neutral in any war, cold or hot. The development of this feeling cannot be said to have followed immediately after the western powers made it known that they wanted to rearm Germany. Early in 1948 in Munich I heard unworldly professors and opportunist politicians put forward the doctrine that the Germans should and must remain neutral in the great power struggle between East and West. At that time, coming from Berlin, the most active sector of the cold war, it was startling to hear Germans in Bavaria, North Rhine-Westphalia and Hesse say that the blockade of Berlin was no concern of theirs, that Germany would do well to keep out of all these quarrels.

Rearmament brought these sentiments to a head. The immediate reaction of millions of Germans to the western desire that they rearm was flat rejection. In the year between September, 1950 and September, 1951, this attitude shifted slowly from rejection to apprehensive acquiescence. Enough uncertainty is left, however, to affect the pace and thoroughness of German rearmament when it comes.

The Germans refused in the beginning to accept rearmament for a number of reasons. The first and most important of these was fear. The Germans feared that if the government of the Federal Republic took the first steps toward rearmament, then, in the autumn of 1950, Germany would be overrun by the Russians. If they overestimated Russian belligerence, the Germans had a clear idea of their own position. The reinforcement of the American, British and French armies in Germany was just getting underway; there was very little in the country to meet a Soviet invasion.

The idea that rearmament would invite invasion was seized by all those parties and factions favoring neutrality for Germany or opposing the plans of the Allies or the Federal Government. Dr. Kurt Schumacher, the leader of the Social Democratic Party, demanded that the defense of Germany on the Vistula River, in Poland, be guaranteed by the Allies before rearmament began. Other politicians warned that rearmament would bring on a war in which West Germany would be the main battlefield.

As I have mentioned earlier, such ideas were embraced by a very large percentage of the students in Germany. They were opposed to war and to them war meant rearmament. This opposition was not based on theory. Most of them had grown up during the war and postwar years. They knew what World War II had done to their country and they had had enough. Besides, for five years they had been told that militarism was a German vice and that the new masters of the country were there to cure the German addicts.

Neutralism was and is strong in Germany. It will continue to be because it is tied to another extremely important issue in German political life; an issue charged with emotion, affecting great masses of the people. This factor is unity.

Germany has been divided between East and West since 1945. The division is unpopular. When the West asks the people of the Federal Republic to rearm it is asking them, in the belief of many, to give up their hopes of unity with their friends and relatives in East Germany and ally themselves permanently with the western powers against the Russians and their own compatriots in East Germany. No amount of persuasion by the government of the Federal Republic or the governments of the United States, Britain and France can destroy completely this belief.

The argument that the integration of the Federal Republic with the West and its rearmament as part of a European Defense Force is an absolute prerequisite to the future reunification of Germany does not ring as true in German ears as it does in the western capitals. For a great many Germans want unity now. They do not want to wait. Nor are they as afraid of the dangers of hasty reunification as are the Federal or the western governments.

The pursuit of unity also affects rearmament through unity's close connection with the concept of neutrality. The Germans who advocate neutrality realize that a united Germany would be much more powerful than either West Germany or East Germany is today. So powerful, they believe, that it could afford to remain outside the struggle between East and West. Reunited and independent, Germany could bargain with both Russia and the United States and might even become the leader of a group of neutral states including Sweden, Switzerland and Austria.

To anyone understanding the depth of the quarrel the Soviet Union has picked with the West, such ideas are curiously old-fashioned and unrealistic. Yet much German political thinking is old-fashioned and unrealistic, chiefly because the Germans have been more or less willing prisoners, first of Hitler and then of Allied rule.

Both unity and neutrality directly affect the German willingness to rearm. They present grave problems for the West. But there are equally grave problems resulting from other factors in the twisted, disjointed German political scene. Moreover, none of these stands alone; they affect each other just as the desire for unity and the desire for neutrality are mutually supporting.

The Federal Government, pushing West Germany toward economic, political and military ties with the West through the Schuman Plan, the Council of

Europe and the General Agreement with the three western occupation powers and the European Defense Force, has been taking advantage of one of the most gratifying features of postwar German political development. This is the realization by many Germans of all classes that in the troubled world of today, Germany cannot stand alone. This knowledge has been strong enough to push the Federal Republic toward integration with the West despite the counterattractions of unity and neutrality which also enjoy the support of Germans of all classes, political parties and religions.

But progress toward integration also has run counter to the powerful impulse to revive Germany's old power on strictly national terms.

The proponents of German nationalism—and they come in many shapes and sizes—never have liked the idea of integration with the West. They see Germany growing stronger every day in relation to other continental powers. They think this strength entitles Germany to control of its own destiny, including the use of its armed forces, and, licking the wounds of 1945, they have decided that next time it might be different.

The spate of books by former German staff officers and field commanders, each "proving" that Hitler and not the Wermacht lost the last war, can be attributed to more than a desire to whitewash the army. They are also a consequence of the reviving national pride in the accomplishments of that army and of national belief in the greatness and power of Germany, a country in which the two words are synonymous.

The Germans in 1945 were a tired people, weary of war. They are not so tired and weary today. Nationalism, with its overtones of future revenge, thus far has failed to win majority support. But it has affected the ability of the Federal Government and the three western powers to achieve enthusiastic support for rearmament within the framework of a European Defense Force.

Another factor affecting the progress of the Germans toward the sort of rearmament the western powers desire is the pronounced German dislike of foreign leadership. After six years of occupation this is natural enough, so natural that foreigners in Germany sometimes forget that it is important.

In Germany we are not facing anti-Americanism alone. We also are meeting anti-British and anti-French sentiments. And these latter result from psychological motivations much deeper than the events of the last six years.

Anti-Americanism in Germany differs from that in Britain or France. It is not due entirely to the fact that in Germany, as in other European countries, people fear and dislike American policy because they believe it is leading the world to war. In fact, the Department of Public Affairs of the United States High Commission has done a very good job in explaining United States and Federal Government policy to the Germans, a much better job, incidentally, than Chancellor Konrad Adenauer's government has done.

But anti-American feelings also feed on conditions that do not exist in other countries, chiefly large-scale occupation and the conditions under which the occupation continued from 1945 to 1951.

The Germans do not want to have soldiers quartered in Germany, they do not like the requisitioning of hotels and apartment houses and homes, they do not like special privileges for Allied soldiers in Germany. Their complaints have been exaggerated, wildly so in many cases, but even when this exaggeration is taken into account, there remains a residue of ill feeling which no amount of speeches by statesmen can completely remove.

Finally in Germany, and in other European countries, there is a cultural basis to anti-Americanism. Broken and poor in 1945, the Germans consoled themselves with stories of the barbarity of the Americans, their habits of chewing gum, their lack of appreciation of the arts, their "new rich" attitude toward the servants and the fine houses to which they, as the conquerors, fell heir when they arrived in Germany.

Since then it has become almost a cult.

"You mean you have read Latin?" a German woman said to a friend recently. "Are those things really studied in the United States? We heard your universities taught only farming and the best way to sell underclothes."

Finally, of course, we have crammed democracy down the throats of the Germans. This is not the place to discuss how long they will continue to use its forms in government. But the majority of educated Germans do not, nor did they ever, think that democracy is the most efficient or intelligent form of government.

It can be argued, as many American officials in Germany do argue, that these are all "small things" connected with internal German politics, not to be considered as affecting the major objectives of United States policy. But the major objective asks a very great deal of the Germans. We are no longer asking the Germans merely to live in peace under democratic rule. We are asking for much more. We are asking them to join the West in a military alliance which, it is hoped, will deter a Soviet attack but which, if this fails, will fight the Russians.

Under those circumstances the drives toward unity and neutrality in Germany, the strident voice of rising nationalism, the anti-Americanism, become dreadfully important. For we are not asking Germany to be a friend. We are asking it to be an ally, and the question we must ask ourselves is whether, while those internal conditions endure, Germany can be a valuable, reliable ally.

As this is written the European Defense Force, in which Germany is to have an important place, has not yet fully taken final shape. We do not know how it will work and there are serious doubts among military men of the highest professional qualifications whether it will work. But we know what it is trying to establish and this, I think, is the secret of its importance to Europe.

Eventually the European Defense Force will take over from each of the nations involved—at present France, Italy, West Germany, Belgium, the Netherlands and Luxembourg—the European defense of those countries. Loyalty will not be to German or French or Dutch commanders in chief or armies, navies or air forces but to the European Defense Force and its commanders. Promotion will not be won as a result of assiduous care in furthering the military interests of the nation to which an officer belongs, but to the furthering of the interests of all the nations in the European Defense Force.

This is a brilliant conception. Even at SHAEF, Allied Supreme Headquarters during the war, the first loyalty was owed to the United States Army or the British Army. The same is true at SHAPE, General Eisenhower's present headquarters in France, and it will remain true as long as such headquarters represent staff officers serving in individual armies brought together for a common purpose.

The European Defense Force will have another great advantage. I have referred frequently to the urgent need for standardization of arms as the first step toward standardization of military organization and tactics. But standardization of arms has another important bearing on Europe's ability to defend itself: it is one of the sure ways in which the expenditure necessary to raise and maintain adequate defense forces can be reduced.

The economies of the nations involved in the European Defense Force just cannot bear the initial cost of equipping individual armies plus the costs of supply once the armies are in being. Nor would it be economically possible, in war or peace, to supply ammunition for six different types of field gun or three different types of rifle through a central organization.

By standardizing equipment throughout the European army, western Europe can apportion the manufacture of that equipment to those countries best prepared to make specific articles of equipment. Thus instead of every nation making or buying individual rifles, the Belgians could make all the rifles for the

European army while some other nation could make all the ammunition for the rifles.

This will cut costs and costs are terribly important. But it also will serve to reassure other continental countries about the Germans. For under the European Defense Force scheme, no single nation will become the armorer of Europe, just as no single nation can dominate the European Defense Force's army, navy or air force.

There are some alarming military weaknesses in the European Defense Force. But the conception does provide for cheaper rearmament, ultimately, and a method by which Germany can be harnessed to the task of defending Europe without arousing the fears of the rest of the continent.

Thus far we have covered the strains and stresses of Germany in the pre-rearmament period and the mechanism, the European Defense Force, through which Germany will be rearmed. What happens when rearmament begins?

The first step will be the raising of the twelve German divisions, or *groupements* as the French call them, which will make up the Federal Republic's contribution to ground defense.

It may be possible to raise these divisions by volunteer recruiting, but because the essence of the concept of German rearmament is that this is to be a popular effort, it probably will be wiser to conscript the divisions. For recruiting inevitably would bring to German colors a great many old soldiers, vengeful refugees and unrepentant Nazis. Such men do not have a real stake in the Germany that the West has tried to fashion since the war.

It will be far better to conscript Germans from every walk of life, men who have a personal investment in the postwar Germany they must defend and who are young enough to be reservists for some years after their initial service is concluded.

Once the men have been sworn in they are to be turned over to the European Command, United States Army, for training although the type of training, like a great many other things, will have to wait upon the final decision on the tactical organization and equipment of the European Defense Force.

There also will be a small tactical air force, trained by U.S.A.F. officers and flying U.S. planes.

Foreign training, of course, is not going to please the former generals and staff officers of the last German army. This is understandable. The old Reichswehr and the armies that fought for Hitler were exceedingly well trained and former German officers believe that their system of basic training was the best in the world.

"We admire much in the American Army," one former army commander told me, "its mechanical ability and ingenuity and its mobility, but we do not regard your training system as adequate for the dirty jobs of war; for instance, the infantry counterattack immediately after a position has been lost. We believe that our *einheit* system, which was developed by Field Marshal Von Rundstedt, remains superior to anything in the armies of the world and we would like to give it another chance in the new army."

The German Army, like the French, is the heir to great traditions. One of the reasons why its former officers are not enthusiastic about the European Defense Force as the instrument of German rearmament is their fear that the German units in that force will have to give up their past and rely on promises for the future.

"Older men, perhaps, understand better the importance of a European army bound together in a common determination to protect western civilization," my German friend said, "but it is difficult to train younger men under such circumstances. For them it is better to say, 'You are now a member of this famous regiment founded by Frederick the Great; be worthy of it.'

"That is frequently attacked as militarism, German militarism, by Americans. But I never have heard the British assailed because they maintain their regimental traditions in just that way. My belief is that such tradition is of very great assistance in training young soldiers."

One important consideration in judging the military feasibility of the European Defense Force plan as far as Germany is concerned is the distaste of professional German officers—and most of the officers in the new army will have to be the younger professionals of 1945—for foreign leadership, especially French.

A young German who ended the war in Hamburg after three years of fighting on both the east and west fronts said he would serve gladly under American or British leadership, but that neither he nor any of his friends would be happy under French command.

"No doubt there are some fine French generals," he said, "but in 1940 and 1941 when we were being trained we learned a good deal, perhaps too much, about French mistakes. And although the French are said to have fought well in the south in 1944, we know nothing about that. And, of course, no German officer is going to be willing to fight under an Italian general."

The same might be said of Italian officers and German generals.

The unhappy fact, however, is that these national animosities are very deep in the military men of Germany and they must be eliminated before approval of the European Defense Force is general. The German professional soldiers are "going along" with the European Defense Force because they understand that it is the quickest route to German rearmament, but the majority of them lack the conviction, held by Chancellor Adenauer and his government and by the western governments, that the E.D.F. is an integral part of Germany's new position in Europe. The old pre-Hitler or prewar position was good enough for them and they hanker after a national army.

This is not wholly out of selfishness. The majority of them are firmly convinced that a national army is the quickest way to German and European security.

Even though they will serve in the European Defense Force, it is obvious that before very long the Germans will have arms in their hands and a much greater measure of control of their own destinies than they have enjoyed for seven years. The French, who pushed the Pleven Plan and the European Army plan which grew out of it, are insistent that "You don't know the Germans until you see them with a gun."

The question which Europe and the world are asking during this present period of transition in Germany is whether Germany can be trusted with arms and independence. What kind of associates will the Germans be in the western community?

To those who have recognized the tremendous threat that the existence of Soviet power raises to western civilization, this question seems picayune. But to those who have been harried by German ambitions, German conquests and, no less damaging, German occupations through ninety years the question is far from academic.

If the defense of Europe is to be erected on a firm basis, there will have to be extensive readjustments of European attitudes toward the Germans and some very basic changes in the German outlook on Europe. But the burden of proof in this period rests with the Germans. It is symptomatic of the psychological condition of the German people during the present period that they cannot understand this.

Our newest, and if all goes well our most decisive military allies, in the sense that Germany's addition to the West will swing Russia from war, are now going through the final phase of the transition from an utterly defeated nation to a partner and ally of the West.

The first phase lasted roughly from 1945 to currency reform in June of 1948. During that period the Germans were dispirited and apathetic, politically and economically.

From currency reform to the establishment of the Federal Republic in the autumn of 1949 the Germans were much more intent on restoring their economy than on internal or foreign political affairs. But from 1949 until the present the Germans have been feeling their way into the center of European politics and

have been taking a good, hard look at the Europe produced by the cold war.

Germany is now all but sovereign. It has 50,000,000
people, highly industrious, skillful technicians, virile
and proud. This is the most populous state on the
continent, the richest in industrial resources. The
Germans know this. It is not surprising that as they
recognize their strength they look at Europe and at
the Europe that might result from the reunification of
Germany.

"Here we are," a German leader might say. "We
were totally defeated in 1945, but today our industry
and commerce are flourishing, our people are working
hard, internal communism is not a menace. There are
eighteen millions of our compatriots in the East asking to join us.

"The French are divided and uncertain. The British
are broke. The Italians don't count. The Americans
like us. They must. Look at the way they have helped
us. Of course, they talk a lot about democracy and
cracking down on the Nazis, but they like us and they
need us."

· What are the disquieting factors in an analysis of
Germany's ability to play the role of a partner in
Europe's defensive alliance? Here are some of the
important ones.

(1) The Germans still do not, or perhaps cannot,
understand the suspicion and mistrust with which
their European neighbors view them.

There is little novel in this. Nietzsche wrote in
The Genealogy of Morals: "The profound and icy
mistrust which the German arouses whenever he gets
power into his hands is the aftermath of that vast and

horrible fear with which for long centuries Europe
dreaded the wrath of the Teutonic blond beast."

But this mistrust, this loathing of the Germans, are
not understood by the mass of the Germans themselves. This may be due to an unconscious national
effort toward mental disassociation from the excesses
of 1933–1945, a feeling that since nothing can be done
for the victims it is best if the Germans, and everyone
else, forget about them.

This attitude will have to be changed if complete
co-operation, which in defense no less than war is the
only kind that counts, is to be obtained. The Germans
must learn to understand and combat the dislike
of other nations, they cannot remain the Ishmaels
of Europe forever. They cannot afford it. Neither can
Europe.

(2) German nationalism, trying its wings at the
same time that German soldiers shoulder arms for the
first time in over half a decade, is a disturbing factor
in the inclusion of Germany in the European defense
community.

Nationalism has been accompanied by the revival
of Naziism and by the return to office of thousands of
former Nazis. Unfortunately for the Germans the best
aspects of nationalism, which, a British general remarked, would be called patriotism anywhere else,
have been confused with the rantings of such fascist
organizations as the Socialist Reichs Party.

Nationalism at its best is a pride in country and a
concern for its safety. This is compatible with the
German insistence on equality in defense.

Equality is a goal sought not only by ex-Nazis or
the new parties of the radical right. It is the objective

also of Dr. Schumacher and his socialists, whose antagonism to both the army and the Nazis under Hitler
is a historical fact, and of Chancellor Adenauer and
the parties of the government coalition.

A Frenchman, a Belgian or a Dane would answer
that this is all true today, but what of the morrow?

For the history of postwar Germany shows that
each new grant of sovereignty, each relaxation of Allied power, has been followed by a sudden upsurge
of German nationalism.

The currency reform of 1948 which helped restore
Germany's economic structure was followed by the
first postwar expression of rabid nationalism. The establishment of the Federal Republic in September,
1949, was followed by another nationalist renaissance
and the return to state and federal office of many
former members of the Nazi party.

With the Federal Republic stronger politically and
economically than it was two years ago, there is little
wonder that its prospective European allies fear another and perhaps more violent nationalist explosion
once German troops are in the field, no matter what
organization they may serve.

(3) This fear is acerbated by the explosive entry into
German political life of the veterans' organizations.

Now the veterans' organizations of post-Hitler
Germany are not a group of ex-soldiers, rear rank
privates and generals joining in fraternal and beery
reminiscences of the good old days, but large groups
of soldiers led with firmness and discipline by former
generals.

In the United States, a German diplomat pointed
out, "The generals have better things to do than pre-

side over the meetings of veterans. They have important jobs as chairmen of boards or in the government.
In Germany, they have nothing to do but twiddle
their thumbs or go out and make speeches to veterans."

The veterans' organizations in Germany were
formed first to work for the welfare of the survivors of
various units: the Afrika Korps, the Parachute Army,
the Gross Deutschland division. Slowly they were
brought together under a single "roof" organization,
The Association of German Soldiers.

The best introduction to political life in Germany,
or anywhere else for that matter, is a stern declaration
of aloofness from politics. Having made this declaration the Association plunged into politics up to its
neck, demanding the freeing of war criminals and
insisting on complete equality in armament.

The French and the other continental powers had
not been too alarmed when Dr. Schumacher and Dr.
Adenauer made such demands. They were pretty worried when the men who knew what war was all about
made them.

(4) The French and other European powers are
deeply concerned over the vengeful, irredentist attitude of the Germans toward the areas they lost as a
result of the second World War.

The French fear of the Germans "with guns in their
hands" is based as much on this as the fear that the
Germans might turn on them.

"We hope to control the Germans through an international structure once they are rearmed," a French
official in Germany said. "Not because they would
turn on us again, but because we French do not want
to be lured into a war in the East to recover the ter-

ritories beyond the Oder and Neisse rivers or East Prussia."

To Americans this seems a very remote possibility. But to the French or the British or the Dutch, who hear German speakers proclaiming that these lost territories must and shall be German again, this is very worrying. They have no love for the Russians. But they do not want to be drawn into a European war against the Russians solely because the Germans want to recover some territory.

These are all disturbing factors in the acceptance of Germany as an ally. But there are reassuring circumstances.

The first is the constant desire of the Federal Government to be "good Europeans" and to participate in all the plans that call for a greater integration of Europe by political, economic and military means. The persistency with which such plans have been pushed by the government at Bonn shows that, as far as it is concerned, the ideas of German domination of Europe are over. In their minds the idea of Bismarck's powerful Reich has given way to the concept of Germany as one of the foundation stones of a united Europe.

This is a revolutionary change in political thinking. Unfortunately the change has affected only a very small group of political intellectuals in a country where politics are mainly emotional.

The change results from the recognition on the part of this group that Germany's power of unilateral decision has vanished. Here, the group has led public opinion. The idea has been sold to tens of thousands of influential Germans in all the social groups.

Cynics attribute the growth of this idea to German

realization that the rise to world power of the United States and the Soviet Union has impressed all but the most chauvinistic Germans with the bitter truth that Germany no longer can attain the power of decision, although it can combine with other states to build power blocs.

It is almost axiomatic that a democratic Germany will be a good partner in Europe and a totalitarian Germany a bad one. The government of the Federal Republic has been of the conservative right, it has raised to high position too many former Nazis and it has, at times, betrayed its distaste for the practice, if not the forms, of democracy. Nevertheless it is a democratic government, democratically elected and kept in line by the critical, bitter opposition of the Social Democrats and the dissenting elements within the government coalition itself.

One of the most important factors insuring the continuation of democracy in Germany and, consequently, that nation's ability to use military power with restraint and intelligence is the labor union movement. This is *not* the Social Democratic Party, which differs with the union movement on many important questions. But all the political parties have to respect the democratic, egalitarian policies of the unions and the unions themselves have been as alert watchdogs as the Socialists and the smaller parliamentary parties.

Two examples: It is the unions who have led the German side of the fight against reconcentration of economic power in the Ruhr and that have warned the Federal Government most sharply on the consequences of continued economic inequality in Germany.

Do these reassuring factors cancel out the disturbing ones? At the moment I think they do. The union movement, the growing belief in democracy as a workable system of government among young people, the movement toward integration with Europe, are stronger at the moment than German inability to "win friends and influence people" in Europe, the rising tide of nationalism and neo-fascism, the growth of the veterans' organizations and other worrying developments in postwar Germany.

The operative words in the preceding sentence are "at the moment."

For tomorrow, not today, is the danger period in Germany's relations with the West. One overall factor which I find discouraging is that the disturbing influences in German public life today are all primarily emotional, springing from roots deep in the mystique of German legend and from the pride and nationalism that bred Hitler. Temperamentally the Germans are not yet accustomed to democratic processes and it may be that not until these emotional influences are finally curbed, as far as such things can be curbed, can Germany be greeted as a reliable ally and partner.

Conversely the elements which seem most reassuring in German life today have intellectual rather than emotional sources and they do not pervade German thought to the extent of the emotional factors mentioned above.

In another period of history, the disquieting factors would have been regarded as paramount in view of Germany's historic impulse toward European dominance. But in this postwar period conditions have changed.

The threat today is not so much that Germany will build a mighty military machine and overrun Europe as it is the possibility that Germany may use her manpower and industrial strength to wring concessions from the western powers that will permit her to regain economic dominance in western Europe. Or even worse, that a revived and arrogant Germany might—as the Germans have done before—make a deal with the Kremlin that would tip the whole balance of power in Europe.

Certainly there are grave risks in rearming Germany. But they are risks we have to take if an effective defense is to be constructed for Europe.

An independent, rearmed Germany will be powerful, perhaps the most powerful nation in Europe, even if its economy is tied to the Schuman Plan and its military strength part of the European Defense Force. An independent, rearmed Germany will contain nationalist and militarist elements that can wreck democracy in Germany and thus help to wreck the whole European defense structure. Above all an independent, rearmed Germany will be in a position to play the East off against the West unless—and here is the heart of the matter—it is bound so tightly to the other nations of western Europe that this is impossible.

The military, political and economic integration of Germany into western Europe is a great goal. But it can prove a sham unless the democratic elements in Germany are sustained continuously in deed as well as word by the West, the militant nationalists and militarists are discouraged and the best characteristics of nationalism harnessed for the good of Germany and Europe.

We need the Germans. But they need us, the United States, Britain and western Europe, far more than we need them. They are not going to be easy partners but it is worth the effort on both sides to bring them into the Atlantic alliance which is Europe's only hope.

From the standpoint of the United States, there is a selfish reason for bringing the Germans into that alliance as an armed and independent ally. Only if Germany makes a contribution to western defense commensurate with its size and importance, can Americans look forward to the day when the bulk of United States troops will be able to leave the continent and return home.

Until the capitol in Washington stands empty to the sky and our hour is passed, it will be an American responsibility to help police the world. But there are cheaper ways of doing it than sending six divisions to Europe, if the rest of the free world can be organized to help.

And the free world means all the free world, not solely the three great European nations whose physical and moral armament we have been discussing. The responsibility of defending Europe rests also on other nations, hard used by war and hard pressed in peace, but nevertheless containing those hardy seeds of freedom which is the West's best weapon against the East.

11. From Scandinavia to the Mediterranean

Up to now we have been concerned with the defense of central Europe, the westernmost end of the great Eurasian land mass which lies between the Danish peninsula on the north and the Alps on the south. In this area are the greatest industrial and military prizes, it thus has to be the site of our most comprehensive defensive efforts. But in a global conflict the central area itself is no stronger than its flanks. Conversely if the western powers can attain a position of strength on one or both of the flanks, a lesser investment in men, money and material may be necessary in the center.

The emphasis for the past year has been on the southern or Mediterranean flank. But the strategic importance of the northern or Scandinavian flank also is great. If the Russians could overrun Scandinavia they would win important strategic rewards, the greatest of which would be the outflanking of the Allied forces on the central front in Europe.

Occupation of the Norwegian coast by the Soviet Army would give Russian submarines and long-range bombers harbors and airfields from which the convoys of men and material steaming into Britain from the United States could be attacked. It would also complicate the air defense of Britain; it is only 500 miles from the industrial Midlands to the southern tip of Norway.

From the economic standpoint, occupation of the Scandinavian peninsula would cut off from central Europe the iron from the Kiruna and Gaellivare workings in northern Sweden and effectively close the Baltic to all but Soviet shipping. The ancient dream of the Baltic as a Russian lake safe from foreign invasion would come true. These are high stakes in a world war.

Should the western powers construct in Scandinavia a defensive system adequate to check Soviet aggression in the area, then important strategic gains would be theirs although these would be largely defensive.

First, the main Russian effort would be channeled into the central area where the western powers will be strongest. Second, the right flank of a Soviet advance through central Europe would be exposed to air attacks from the Allied bases in Scandinavia. Third, free access to the Baltic, insured by holding Denmark and Sweden, would enable the Allies to land airborne or seaborne forces in the rear of the Soviet armies rushing westward toward the Atlantic coast.

Do we have a chance of achieving these tactical successes? It is very doubtful. The northern flank is the weakest of the European flanks.

To begin with, the three Scandinavian countries, Norway, Sweden and Denmark, have a combined population of only 14,500,000 people; Sweden, the largest, best armed and most vulnerable of the three, is not a member of the North Atlantic Treaty Organization.

Each country is vulnerable geographically. Norway has a common frontier with the Soviet Union, Sweden has one with Finland and its coast is only a hundred miles from the German shore of the Baltic and the Russian group of armies and air forces in East Germany.

The entrance to the Danish peninsula is only a stone's throw from the forward Soviet Army positions along the East German–West German frontier.

Under these conditions, in any general war, the West would be doing very well, after six weeks' fighting, to hold southern Norway in the face of a determined Soviet attack. Much of the terrain in Norway and Sweden is suitable for defensive fighting, Denmark is an invitation to an invader.

Norway is a doughty ally. When General Eisenhower completed his first tour of the North Atlantic capitals early in 1951, an officer on his staff remarked that it would be a little difficult to sell the United States Congress the "fact" that, in his words, "the only two peoples who look as though they would fight to the last if the Russians moved are the British and the Norwegians, and both of them have socialist governments."

The Norwegians began their defense efforts with a national militia plus a small navy and air force. Few small European nations made a greater effort in World War II. Peace found Norway, a poor country in the best of times, economically exhausted. At the start of its rearmament, the only effective Norwegian fighting force was the infantry brigade attached to the British Army of the Rhine in Germany.

It was then well under strength. Its numbers have been increased since and the Norwegians have raised another full-strength brigade to be stationed in the far north of Norway along the frontier with the Soviet

Union. Eventually the Norwegians hope to have a total of twelve brigades, ten of which can be mobilized on three days' notice.

The Russian bear has been huffing and puffing at Norwegian rearmament from its outset. Diplomatic notes about supposed rearmament plans for Spitzbergen, protests over the alleged desecration of the graves of Soviet Army dead in northern Norway and the customary vilification and abuse in the Moscow press have been employed in the hope that they would induce the Norwegians to weaken the country's support of the Atlantic Pact.

Of course, the Russian propaganda campaign failed. The Norwegians had some misgivings about the extension of the pact to the eastern Mediterranean but they are neither cowards nor fools and the uproar in Moscow apparently has only strengthened the determination of this tiny people (the population is about 3,233,000) to stand with the West.

This was another example of the ineptness of Soviet diplomacy in meeting western rearmament measures. It is customary in the United States to regard the Russians as wily and guileful negotiators always slipping something over on the West. But the whole Soviet campaign to halt rearmament, even in Germany, has foundered.

Why? The reason is that Stalin's totalitarianism has reached the point in the development of such organizations where even the tiniest hint of compromise, concession or withdrawal is treason. Since these three are essential to any successful negotiation, true diplomatic negotiation is becoming impossible for the Soviet Foreign Ministry.

Denmark sticks up out of northern Europe like a thumb and it is a very sore thumb at the moment. As this is written the Danes stand last on the list of NATO countries in point of overall defense effort and as an American diplomat said, "If you talk to them about defense, they suggest you go out with them and have a nice lunch."

Lavalism, which is very much alive today and flourishes in many continental countries beside France, is well dug-in on the Danish peninsula.

The Danish attitude seems to be: There's nothing we can do to stop the Russians if they come. Even the protestations of NATO leaders that there is no intention of throwing Denmark to the wolves, that there are plans for the country's defense, have not dispelled the gloom.

The Danes have an infantry brigade in Germany attached to the British Army of the Rhine. Their main reliance in time of war would be on a national militia organized on Norwegian lines. Their weakness is their geographical vulnerability; Denmark could be attacked by land from Germany and by sea and air from Poland or the Soviet Union itself. If the Russians start a war, such an attack is inevitable. For in the event of war, the Soviet General Staff would regard it as essential to close the Baltic by grabbing Denmark.

There is reason for the melancholy of the Danes.

It may be that the steady growth of the western defense effort will encourage the Danes. That is the theory at SHAPE. But at the moment the Danes wait shivering in the fogs, looking eastward to the Baltic. The sort of strength that will encourage them is not yet in sight and, like other small nations of western Europe, Denmark will not feel secure until its conquerors of yesterday, the Germans, are rearmed.

Sweden is the largest and most populous of the Scandinavian nations. She is also, although outside NATO, the best armed. Military service is compulsory, the army is well trained and well armed, although with the crying need for equipment in western Europe, it is probable that the Swedes henceforth will have to rely more and more upon their own armament industry.

There is an air force of twenty wings and a comparatively large navy. There also is a national disposition to remain aloof from any group like NATO which seems to the Swedes liable to provoke the Russians to war. It has been well over a hundred years since the Swedes last fought a war. In Sweden there is an almost fanatical isolation which exists side by side with the inner understanding of many Swedes that war is no respecter of either isolationists or neutrals and that, if Russia moves west toward the Atlantic, Sweden is in the way.

"What would Sweden do, if the Russians attacked?" I asked a young Swede.

"Of course we would fight and we are much better prepared to fight than you think. And we would make common cause with the West and try to co-ordinate our defense with that which General Eisenhower is trying to build up. But we hope and believe that we will not have to fight. Many of us believe that it will be in Russia's interest to keep Sweden a neutral in case of war.

"We have not fought in the last two wars," he continued, "but remember that Sweden has a great military tradition. All of us do our military training, we have good weapons and we are tough. If the Russians attack us we will give them a taste of real fighting—after all, we have defeated them in the past."

"If the Swedes or the Danes had half the pluck and determination of the Finns," an American Army officer said recently, "they could hold the Russians forever."

The most vulnerable of the northern tier of nations —Finland—through nationwide self-denial, hard work and national pride has made a brilliant recovery from the effects of two wars with Russia. Almost surrounded by Soviet power, an apple in the grasp of the Russian bear, the Finnish people are bitterly determined to fight the Russians to the last should there be a third war with the Soviet colossus.

The Finnish defense forces are limited to a total of 34,400 of all arms by the Peace Treaty of 1947. Every male serves a year in the army on becoming twenty-one and the cadres of the force include a high percentage of veterans of Finland's forces in the two wars against the Soviet Union between 1939 and 1945. The Finns are, of course, excellent shots, good woodsmen and a hardy, courageous race.

Should war begin, the Finnish Army would be too small to do anything but withdraw into the forests and from there wage a guerrilla war against the Soviet forces. Communism, according to American intelligence reports, has been practically eliminated from the army.

There is also a tiny air force and navy.

The Finns, not a bit daunted by two defeats by the

Russians, will fight again for their country if war begins.

The northern flank is at best an uncertain quantity in Allied defense calculations.

Sweden, the most powerful of the four countries, is outside the NATO and likely to remain so, half out of fear of what the Soviet Union would do if Sweden joined, half out of the delusion that in a new world war Sweden could retain its neutrality. Norway and Finland have tough, experienced fighters but there are very few of them. Denmark combines an inviting vulnerability with a psychological distaste for the whole system of rearmament, an attitude which the government is desperately trying to overcome.

Ultimately the successful defense of the north, in the event of war, would rest upon the ability of United States air power and British seapower to reinforce the national forces of the three countries with troops from Britain or the United States. Such forces need not be very large, five divisions at the most. The Russians would not be able to maintain a large number of divisions at the outset of a campaign in Scandinavia.

It would be vital however to keep a defense alive in case of war. What would have to be avoided would be the sort of blitz tactics which won Norway, Denmark and the Netherlands for the Wehrmacht in 1940. That means constant alertness, a very efficient mobilization scheme, the closest liaison with the Royal Navy and the U.S.A.F. so that both ports and airfields will be familiar to these Allied forces.

The northern flank, as we will see, does not offer as many opportunities to an ingenious command as does the Mediterranean flank. But if war came the possibil-

ities of the Baltic as a road to Russia could be explored
only if the northern flank is held.

The strategic importance in a European war of Belgium and Holland is obvious. Here are two highly developed peoples living in relatively small areas which
include a considerable share of Europe's heavy industry and some of the best ports in Europe, within easy
reach of Britain.

For centuries, Britain's prime consideration in foreign policy was the denial of the channel ports of
Holland, Belgium and northern France to any hostile
power. In view of Britain's supreme importance to the
whole system of Atlantic defense, today this must be
a prime consideration of United States power as well.

In the current situation, when there is never enough
of anything—men, arms or planes—there is a tendency
to dwell on the importance of the larger powers, the
United States, France, Britain and Germany, to the
defense effort. But smaller nations like Belgium and
Holland, whose military contributions will be comparatively small, have an importance of their own.

It is their presence in the North Atlantic Treaty Organization that proves that this is not simply a big-
nation bloc planning an aggressive war against the
Soviet Union but what it really is, an association of
like-minded nations, large and small, earnestly, almost
desperately banded together to build strength to deter
a Soviet attack.

The Dutch entered NATO in a mood of surly
self-assertiveness. They realized the need for the organization, but they were then (they are slightly more
friendly now) extremely bitter over what they charac-

terized as "American interference" in Indonesia which, they believe, cost them their control over much of that rich area. The attitude seemed to be: We'll join this thing the Americans and British are organizing because we have to but no one can make us like them.

There was deep popular resistance in the Netherlands to the sacrifices entailed by rearmament. Nevertheless the government drew up both short- and long-term plans for rearmament. As this is written the implementation of these plans is being delayed by a shortage of weapons and equipment due, as in so many other cases, to the deficiencies in the United States production system of the moment.

By the summer of 1951 the Dutch had placed one infantry brigade at the disposal of General Eisenhower and had the cadre for a reserve infantry division in Holland. By the autumn of 1952, the Dutch hope to have two more reserve infantry divisions ready plus a number of internal security battalions capable of guarding lines of communication and industrial and military installations against airborne attack. The Dutch have not forgotten 1940, when the Germans defeated Holland almost in a day by seizing with Fifth Columnists and airborne troops the country's vital installations.

This is the short-term plan. A second plan projected further into the future calls for an army consisting, by the end of 1954, of five infantry divisions organized into an army corps and two independent divisions. In addition there will be a greater number of defense battalions to safeguard communications and an antiaircraft command. The Dutch expect the total force to be around 250,000 men.

Here again the difference between regular and reserve divisions is emphasized. Of the five divisions in the corps four will be reserve divisions which can be mobilized, according to Dutch officers, "in a few days." These officers point out that the men of these divisions will have had extensive training and will live near their supplies and personal equipment and they assert forcefully that in the case of the Netherlands Army "a few days" means three or four days, no longer.

The fifth division of the corps will be maintained at full strength under arms and ready for action. One third of this division became available to SHAPE in the autumn of 1951, another third is to be ready by the summer of 1952 and the organization of the entire division will be completed by early 1953. As report cards said in my boyhood: *Shows zeal but is too slow.*

The Dutch also have long-term plans for naval and air expansion.

By 1954, the Netherlands government hopes to have a navy boasting an aircraft carrier, two light cruisers, twelve destroyers, six destroyer escorts, four submarines, forty-eight minesweepers and about one hundred aircraft of the naval air service plus patrol and auxiliary vessels.

The expansion of the air force, again with a target date of early 1954, will result in a force of twenty-one fighter squadrons, including day and night fighters, an undisclosed number of ground support squadrons and a number of reconnaissance, army liaison and transport squadrons.

It is far too early, of course, to assess the quality of the new Dutch forces. Those that participated in the British and French maneuvers in the autumn of 1951 were still learning. The young soldiers were enthusiastic and serious, the officers were eager to learn but the snap and precision noticeable in veteran units was absent.

"If we had our own way," a Dutch officer said, "we would like to move a little more slowly. In other words, I should like to concentrate on our long term objectives, rather than hurrying things along to meet our immediate commitments. However, General Eisenhower is the boss, and General Montgomery, whom we respect as a very experienced combat commander, is most optimistic about our progress, so we will try to do both at once.

"In time," he continued, "we can merge our short-term plan with the larger one. What is necessary is to give hard, rigorous training to the young men now so that later, when they become reservists, they can be counted upon. Reserves are the answer and in the case of my country we intend, if there should be another war, to have both the reserves and the means to equip them in a hurry. We will never fall to a blitz like 1940 again."

The Dutch, like everyone else in Europe, are short of training areas and hope to be able to train their divisions in northern Germany. The Germans, who someday will have their own divisions to train, don't like the idea. Where and when the armies of western Europe are to be trained is another SHAPE headache.

The Belgian contribution of ready divisions will be a good deal larger than that of the Netherlands. The Belgians have maintained an army corps, in actual strength something less than a division, in the Rhineland since the end of the war and with the start of

rearmament under SHAPE, a start was made on bringing this corps up to strength. By early in 1952, Belgium hopes to have one ready infantry division and
one ready armored division plus a single reserve infantry division.

During 1952, Belgium plans to increase this force
until by July, the country will have available two
ready infantry divisions, one ready armored division
and two reserve infantry divisions.

The Belgian air force is weak. As this is written it
has only seven fighter squadrons, two fighter bomber
squadrons and some transport planes. By the end of
1952 it is planned to raise the strength to eleven
fighter squadrons, nine fighter bomber squadrons and
two transport squadrons.

During the maneuvers of 1951, the Belgian troops,
especially the infantry, made an excellent impression. They were obviously well trained, their equipment carefully maintained and their ability to co-
ordinate with other units was evident.

Since the war Belgium has been the best off of the
smaller nations of western Europe. The economy is
sounder than most, despite frequent predictions of a
coming crash. Labor difficulties are less important
than in France and austerity almost unknown. Belgian morale, then, could be expected to be very good;
that in the army appears excellent. But Belgium has
its neutralists and it also, despite involvement in two
world wars or perhaps because of it, has many who
feel that anything, even subservience to Moscow,
would be better than a war in Belgium.

On the whole these sentiments have not affected
the mass of the people. The expectation is that in the

event of war Belgian morale would be good, and the Belgian military contribution to the defense of the West small but well trained.

In considering Belgium, and almost every other country on the continent, however, we must think of morale not only at the outset of war but after some weeks or months of war.

The rearmament of western Europe and Scandinavia undoubtedly will benefit the West in a strictly defensive manner. We can expect that, if the re- armament programs now under way are completed within a reasonable time, the Soviet Union may be deterred from attacking in central Europe.

But there is one area, the Mediterranean, where rearmament can do more than deter; it can, if properly carried out with the proper emphasis placed on those Allies we know to be combative and militant enemies of Russia, force the Soviet Union to re-examine its whole military strategy in western Europe and, in the event of war, force the diversion of Russian military strength from central to southeastern Europe.

Here, from Gibraltar to Suez and from the Alps to the Atlas, is half a world in ferment. Here are proud, defiant peoples like the Yugoslavs, Turks and Greeks. Here are the Italians. Here are restless, unknown millions whose hatred for the western world, symbolized by Britain, is exploding.

The colonial powers of yesterday, Egypt and Morocco, are becoming the nationalist powers of today, just as in Europe the great nationalist states of France and Germany now are as dependent on the

bounty of the United States as colonies of the past
have been on them.

Because of the strategic importance of the Mediterranean, it is strikingly evident that these new
nationalist powers must be induced to join the West
in its effort to rearm and halt the new imperialists of
Russia. It is clear, I believe, that although it may not
be possible to win a war in the Mediterranean, any
European conflict could be lost there.

Of the western powers in the Mediterranean, Italy
is the largest, the best established as a member of
NATO and, I suppose, the least stable as an ally.
Here is a poor country where shocking inequalities
between rich and poor breed communism and fascism, a tired country, a nation weary of crusades and
wars and causes. Yet it is a country whose government is on our side, one into which we have poured
millions of dollars of economic aid and into which
we now must pour further millions of military aid.

When the United States plays power politics in
Europe, as it has been doing for the past six years,
albeit with very little power at the outset, it must
take into account past records. So we must accept
the fact that the record of the Italians in World
War II was shocking. The army was corrupt, ineffi-
cient and timorous, the air force negligible, the navy
a joke. We are now in the process of rearming the
army, navy and air force in the expectation that once
they are rearmed, Italy's strength combined with the
strength of all the other NATO powers will deter
the Russians from attacking, give Italy and the other
states greater independence and, should the worst

happen, enable the West to check the Soviet on-slaught.

It is, in Italy's case at least, a very long chance. Since we have already taken it, let us see what has been done and what is planned. For in Italy we are betting on a cart horse as though it were a Derby winner.

In June of 1951 the Italian Army was composed of three infantry divisions at 90% strength, four infantry divisions at 80% strength, two infantry divisions at 66% strength, one armored brigade at 90% strength and one armored brigade at 45% strength.

By June of 1952 it is expected that four infantry divisions will be at full strength and that the supporting units, heavy artillery, engineers and the like, also will be established at full strength.

The overall goal, by the end of 1952, is twelve divisions as part of the European Defense Force, depending on what progress is made toward lifting the Italian Treaty Limitations which restricted Italy to an army of 250,000 including 65,000 Carabinieri.

Defense Minister Randolfo Pacciardi asserts that the twelve divisions in 1952 will have the same firepower as sixty to seventy divisions in 1939; a questionable statement.

The Italians have placed at Eisenhower's disposal three infantry divisions, one tank brigade and one Alpini (mountain) brigade.

The Italian air force is being built up by the inclusion of jet fighters. As this is written there are sixteen fighter wings, including six jet wings, and Italian factories report they have begun the production of jet fighters.

The Navy is expanding from a base of two battle-ships, three cruisers, eight destroyers, fourteen tor-pedo boats, twenty-three corvettes, six gun boats and eleven antisubmarine trawlers.

More than most NATO nations Italy depends on arms from the United States. Major General John K. Rice, chief of the United States Military Assistance Group in Rome, estimated in the autumn of 1951 that only 75% of the arms authorized in 1950 and 13% of those authorized in 1951 had been received by Italy by September 1951. The standard Italian rifle is a weapon first made in 1891, and much of the equipment has been salvaged from piles of discarded American, British and German military stores.

It is not surprising that the estimate of the capacity of the Italian Army to maneuver—or fight—at the same pace as other Allied armies is low.

Obviously, if the United States gives Italy arms and helps Italy to make more arms and equipment, the new Italian Army will be able to take the field tolerably well equipped. But the equipment needed for twelve divisions, starting from scratch, is enor-mous. So military men, unimpressed by the Italian record in World War II and skeptical of the value of the Italian Army as a makeweight to deter Russian aggression, sometimes wonder whether it would not be a good idea to give this equipment to nations whose fighting capacity is not in doubt.

There is very little possibility that this will be done. As this is written, the United States is firmly com-mitted to the idea of an armed league to deter Soviet aggression or meet it if it comes. This commitment means, of course, that we must take the weak nations and the strong. Politically, it probably is the wisest course. From the military standpoint of the number of troops available, their quality and morale, it often appears wasteful and slow.

Many Italian units fought exceptionally well in World War II. But the Italians did not fight well as armies in Greece, Africa, Sicily or Italy. It may be that, by using Italian divisions in corps with French or other European divisions, their efficiency will increase and, if the worst comes, they will fight well. Italy could participate in a short, successful war. Like France, her ability to withstand a long conflict involving not only the obvious horrors of bombing but prolonged rationing, mass conscription and labor direction is doubtful.

The military prospect improves as we move eastward along the north shore of the Mediterranean. East of Italy there live three valiant peoples, the Yugoslavs, the Greeks and the Turks. Here, if anywhere in the Mediterranean, is real military support for the western cause.

"I wish to God we could forget about the Italians and the Belgians and some of the others," an American diplomat remarked in an unguarded moment, "and leave the military side to those who know what it's all about. What is the sense in giving jets to the Belgians or the Italians when the R.A.F. is short of planes? And why in the name of all that's holy are we arming the Italians when the same investment in Yugoslavia, Greece and Turkey would mean so much more to our security?"

First, the Yugoslavs, a valorous people. They have fought the Germans, the Austrians, the Turks, and undoubtedly they would fight the Russians, as they would fight any invader.

Here is the land of the guerrilla and the partisan. Here we could help build an army of tough fighting men who with modern equipment could do a lot more than hold out in the mountains. These people could engage the Russian or satellite armies on even terms if they had the guns and the tanks and the planes.

Can the Yugoslavs be trusted? In the event of an invasion of their country by the satellites or by the Soviet Army, I believe the Yugoslavs would fight bravely and resourcefully whether they had no allies or twenty. The seriousness of Tito's break with Moscow cannot be questioned, although there were plenty of western intelligence officers who did question its authenticity when it occurred, nor can we doubt the antagonism built up in Yugoslavia toward Russia by the usual stupidities of Soviet diplomacy and propaganda since the break.

Are the Yugoslavs questionable political allies? They are. The regime, despite some slight movement toward a more liberal view of human rights, remains a totalitarian one, probably more totalitarian than Franco's government in Spain.

The Yugoslavs then are questionable in the sense that they are not the pure-hearted democrats with whom we would *like* to be associated in the defense of Europe. But the time is long past when the United States, in its world struggle with communism, could afford to select its allies through a political purity test.

What counts today is not whether a people goes to

town meeting, admires the Constitution of the United States or keeps its jails clean but whether it will stand with us, whether it can use the arms we give it and whether, in the last analysis, if war starts, it can be counted on to fight by our side.

This is a long way from the crusading idealism of 1917 and an even longer way from the principles of democracy that animated the founding fathers. To such a moral impasse have Americans been brought by two world wars and six years of world crisis. But it is useless to hide in the past or even in our isolation. This is the world we live in. And if we want to continue to live, we had better make the best of what we have.

The Yugoslav government suffers, like all totalitarian regimes, from an advanced case of spy phobia, understandable in view of the fact that the satellite nations to the north and east, Hungary, Rumania and Bulgaria, are rearming at top speed and are telling the world what they are going to do with Tito and his supporters when they catch them. However justified, the spy phobia prevents the gathering of reliable information on the Yugoslav armed forces and even prevents the exchange of information between the Yugoslav general staff and the American and British general staffs in Europe.

The army is believed to number over 600,000 men. Next to the Russian Army this is the largest in Europe. By all accounts the troops themselves have the same qualities that make the Russian soldier feared: they are brave, they have great physical stamina and they are resolute, unimaginative fighters.

The standard of mechanical ability in the Yugoslav Army is slightly higher than in the Soviet Army, according to Allied officers who have studied both forces.

The gravest weakness in the Yugoslav Army is the lack of equipment. At the end of World War II, when Tito still was a Soviet ally, the Yugoslav Army received considerable quantities of supplies and weapons from the Soviet Union. This materiel was not as good as that now going from Russia to the satellite states, a great deal of it was old or of inferior quality, and inadequate maintenance facilities in Yugoslavia and the passage of six years has not improved it.

The worst feature of the equipment situation, however, is that spare parts, ammunition and replacements must come from Russia. None of these have entered Yugoslavia since the break between Tito and the masters of Russia. Today the Yugoslav Army, in the words of one American general, is "held together with pieces of string."

The cost to the United States of re-equipping Tito would be formidable because the job would have to be done from the shoes of the soldiers to their helmets. But it is worth it since the military power of the western world receives a formidable reinforcement.

For Yugoslav co-operation in any alliance against the Soviet Union, once the Yugoslav forces are re-equipped, would not be measured in defensive terms alone. Twenty-five Yugoslav divisions perched on the southern flank of any possible Russian drive westward would be a greater deterrent to Soviet aggression than twelve Italian divisions in the Po valley or fifteen French divisions on the Rhine.

Despite all the Soviet claims of unity of purpose among the satellite peoples, there must be on the part of the Soviet General Staff deep suspicion of how well the satellite forces would fight in the event of war. If the Bulgars, Rumanians and Hungarians had to fight the Yugoslavs they would encounter a foe who is dangerous both militarily and politically to the Russians.

For in the Balkans, where Soviet communism has tried for six years to eliminate national patriotism, Yugoslavia is the exception to the rule that all must bow to Stalin or be eliminated. The Yugoslavs are still there, defiant and independent. The Russians would think twice before sending other Balkan troops to fight against a nation so imbued with the importance of its independence.

Like most of the nations on which the United States can count for determination to safeguard their independence by rearming and for combativeness in war, if that should come, the Yugoslavs will not be easy allies. They will haggle, they will be suspicious, they will cling to their own military customs; they can be helped but they cannot be bossed. Here again, the United States faces the problem: Does it want allies or vassals?

Moving further eastward along this vital northern shore of the Mediterranean we come to those gay, great people, the Greeks. Here, in Greece, are many of the problems that exist in Italy: abject poverty side by side with ostentatious wealth, a poor country and a poor people. Yet there is something else be-

neath the surface, something that shone with an
antique splendor when, in the autumn of 1940, the
Italian blackshirt bravos attacked the Greeks.

"The Greek soldier will give you everything you
ask for," a British officer said; "endurance, bravery,
common sense, all that plus something that goes beyond phrases like good morale, a sort of fury at the
idea that anyone should put a foot in his country
without his invitation. God's boots! I saw them in the
winter of 1940–1941, with damn all to eat and very
little in the way of equipment, sail into the Italians
like tigers."

The Greeks are another "victorious" power impoverished in victory. The army has fine fighting
qualities proven not only in the war but in the long,
bitter, unspectacular battle against the Communists
in northern Greece. For it fell to the Greeks, having
given Mussolini the first sound drubbing suffered by
an Axis army in the autumn of 1940, to hand the
colossus of postwar Russia its first military defeat by
wearing down and wearing out the Soviet-sponsored
guerrillas.

The Greek Army has been trained by the United
States Army and it has a high percentage of officers
and men with experience in all sorts of warfare from
the sneak raids and rough and tumble flare-ups on
the frontier to the great battles of the British Eighth
Army in Africa.

The core of the Greek Army is nine divisions of
good, experienced infantry. Eight of these divisions
are disposed to meet any attack across the Bulgarian
frontier, an attack from tiny Albania is unlikely, and
one division is stationed near Athens. In addition a

small frontier force, specially chosen for the job, patrols the frontiers.

The valor of the Greek private soldier seldom has been questioned. But in this century Greek armies too frequently have been poorly trained and ill fed. Since the United States Army's military mission took over the training of the army, first under General Van Fleet and latterly under Major General Reuben Jenkins, both the training and the leadership have improved.

Young Greek officers have been sent to the Infantry School at Fort Benning, and experienced United States officers have been added to the Greek divisions as advisers. The Americans have sold their own doctrine of incessant training to the Greeks and the efficiency of the field divisions is higher today than it was during the protracted frontier war with the communists.

The Greek Army is short on modern heavy weapons although machine guns, mortars and rifles were supplied in quantity during the struggle with the communist forces in the north. But a more desperate need is for field equipment, clothing, field kitchens and the like.

The admission of Greece to the North Atlantic alliance will insure military aid for Greece. Few armies are better equipped, today, in training and leadership to use it effectively.

Field Marshal Papagos purged the staff and the higher field command to restore experienced soldiers to control of military matters and to eliminate the politicians in uniform.

Any Soviet move in the Balkans would involve the

Greeks. They know it and they are ready for it. They have a much lower opinion, incidentally, of the satellite forces than do some excitable pundits in Washington, holding the Bulgars, whom they regard as only slightly more intelligent than horses, in low esteem. Greece and Turkey are necessary to hold the Mediterranean, as General Bradley has pointed out. But an adequate, well-equipped Greek Army added to the larger armies of Turkey and Yugoslavia can raise second thoughts in Russian minds over the advisability of plunging westward in central Europe.

East of Greece, their frontiers meeting in Thrace, lies Turkey, once the suzerain of both Greece and most of Yugoslavia, now united with them in a determination to maintain national independence. With its admission into NATO, Turkey became the extreme right flank of Eisenhower's command, and like Norway on the extreme left flank, it has a common frontier with the Soviet Union although the length of the frontier is much greater, approximately 376 miles.

For five years the Joint American Military Mission for Aid to Turkey has been assisting in the training and equipment of the Turkish fighting forces. Partly because of this help, but mostly because the Turkish soldiers, brave, hardy peasants, are excellent material, the Turkish military position is extremely good.

But the purely military situation as usual is only half the story, morale is an equally important part and here too the situation in Turkey is reassuring. Having fought the Russians thirteen times in the past four hundred years the Turks are neither awed by Russia's military might nor terrified by stories of

Russian cruelty. The Turks, themselves, have no light hand in war.

Turkey has received over $500,000,000 in military aid from the United States since 1947 and advice in training, organization and tactics from the Joint American Military Mission. The result is a stream-lined army of just under half a million men with a spearhead of six armored brigades. (At the end of the second World War, which Turkey entered on the Allied side in February, 1945, the army was an un-wieldy force of close to a million.)

The Turkish Army has received signal equipment, bazookas, howitzers and field guns, anti-aircraft and anti-tank guns, tanks, trucks, jeeps and machine guns from the United States.

This was a big mouthful for an army which was almost unmechanized. The Turkish soldier or *asker*, like the peasant soldier anywhere in eastern Europe or the Near East, has little knowledge of machinery and it takes time, and an appalling number of mechanical mishaps due to his ignorance, until a minimum of mechanical efficiency is attained.

Discipline has been tightened and training im-proved. The soldiers are brave and hardy. It has been difficult to induce generals and staff officers to dis-card tactics and organization more suited to plod-ding infantry and horse cavalry than mechanized formations, but the job is being done.

The air force has been strengthened with United States bombers and transport planes; and some British fighters, submarines, destroyers and minesweepers have been sent to the navy.

Yet despite all this aid, one gets the feeling that

the western attitude toward Turkey's role in any new conflict emphasizes the defensive rather than the offensive. "On the other side of the hill," it seems to me that the rearmament of Turkey, even more than that of Yugoslavia, poses a real question for Russian strategists: Is it safe to move west with the Turks on the left flank?

Such a question involves, of course, not only the Turks but the prospect that the Turkish Army would be strong enough in time of war to mount offensive operations against the Soviet Union with a minimum amount of assistance, most of it in the form of air and sea power, from the United States and Britain.

The whole strategy of the United States in the eastern Mediterranean seems to be obsessed with the idea of *holding* this country or that, so as to extend the area of friendly air through which American bombers would have to fly to strike at the industrial area of the Donetz Basin in the southeastern Ukraine or the oil fields and refineries of the Caucasus.

This is naturally important to the Air Force generals but it may be that insistence on confining the offensive to the air may be diverting our attention from the rewards to be won, if the Russians should strike, from more ambitious plans in the eastern Mediterranean.

In two wars, Britain and the United States have failed to take the opportunities which their sea power offered them in that area. In the peculiar circumstances of a war between the West and Russia, it would be folly to miss the chance again.

It is obvious that in such a war the West could not invade the Soviet Union on a wide front and probably would not want to even if its high command had at its disposal the enormous numbers of men necessary for such an operation. But it is highly probable that the western powers would wish to launch limited operation against various points of the periphery of the Soviet Union.

Turkey is the only number of the North Atlantic alliance close to areas of Russia where such operations would hurt. The Dardanelles hold the key to the Black Sea and if a war with Russia is to include some "nibbling" operation, the Black Sea coast becomes very important.

The three nations of the extreme right or southern flank, Yugoslavia, Greece and Turkey, thus seem much stronger from the military standpoint than do the Scandinavian nations on the northern or left flank of Eisenhower's continental command. They are of course much further from the main source of industrial supply, the United States, than are the Scandinavian nations and even less capable of making their own weapons.

Turkey's major contribution to its own weapons, for instance, is the Ankara, an old 7.92-mm bolt-action rifle modeled on the obsolete Mauser.

This almost absolute reliance on the West for military equipment means that the Mediterranean must be open. Yugoslavia, Greece and Turkey all have ports on the inland sea, hence the fall of one of these nations and the subsequent thrust of Soviet power to the Mediterranean would mean eventual interference, by bomber or submarine, with supplies to the other two.

The exercise of sea power in the Mediterranean, in

the sense of the passage of merchantmen through the sea from east to west or west to east, was only barely possible in World War II when the Axis retained bases for aircraft in Sicily, Sardinia, Southern Italy and Patellaria. With the extension of the range and bomb load of land-based aircraft since then, it is all the more important that all the powers in the eastern Mediterranean receive the fullest American support, so that none falls to Soviet aggression.

There is another danger in the Mediterranean which may in time be more important than the present danger to the independence of Turkey, Greece and Italy of an aggressive Russian government. This danger is the increased nationalism of the nations along the southern shore of the sea from Egypt to Morocco.

The political danger is that if the West fails to reach agreements with these aroused peoples, agreements which must be more than large-scale handouts and the retention of quasi-colonialism, North Africa will drift from aggressive nationalism into anarchy. If the United States, Britain and France attempt to suppress the nationalist movements by force, they will only increase their virulence. If they do not, then the Communists will win a foothold in an area of supreme strategic importance to the West. Either way, the Atlantic powers face perplexing problems.

You cannot defend Europe without defending the Mediterranean. But you cannot defend the Mediterranean by defending the northern half of it. If the rearmament of friendly European nations bordering the Mediterranean is to mean anything, it must be accompanied by a series of settlements with the

Moslem powers of North Africa. And because in North Africa the Atlantic powers will have to deal with peoples holding political and religious beliefs totally different from theirs, the political job in North Africa will be as complex and as difficult as any facing the Atlantic alliance in Europe.

We have been discussing nations whose strength relatively is less than that of the Big Three of the Atlantic alliance, the United States, Britain and France. But there is an adage about a chain and its weakest link.

12. The Economic Problems of NATO

The military and morale problems besetting the various countries belonging to NATO are, as we have seen, extremely complex and serious. But they are not as important, in any single instance, to the overall task of rearming Europe as the general economic problem that arose out of the rearmament conception.

By the autumn of 1951 these issues overshadowed all others as two fundamental difficulties developed.

(1) Eisenhower had found divisions sufficient for the initial NATO force. The divisions were being formed but there was a drastic shortage of equipment.
(2) The rearmament effort of certain countries, measured in terms of those countries' industrial contribution to rearmament, had seriously affected the entire economic outlook in those countries.

These difficulties were increased, they certainly were not helped, by the fact that the whole military, political and economic machinery of NATO had become so vast, intricate and complex that only a very few men could see the entire picture.

As is customary among bureaucrats, each new problem inspired the formation of a committee which

in turn spawned a subcommittee. Large numbers of
purposeful young officials, eyeglasses gleaming and
brief cases bulging, hurried around Europe uttering
Gobbledookian statements.

In European history the autumn of 1951 probably
will be remembered as the period of the great Washington invasion when the confusion, self-assertiveness
and basic uncertainty common to our bureaucrats
was transferred to Paris and thence to the rest of
western Europe on such a large scale that several
innocent nonofficial Americans were pre-briefed,
briefed and de-briefed before they had a chance to
protest.

The original NATO structure just grew and grew.

In May of 1951 it had been simplified. At the top
stood the North Atlantic Council of Foreign Ministers and just beneath the top the North Atlantic
Council Deputies. Their work was correlated by an
international staff in London.

Four agencies were directly responsible to this top-
most echelon. They were, first, the Military Committee formed of the Chiefs of Staff of the NATO
nations, which met infrequently but whose functions
really were carried out by two bodies in permanent
session in Washington, the Military Representatives
Committee and the Standing Group of Representatives of the United States, France and Great Britain.
Originally SHAPE was subordinate to these groups.
As a result of Eisenhower's personal drive, influence
in Europe and mounting international importance,
SHAPE became coequal with these permanent
groups; Eisenhower, for instance, talked directly to
the North Atlantic Council.

On the economic side there were two groups in permanent session, the Defense Production Board in London and the Financial and Economic Board in Paris.

The Defense Production Board was headed by William R. Herod, a former president of the International General Electric Company, who in June of 1951 appeared to be more aware of the economic storms ahead than some of the politicians of western Europe.

He pointed out then that dual pricing policies, used in Europe to discriminate between home and foreign users, and the uncertainties of national control policies had weakened the willingness of nations to depend on each other for raw materials or finished products for military or civilian use.

"If the NATO defense efforts are to be complementary and dovetailed for maximum effectiveness," he said, "compensatory production and transfer must not be restricted to military items, such as would tend industrially to limit the realization of collective results to a ceiling considerably below the optimum potential with considerable strain on the payments mechanism and a less equitable sharing of the burden."

At that time Herod was looking forward to a rise in the standard of living of the NATO nations in two or three years. This could be accomplished, he believed, even under the conditions imposed by the economic consequences of rearmament.

This prediction, which reads rather strangely in the light of what has happened since, was qualified by several conditions. To reach the goal of a rise in living standards simultaneous with rearmament production programs Herod stipulated that there must be greater austerity and more economic controls in Europe plus better allocation of raw materials.

So the troubles that came upon NATO that autumn were not unforeseen even though sufficient weight had not been attached to them.

Up until the meeting of the Atlantic Council in Ottawa in September, 1951, the affairs of NATO seemed to be moving fairly smoothly. The Financial and Economic Board, the Defense Production Board, and the Military Standing Group in Washington had completed their planning. So had SHAPE.

The Standing Group, on Eisenhower's advice, had agreed on the number and type of troops to be contributed by the member nations if the Soviet Union was to be deterred from invading Europe.

The Defense Production Board had decided how much equipment could be produced in Europe under the original organization of the economic sections of the NATO structure, that is without greater coordination of European industrial programs or purchases by the United States to stimulate such production.

The Board found that there was surplus industrial production to be drawn from Europe. But it also found that financial stimulus would be necessary if this additional production was to be used to meet the shortages in military equipment. In none of the member nations, except perhaps in Britain, was there any willingness to assume new financial burdens.

In fact, as an American said, "It's all very much like Mark Twain and the weather. Everybody I meet talks about rearmament but no one seems to want to do anything about it."

Meanwhile the Financial and Economic Board were gravely concerned by what was happening to the European economies under the impact of rearmament. The cost of living was rising in France. The British balance of payments position sagged seriously. The Board was told repeatedly that if the plans for industrial production for rearmament were to progress much further, economic aid must come from the United States.

All this worried Eisenhower very much. In early September in Paris he felt that the first impulse toward rearmament, which he had done so much to create, was slowing down.

The General understood the economic difficulties. But he blamed some of these difficulties on the lack of courageous leadership.

"That's what these countries have to have," he said, "someone to go to the people and hammer home the lesson that they have to take financial risks, that they have to make sacrifices if this thing is going to work."

At that time he contemplated going to the Ottawa conference himself. He changed his mind and instead sent a personal message which was very strong, even for Eisenhower.

As so often happens, the difficulties produced more committees. At Ottawa it was decided to form a Temporary Committee of the Council, composed of members from the twelve NATO countries. They in turn appointed an Executive Bureau, the "three wise men," a group composed of men of influence both in their own countries and in the rest of Europe. W. Averell Harriman of the United States, Jean Monnet of France and Sir Edwin Plowden of Britain were the three selected.

The "three wise men" in turn appointed two advisory groups, an Economic and Financial Committee and a Screening and Costing Committee.

But the principal task remains with the trio. They must find a way to reconcile the economic part of the drive for military strength with internal economic stability in the member nations. Success in this depends to a large degree in setting a better time schedule for military production, one which will not bite so heavily into existing commitments for civilian output. But here "the three wise men" encounter the military necessity of completing the equipment of the minimum number of divisions, about twenty-five, which Eisenhower considers essential by the summer of 1952.

Yet the information gathered by the three wise men indicated that what many people had feared actually was happening. Rearmament was seriously threatening the economic health of western Europe. And if economic stability was lost, political chaos giving communism the opportunity to recoup its losses since 1946 was a probability.

Now although all the reports and recommendations flow into the central agencies such as SHAPE and the Executive Bureau, the real battle to save Europe's economic stability has to be fought on twelve different fronts, the economies of the twelve NATO members.

In almost every case the remedies which may re-

store stability are those which the individual governments are loath to take. Financial policies which
involve increased taxation, controls of such production as consumers' goods, controls on imported products—all meaning an increase in austerity—never are
popular with the people on whom they are imposed
and hence less popular with the politicians who have
to impose them. When the lukewarm attitude of
some of the populations of the NATO members
toward the whole rearmament program is considered,
it is not surprising that the government officials called
upon to enforce these policies will see their political
defeat as the outcome of the policies.

One way in which the cost to the member countries of rearmament can be reduced is through a
co-ordinated arms program and a great increase in
standardization of armaments.

Here is one of the encouraging aspects of the
European Defense Force, which in time will develop,
if present planning is followed, into a force in which
the troops of six nations will use the same arms, the
same ammunition and wear the same uniforms. Such
a force then could be equipped as a unit with a cor-
responding saving both in the initial outlay and in
subsequent supply and replacement.

The crisis in the economic aspects of NATO
reached a climax in the autumn of 1951. It resulted
from the following factors:

(1) The Congress of the United States had cut
    foreign aid.
(2) The weapons promised member nations by
    the United States to make up their own

deficiencies in arms production just had not been delivered.

(3) There was a shortage of machine tools in the United States impeding American efforts to rearm ourselves and rearm Europe.

(4) Europe itself, under the most favorable use of present industrial plant and labor, could not produce more than 48% of the equipment which European forces will require by early 1954 when, it is hoped, over 55 divisions will be available to the Supreme Commander.

(5) At that point European production was turning out only about 25% of the necessary military equipment.

(6) It was clear that to make more equipment, industrial production would have to be diverted from consumers' goods to weapons.

(7) If expenditures for armaments increased, inflation—already well established in France and Italy—might run wild.

The looming economic crisis had its political connotations. If the standard of living in Britain fell further as a result of rearmament and more of the social benefits of the welfare state disappeared, Aneurin Bevan's prediction that Britain could not both rearm and maintain the social program instituted by the Labor Governments of 1945–1951 would be proven right.

In Italy and France it was obvious that a fall in the standard of living would help Moscow and inter-

national communism. In other nations where communism is weak but apathy toward rearmament
strong, public opinion would move further towards
neutrality in the face of the Soviet danger.

This was a period of re-examination of what Europe had done, what it was doing and what it could
do in the future. In reviewing the past year and a
half when Europe's rearmament was getting under
way, the "three wise men" found four conditions that
had complicated the process of rearmament and
produced the factors that in turn produced the crisis.

The first, and perhaps the most important, was the
jump in the price of raw materials resulting from the
increased buying which followed the start of the war
in Korea and the start of European rearmament.

Another was the cut in European exports as production was diverted to armament. This meant a
drop in earnings abroad at the precise moment when
money was needed for raw materials and other key
imports.

There was, is and will be a shortage of both coal
and steel in western Europe.

The rise in the costs of imports coupled with increased employment spurred inflation. By December
of 1951 it was estimated that the price level in western Europe had risen 25% since the middle of 1950.

As this is written, no final plan for dealing with
all these difficulties has been completed. It is evident
however that the solution will have to include two
processes: a scaling-down of European production
for rearmament during the first half of 1952 and an
increase in both the amount and the rate of flow of

American armament supplies during the correspond-
ing period.

Another solution is the placing of American armaments contracts abroad. This might help rebuild the
European arms industry and at the same time provide the dollars necessary for raw materials. But a
snag is that such a program would be opposed violently by the United States industries now involved
in rearmament.

This book has dealt chiefly with what Europe and
the Europeans are doing to construct a military force
large enough and efficient enough to deter the
Soviets. But what the United States does and doesn't
do is inextricably connected with the European effort.
And the plain facts brought to the surface by the
crisis in NATO in the autumn of 1951 showed that
the United States was not without blame.

Our own deficiencies naturally were overlooked by
table-pounding Congressmen junketing around Europe and making themselves popular by telling
Europeans they had to do more. Nevertheless it was
true that, measured in dollar value, the United States
had delivered about 65% of the amount it promised
under the Mutual Defense Assistance Program for
the fiscal year ending June 30, 1951, and little of what
had been promised for the next fiscal year.

Here is one reason why continental air forces are
flying superannuated *Spitfires* and the French Army
in Germany is nursing ancient Sherman tanks.

The American production picture was particularly
gloomy regarding military aircraft. Aside from the
British aircraft industry, whose production is high in
quality but less impressive quantitatively, there is no

important aircraft industry in western Europe. The
United States must make up the difference.

Yet in November, 1951, the United States was still
far short of Defense Mobilizer Charles E. Wilson's
goal of a production capacity of 50,000 planes a year
and it did not appear that this objective, which Wilson had hoped in the preceding January to reach by
the end of 1952, would be won by the end of 1953.
It is probable that military aircraft production in
1951 was no more than about 5,000 aircraft of all
types.

So it appears that despite the flood of criticism
from across the Atlantic the Europeans are not the
only people who have failed to put their full weight
into rearmament. I asked an American industrialist
visiting West Germany what he thought the trouble
was.

"Well, one thing is, everyone is trying to blame
someone else. In industry we think the services are
to blame, they think we move too slowly, everybody
blames labor and labor blames everyone else. I think
that the real trouble is that we're going through one
of those periods in the United States when no one is
worried about anything. There's no pressure as there
was in the first months of the Korean war; the Russians are pretty quiet. Perhaps you can blame this
apathy on the government. It kept people whipped
up so long with all sorts of warnings and predictions.
But the effect is wearing off. Somebody says the
Russians are making 12,000 planes a year, don't believe it myself, and the usual answer is 'ho-hum, so
what!' "

This attitude has its counterpart in Europe. It has

contributed a great deal to the laggard pace of the European rearmament effort.

Has the United States done all it could to stimulate European arms and equipment production? Probably not and mainly because it is tied so tightly by its own major allies in its approach to Germany, the most powerful industrial nation on the continent and the one, up to now, which has contributed less to the continent's industrial rearmament.

The French, Dutch, Belgians, Norwegians and others are worried equally by German soldiers and German industrial rearmament and they are naturally frightened of a combination of the two. As a result the German industrial production was prevented, throughout most of 1951, from making a larger contribution to industrial defense needs. Some of the blame, of course, must be borne by the Germans who for two years tried to slip industrial expansion schemes past the Military Security Board, organized by the Occupation Powers, and hence made the Board warier and stricter than it would have been ordinarily.

An instance of German heavyhandedness occurred in November of 1951 when the August Thyssen Company, one of Germany's biggest prewar steel producers, applied to the Military Security Board for permission to construct extensive additions to its plant at Duisburg-Hamborn. The new construction would include a blooming mill and would raise the steel output of the plant to nearly 1,000,000 tons a year.

The Thyssen company was confident. It knew, as most Ruhr firms knew, that although the Allies resolutely rejected all applications for increases in output in the restricted industries, they were eager to raise European steel production. Indeed a few days before the application was made, United States Defense Mobilizer Wilson had made a speech urging a 25% increase in European steel output.

So the company, even before the application was made to the Military Security Board, had begun work on the additions to the plant. When the application was rejected by the MSB there was a national outcry against unintelligible Allied policy.

The incident is of a type inseparable from the dissolution of Allied Occupation in Germany and as such not terribly important. It is important however in indicating the duality of United States policy in Europe during a crucial period for the economic rearming of the continent.

For while on one hand the United States was doing everything it could to increase industrial output in Europe for Europe's defense (and striving mightily to bring Federal Germany into that defense system) it was at the same time maintaining the checks, first established in 1945, against the expansion of German industrial output.

By the time this book is published, the conditions for Germany's final emergence from the status of an occupied power, agreement with the Allied nations on a General Agreement and attached Conventions covering their relations and agreement on the European Defense Force, should have been met.

It is reasonable to believe that this change in the status of the Federal Republic will be followed by the sudden discovery that a great many of the things needed for European defense, products not essentially military in nature, can be bought in Germany.

From the time German rearmament was first projected, John J. McCloy, United States High Commissioner in Germany, urged American officials and business men to start buying in Germany. There were plenty of German products, such as chemicals, whose increased production did not run counter to the restrictions of the Military Security Board, which the West could have been stock-piling from Germany during the long period in which the Allies and the Federal Government stumbled hand in hand toward rearmament.

The economic crisis that struck the NATO nations in the autumn of 1951 undoubtedly had some serious consequences. But it also was responsible, I found, for a much clearer appreciation on the part of many American officials of what Europe is up against in its attempt to both rearm and maintain standards of living high enough to check communism. It became apparent, even to some of the generals at Heidelberg, that it was not simply because Europeans spoke different languages or lacked "know-how" that rearmament production had been delayed, but that solid economic causes were at the bottom of a great deal of the delay.

The gift that the crisis brought was a sense of balance in the European program for rearmament. The Soviet military superiority in central Europe had been slightly reduced by the time it occurred. But there was evidence, which the crisis brought to a head, that if the United States and its Allies continued to rush pell-mell toward exaggerated production and mobilization targets the resulting economic difficulties would open the way to new communist gains.

It is customary these days to arbitrarily select a year as a "critical year" in our relations with the Soviet Union. That's nonsense. Every year is a critical year because of the character of Soviet Foreign Policy. This seeks to exploit every crack in our defenses, whether that crack is economic, political or military, whenever and wherever the crack occurs.

In late 1951 we came very close to paying so much attention to the military side of our effort that the economic and political aspects were overlooked.

That danger was averted. But granted the Russian policy mentioned above, it will recur whenever one type of rearmament—military, economic or political— is favored over another. Whenever we believe that a single type of rearmament, rather than the combination of all three, can do the job we are in danger.

13. If War Breaks Out Tomorrow

Russia forced the West to rearm. But the burden is heavy in those European nations impoverished by World War II. It is natural then that western Europe listens anxiously for any word that the Soviet Union is ready to abandon its policies of the last six years and try to co-operate in Europe. Granted the dread of war that pervades the continent, it is understandable that the various Russian "peace offensives" of the last two years receive a warmer, less skeptical welcome in Europe than in the United States.

Under these conditions, the plan for world disarmament presented to the General Assembly of the United Nations by the United States, Britain and France in the autumn of 1951 was a shrewd stroke of propaganda. It won for the three leading western powers the propaganda initiative by countering the insidious propaganda line of the communists in western Europe that the United States, hell-bent for war, was dragging Britain and France along in a race to rearm, and attack the Soviet Union.

But it was no more than that. If it was intended, as some officials claimed, as an approach to the Soviet Union for an armistice in the cold war then the State Department, the Foreign Office and the Quai d'Orsay have learned nothing about the Soviet Union. The rulers of Russia, if they ever do negotiate with the West in a serious attempt to end the cold

263

war, will not do so before the General Assembly of the United Nations. The whole record of postwar Soviet diplomacy indicates that whenever Russia sought serious negotiations with the West, the approach and negotiations were secret. The conversations that led to the lifting of the blockade of Berlin are a case in point.

The disarmament proposal was good propaganda, but no more than that. As a serious effort to induce the Soviet Union to disarm it was quite useless. And as long as the government of Russia retains its present character, that of a ruthless totalitarian dictatorship, all such attempts will be useless.

For the subjection of the Russian people and all the peoples of all the republics of the Union to the Stalinist dictatorship rests in part upon the ability of the government to convince the people of the existence of a world-wide conspiracy against the Soviet Union.

Only by preserving this fiction can the Russian people be driven, year in and year out, to toil under shocking conditions for low wages and a tiny trickle of consumers' goods, to yield its sons to the armed services. The concept of a Soviet Union encircled by enemy states is absolutely necessary to the maintenance of the extensive apparatus of repression, the troops of the M.V.D. and the M.G.B., the hundreds of thousands of spies and informers and plain-clothes men.

The government of the Soviet Union must maintain them for use against the "spies" and "saboteurs" sent to Russia by "the imperialist war mongers" or against those mutinous Russians who, for propaganda purposes, are never motivated in their crimes by anything but foreign or "Trotzkyite" influences.

A government that is totalitarian has one salient weakness. It cannot admit its mistakes to the people. Therefore there must be an enemy on whom all mistakes and all political deviation can be blamed and whose presence justifies the enormous expenditure for military and internal security purposes.

This does not mean that the tremendous Soviet Army is maintained *only* because of the fundamental moral instability of the regime. The Soviet Army of today, like the Russian Army of the past, is a potential weapon of aggression.

Parenthetically, it should be assumed in the West, I believe, that grumbling over the size of the army probably is less general in Russia than over the size and ubiquity of the security organization. Large armies have existed in Russia since the sixteenth century and a thousand years of invasion by Mongols, Tartars, Poles, Swedes and Germans have led Russians to believe that a huge army is indispensable to any Russian state, be it communist, fascist or republican.

It is not the size of the Russian Army that is the main concern of the West. It is that this huge army of 175 divisions is being rearmed, at as fast a pace as the industry of the Soviet Union can maintain, and that it is the principle weapon of an aggressive, irresponsible oligarchy headed by Stalin.

For these reasons, we cannot expect the Russians, so long as they retain their present system of government, to join the West in any system of progressive disarmament. As long as the Soviet military power exists, the West must be prepared to sacrifice and to work to raise a force strong enough to deter Russia from attacking and, if needs be, halt the Russian onslaught in the first few months of a war until the industrial strength of the United States and western Europe can be mobilized to defeat the Soviet Union. It is only too clear that this strength is not now mobilized and that only an actual war will mobilize it.

The spring of 1952 is a good time to take a look around and see how far western Europe has come along the road to this objective.

Obviously, great progress has been made since the nadir of western military strength four years ago. Divisions, armored and infantry, air groups, depots, and lines of communication exist. A start has been made on bringing the Germans into the defense of Europe. Excluding all other factors, is this progress great enough to deter the Russians? I think not.

It can be charged that it is impossible to exclude all other factors. Especially when one of those factors is our ability to drop atom bombs and another is the development of atom bombs for tactical use. But I think we must accept that the Soviet Union also has that ability. The critical factor is whether the internal air-warning and air-defense system of the Soviet Union has reached the point at which the Russians believe a reasonable defense against United States strategic bombers can be maintained.

To return to Europe. Eisenhower had two military objectives to attain, one immediate, one long term. He had to put western Europe into position to deter or defeat Soviet aggression in 1952, the immediate threat, and he had to plan to expand that military position into one which in 1954 or 1955 would be powerful enough to continue to deter the Soviet High Command and whose power, expressed in terms of available ground and air forces, would be primarily European.

What does Eisenhower have at his disposal today in terms of active divisions?

Granted that progress in mobilization and rearmament is no slower in the first six months of 1952 than in the last six of 1951 (actually a slight acceleration is expected), Eisenhower should have at his disposal by midsummer of 1952, twenty-four full divisions and the equivalent of one and two thirds divisions in the form of brigades.

To this force the United States would contribute six divisions including two armored, Britain four divisions including three armored, France twelve divisions including two armored, Belgium two divisions including one armored. The Supreme Commander also would have under his command two Dutch infantry brigades, one Canadian infantry brigade, one Norwegian infantry brigade and one Danish infantry brigade.

This truly is an emergency force. Save in the American and British divisions and in three quarters of the French divisions, the standards of training and equipment will not be as high as in the Soviet Group of Armies in East Germany. The air groups covering these ground forces will not be numerically equal to the Soviet air regiments in East Germany and in many cases the quality of the fighter aircraft will be well below that of the Soviet Air Force.

Nevertheless the power vacuum that existed when

Eisenhower took over in 1951 will have been filled. Considering the difficulties that SHAPE had to face —apathy, industrial unreadiness, financial timidity, national jealousies and the sheer physical difficulties of raising, training and equipping soldiers—the achievement is a remarkable one, in many ways much more so than some of Eisenhower's achievements during World War II. I do not believe Eisenhower, the soldier of 1942 or 1943, could have done it. Eisenhower, the soldier, diplomat, economist, salesman and statesman of 1951, did it.

This stopgap force, he warns, is just that. "In this job you live a year or two in the future. We have to think of this force as a foundation on which we can build a force that truly will deter the Russians not from one year to the next but forever. That's our goal."

Looking into the future, 1954 and 1955, Eisenhower and the principle planners at SHAPE foresee a force of around fifty-five ready divisions backed by at least twenty-five reserve divisions available to the central command within fifteen days of the proclamation of the emergency.

This force would cover a much wider area than the force (equivalent to twenty-five and two thirds divisions) which Eisenhower will have at his command in the summer of 1952. It will embrace not only the vital central European theatre, from the Baltic to the Alps, but Scandinavia on the north and Italy on the south. The estimate does not include, as this is written, the Yugoslav, Greek and Turkish forces.

The core of this force, according to present plans,

would be the European Army of forty-three divisions: fourteen French, twelve German, twelve Italian and five from Belgium, the Netherlands and Luxembourg. In addition there would be ten American and British divisions and single divisions from both Norway and Denmark.

Such a force, it is thought, would strike the correct medium between large standing armies and the weakness of the past. A most important feature of the military organization, once this force is in being, would be the reliance on reserve strength. The western European reserve force will grow as citizen soldiers graduate from the various standing divisions at the end of their military service into the reserve divisions. Both Eisenhower and Montgomery believe it is essential that these men maintain close connections with the armies in which they have served, that a system whereby reserve formations spend at least a month in camp every year be organized, and that reservists are informed on innovations in weapons and tactics through compulsory attendance at lectures and home study courses.

Regular soldiers whose one idea is to raise as big a force as possible as rapidly as possible find the idea "impractical." But the experience of a year of rearming Europe has convinced Eisenhower that in the absence of any sign of imminent Soviet aggression, and, as he says, "We'll probably never get that," the only thing to be done is to construct first a shield in the shape of regular divisions and second a reserve strength that can be quickly mobilized when war comes.

In other words, it is plainly impractical to try to

maintain European defense on the basis that the Soviet Union is going to attack tomorrow.

If that attack should begin, the burden will fall on the divisions now available. What chance do they have? Are they capable of halting the Soviet attack?

If we confine our answer to a comparison of the twenty-five divisions under Eisenhower's command with the thirty-six to thirty-eight divisions of Chuikov's German "front" then the answer is in the affirmative. The Soviet divisions pushing westward certainly will lose momentum, their supply and maintenance will be subject to all those ills a recently modernized army is heir to, and the Allied air forces, although inferior in numbers and quality to the Soviet Air Force, will hammer the advancing Russians.

But no Soviet drive westward would be powered by an engine of only thirty-six or thirty-eight divisions. We must reckon that the Russian front in East Germany would be very strongly reinforced before any attack was launched, so strongly, it is hoped, that intelligence would get some inkling of what was going on. Some sources believe that the Soviets would not attack until a force of at least one hundred divisions, almost triple the number of divisions now available, had been made ready in East Germany.

This sort of exaggeration is natural to those who think of the Soviet Union's 200,000,000 people as though they were 200,000,000 Americans or Britons or French. Actually, they are nothing of the sort and the rearmament and re-equipment of the Soviet Army on the most modern lines inevitably will reduce the number of men thrown into any conflict while at the same time it increases the fire power and road mobility of the Soviet Army.

My own view is that a Russian attack in the central European theatre will be launched by not more than seventy-five divisions but that a very high percentage of these divisions will be armored divisions and mechanized rifle (infantry) divisions. It will be remembered that the armies that attacked the French, Belgian and British positions in May of 1940 were numerically inferior to the western forces.

To digress, I doubt also that in the event of war the Russians ever will mobilize the 551 divisions which, according to British intelligence, they had available early in 1945.

There are two reasons why such numbers are out of the question today.

The first is that the Soviet Union will not be receiving help in the form of weapons and equipment from the United States. This was *not* the difference between victory and defeat in 1941, despite what some of the professional Russia-haters will tell you. The difference was a blend of German stupidity on the very highest level and the valor of the ordinary Russian.

But then and throughout the war, this assistance allowed the Soviet Union to maintain a larger number of men in the field than would have been possible had Russia had to make all its tanks, trucks, planes, and other equipment used by the Soviet fighting forces. Should there be another war, this condition will no longer be true.

The second reason lies in the change in the character of the Soviet Army. As I pointed out earlier, the Soviet Army since 1945 has undergone an organizational change that has altered its character considerably. Although it is still the largest army in the world, if the Chinese Army is excepted, its fundamental character no longer is that of a mass army. The emphasis is increasingly on quality, of men, equipment and training, and not on quantity. The Russian steam roller is being replaced by the Russian lawn mower, a much smaller and handier instrument.

Such an army can only be equipped and maintained by a tremendous industrial effort on the home front. The men necessary to keep production going in a hundred industrial cities cannot, in any struggle with the primary industrial power of the world, be spared to go out and fight.

The Russian Army will be smaller because it has to be smaller; its weapons will be such that a vast army of industrial workers will be necessary to maintain the Soviet Army in the field. For the first time in thousands of years the mass tactics of Borodino, Balaclava, Inkerman, Smolensk, Stalingrad and Krivoi Rog must give way to a more adroit handling of smaller groups, even though these forces still will be numerically much superior to those they oppose.

So we come down to the prospect that a Soviet drive westward in the central European front will be launched by about seventy-five divisions, all of a very high caliber in training. About half of them will have a lot of armor, although not all of these will be armored divisions in the American or British sense, and the standard of mechanization in all the divisions will be high.

In addition to that force we must consider the

effect of the satellite forces on the general military situation in the event of war.

Those will not be used generally in the forward push of the Soviet armies although I think we can be certain that some units, regiments or brigades from each of the satellite nations will be included in the Soviet front for propaganda purposes.

But the modernized satellite armies will be employed in the subsidiary operations which the Russians will initiate at the same time that they move westward in central Europe. These will be attacks into Greece, Yugoslavia and Italy. There will be about sixty-five satellite divisions ready for offensive operations early in 1952, and in the event of war that year or the next, their mission would be to attack in those important areas.

I do not think the Russians believe that these forces could complete the job. But I believe the Russians hope that these forces plus some Russian air formations would deliver a blow so heavy that there would be no question of the southern members of the Atlantic alliance launching an offensive which would divert Soviet forces from the main theatre of operations.

The main Russian offensive operation westward from central Europe would be accompanied in the south by satellite operations against the southern members of the Atlantic alliance and probably offensives on a smaller scale in the north against Norway and Denmark and possibly against Sweden and Finland as well. This is war on the grand scale, much larger, we must remember, than anything Hitler attempted in 1940.

The numbers dwarf Eisenhower's twenty-five divisions. Yet the odds are not as one-sided as they seem.

To begin with, the offensive, which the Russians must assume, involves certain difficulties. The forward sweep of the Soviet armies periodically will be checked by the necessity of forcing the crossings of rivers and it is during those pauses that the allied tactics of sharp and vigorous counterpunches can best be utilized.

Moreover, the Russian divisions are not going to flood westward easily. They will be tied, as all mechanized units are tied, to the terrain or means of communication over which their vehicles must move. The speed of mechanized divisions depends not only on tanks but on gas trucks, ammunition carriers and all the other vehicles made indispensable by mechanical war in which a day's supply of ammunition or gasoline can be expended in an hour's fierce fighting.

So the Russians, no matter how great their strength, will be tied to the roads and their frontage in attack will be limited by available roads. They will push infantry companies off the roads onto the hills and fields, but the lifelines of the army will be the highways. The nightmare of a great sweep westward of a Soviet horde from the Baltic to the Alps is just that and nothing more. The Russians will have to use certain recognized paths of approach to western Germany.

Now although the force that would oppose them in the event of war is not as big or as good as we would like, it is not negligible. The ten American and British divisions in Germany, for example, are probably as high in caliber as anything the two nations have ever produced in peacetimes.

We are betting very heavily on reserve divisions in Europe and both the United States Seventh Army and the British Army of the Rhine have a percentage of conscripts and reservists in their ranks. But the quality of these men is amazingly high and these can be counted regular divisions, if by regular one means divisions with a high standard of training, a fair amount of experience in the ranks and among the officers, and outstanding morale.

With such divisions a good commander can do almost anything.

The miracle of Dunkirk was attributable in a very large measure to the fact that Viscount Gort, the commander in chief of the British Expeditionary Force, was operating with regular soldiers and regular officers. These are the men who jeer at "God Bless America" or "God Save the King," who have a low opinion of anyone outside their own outfits, but who are the hard dying, hard fighting core of any successful army.

With them an experienced commander can take chances which would be out of the question with newly raised divisions. He can commit them to situations in which other units would be massacred. He can ask them to perform tasks which new divisions would never contemplate.

Divisions like these led by men like Manton Eddy and John Harding are not going to be overwhelmed by any Russian tidal wave. They will not be able to hold the Soviet thrust on the frontiers, nor should they be expected to do so. But they will be able to deliver very sharp and very telling counterstrokes against the Soviet forces in the main battleground between the Elbe and the Rhine.

Of course, if the Germans were to suddenly understand the world of 1952 and discard their dream that this is merely 1942 with the Americans and the British on their side, then it would be possible to think of holding the Soviet forces on the borders of Germany. But until the German people, as distinguished from the government of Dr. Adenauer, are ready to help deter the new Russian imperialism, the first and perhaps the most important battlefield will be Germany.

In the quality of the American and British troops in Germany we find the first "plus" in any assessment of whether a Soviet offensive could be checked. There are others.

One is that the morale, training and effectiveness of the French Army in Germany has risen swiftly since 1950. In the event of war, the French Army on the Rhine would make a real contribution to the defense of Germany. Given the equipment it has been promised, the French Army in Europe generally should develop into a reasonably sound fighting force.

I say "reasonably sound" because no army is any better than the people from which it comes. France is not equipped morally, which is much more important than material readiness, to fight a long war. The French, I am convinced, will fight well in Germany. What they would do if the Russian eruption spilled over into France is a question, a frightening one.

Here is another "plus." The quality of the young men of the United States Air Force and the Royal

Air Force could not be higher. It is a reproach to the people and the governments of the United States and of Britain, that if war began tomorrow these young men would go to war in planes inferior to those of the Soviet Air Force.

"I know all about that," a visiting Congressman said, "but look at the Battle of Britain. The British beat the Luftwaffe, didn't they?"

It is about time that ghost was laid.

There is very little similarity between the Battle of Britain and any air battle which would ensue in Europe if the Soviet divisions moved westward, and it is a criminal mistake to make the comparison.

The British fighters in the Battle of Britain were *Spitfires* and *Hurricanes*. The former was as good as any German fighter that came to Britain that summer. The *Hurricane* was nearly as good as the German best and, of course, it was infinitely better than the second best and a devastating weapon against the ill-armed German bombers, especially the *JU-57*.

True, the pilots of Britain's Fighter Command were superior in training and experience to the pilots of the Luftwaffe although the margin of superiority was not enough to explain the victory.

Finally, those slow, old-fashioned British who are always so deficient in know-how had come up with radar—a good long time before the people with all the know-how had installed it at Pearl Harbor, by the way—and they knew where and when the German bombers were coming.

These conditions do not exist in central Europe today. The two air forces have some very fine and experienced commanders. The quality of the pilots is very high because it will be a long time before the totalitarian world produces anything as good as the young man of middle-class background who, as Kipling's Mulvaney said, has both "brains and bowels."

The best we can hope for during the first weeks of any general conflict will be a series of daring, perhaps brilliant exploits by these young men against the massed might of the Soviet Air Force. These will be enough to win an occasional breathing space for the men on the ground and to permit the mounting of a counterattack.

But we will be buying time with the bodies of young men flying planes that are obsolete because the Smiths got a new television set and the Browns a new convertible.

"The trouble is there's going to be so God-damned many of them," a young air force colonel said. "Look at this. The Russkies fly these *MIGs* (*MIG15's*) into Czecho all the time. Stake out a strip, put them down and take them off. They don't put in any fuel or ammunition. I think those will come along later when they get ready to go. What does it mean? Why, it means they've got an extra hundred strips in Czechoslovakia they can use when the ball game starts."

I asked about his own planes. His are *F84's*.

"Well, you know these aren't the best the air force has. The best are in Korea. They must be better than these. Jesus, chum, we have a hell of a time keeping eight of them ready to go twenty-four hours a day."

By the time this appears in print, some of the forward airfields in the United States zone of occupation in Germany will have been moved westward to areas

where there is something more between them and
the potential enemy than a lot of free air.

In the autumn of 1951 our operational air bases
were almost impossible to defend against enemy air
attacks. The best they could hope for was six minutes' warning. Of course this is not enough.

Now to another "plus," a more concrete one than
the high quality of the fighter pilots, which is balanced by the comparatively low quality of their
planes. The next "plus" is the effect which United
States atomic bombing would have on the Russian
push westward.

If the rearmament of western Europe is viewed
solely through the eyes of the strategic airman, the
advocate of very long-range atomic bombing, its
value lies in one circumstance. This is that a determined resistance to Soviet ground forces by western
troops will force the Russians to expend in battle
ammunition, gasoline and lubricants, to use up all
sorts of other supplies so that the effect of very long-
range atomic bombing of the centers of Soviet production in Russia and centers of distribution and
communication in Russia and the satellite states will
be felt by the Soviet armies in the field very soon,
because their initial stocks of supplies will be exhausted early in the conflict.

This point of view, which was put to me by one
of the highest ranking officers of the United States
Air Force in Washington in 1950, is a cold-blooded
one. For it is based on the idea that the only function
of the ground forces is to make the Russians use their
own weapons so that when the Soviet armies reach
their objectives they will be short of supplies and the

Soviet Union, as a result of atomic bombing, will be so incapable of sending supplies that the whole vast operation will sit still and wither away.

"Then, of course," the high-ranking officer said, "you can attack the Soviet armies."

Fortunately for the civilians, who always fight the wars, great conflicts are not fought along lines laid down by the brass hats of any one service or even by a combination of services. War, as Clemenceau pointed out, is far too serious a business to be left to soldiers.

The "plus" in atomic bombing is not that it would eliminate the reserve stocks of the Soviet armies in Germany, or anywhere else, but that it would paralyze the will to fight of the Russian people and the army that represents them.

I do not suggest that this would represent cause and effect. Ivan's wife is not going to write Ivan from Stalino to say that Voroshilovgrad has been wiped out by atomic bombing, that everyone says Stalino is next and that he had better come home. He'll never get the letter.

What will happen is that while Stalino is being bombed, the Soviet armies in the field also will be undergoing attack from tactical atomic weapons. We put a high value on the effect of atom bombing and in view of the results of Hiroshima and Nagasaki, it is right that we should do so. I do not think the first bomb or the first dozen bombs distributed among the Russian armies and the Russian industrial centers will defeat the Russians. After all we will be fighting a very brave people. But atomic weapons, whether they are dropped from aircraft or arrive in the war heads of guided missiles or are fired as projectiles from guns, inevitably will reduce the advantages which the superiority in manpower now gives the Soviet Union.

We will get a taste of the same ourselves. But in atomic warfare, which is the apex of mechanical warfare, we can count upon the United States being superior. I admit that such confidence is not easily reconcilable with our present inferiority in fighter planes in Europe, but the latter is a passing phase in the struggles for technical air supremacy.

But it must be remembered that for a long time after World War II the only important defense program actively carried out in the United States was in the field of atomic warfare.

The quality of the American and British divisions in the field, the slow but steady improvement in the quality and quantity of the soldiers of France, the high quality of the personnel in the American and British air forces and, lastly, the superiority of the United States in atomic warfare are all factors favoring the West in any conflict with the Soviet Union.

But they are military factors, they concern the results in the field of the national will. What is equally important in any assessment of whether western Europe can check Soviet aggression is the state of political morale and economic strength in the countries concerned once the war begins.

So we come to the political factors. These we must consider in connection with the question, Will Europe fight? rather than, Will Europe rearm? Europe is rearming. The process is not as fast or as complete as we would wish but it is a miracle compared with what was thought possible two years ago and, if you read between the lines in *Pravda* and *Izvestia*, you will see, also, that it is far more than the Russians believed the West could accomplish.

What are the reasons for believing Europe will fight?

One very important one is that there is a developing common European attitude toward the world, a European patriotism which is quite apart from German or French or Greek or Danish national pride.

Ever since, in the summer of 1945, Europeans recognized that their old continent was caught between the two great power groupings of East and West there has been a gradual intellectual movement toward union. The motivation behind this movement, on the highest level, has been a belief in the essential unity of European civilization and a conviction that Europe, which has given so much to the world, can only be saved through its own exertions.

"Europe cannot go on as it has since 1914, a group of comparatively small states each of which is an easy prey for an ambitious big power," Jean Monnet said once during the war. "She must forget her differences, which after all are differences of nationalism, and remember her similarities. We have much in common, ours is a great history."

Out of this belief, held by hundreds of intelligent Europeans, has grown the movement toward European unity. Because it was apparant very soon that Europe could not be rushed into political unity, other forms on which political unity could be built were introduced.

One was the Schuman Plan. Another was the

Pleven Plan out of which grew the formula for the European Defense Force or, as it is popularly called, the European Army.

Of course, the organization of Europe under the Schuman Plan or the European Army was bound to benefit some states more than others. But both plans promise that the energies and resources of Germany, the mightiest of continental states, henceforth will be harnessed for the strength of Europe as a whole.

The progress that the idea has made in Europe owes a good deal to farsighted Americans like High Commissioner McCloy and General Eisenhower, men who argued for the Schuman Plan and the European Army Plan with doubting Europeans. But we are a hasty nation, and it may be that less diplomatic but equally enthusiastic advocates of European unity did as much harm as good.

The practice of grabbing a European by the lapels and shouting, "Damn it, you've got to integrate," got us nowhere. The impulse must come from within. Because of the depth of some of the national antagonisms, progress cannot be hurried too much.

Unhappily, the concept of a united Europe thus far has not permeated through the peoples of western Europe. This is partly because politicians continue to stress old national antagonisms and partly because the original conception was confined to a group of men like Monnet in France and Adenauer in Germany whose political appeal is negligible. They are technicians of government, not politicians.

When the idea of western European unity is fully understood by the peoples of western Europe, it will be warmly accepted. The farmer in the Champagne and the farmer in Bavaria, the miner of the Ruhr and the miner of Lorraine are not, in the outworn phrase of nationalism, natural enemies.

Their economic masters were natural rivals, a condition that helped breed two world wars. Now a terrible world war and the rise to awesome power of a great, essentially non-European nation beyond the Elbe has forced even the masters of Europe's people to consider the idea that they must unite or die.

But the industrialists of Europe still lack the vision and enthusiasm of men like Monnet.

Not long ago I sat at dinner in an elegant private dining room of the Breitenbacher Hof in Düsseldorf with six leaders of Ruhr industry. They were serious, forthright men whose minds seemed to have been molded in the days before World War I. They were, of course, violently anticommunist, but at the same time they were shockingly ignorant of their own danger.

"After all," one of them said, "you know we Germans are anticommunist but I think you Americans should allow us to judge for ourselves whether there is any military danger from Russia. Certainly we wish to sell steel and machines in the East. But you must believe us when we tell you that we understand the Russians and that we would not sell a single ton if we thought there was any danger that it would be used against the West."

I asked about the Schuman Plan. They smiled and one man said that "it's a good idea for France, but not for us."

"Of course we are for European unity," another said, "but it should be political unity. The politicians should concentrate on that and leave the economy of Europe to those who understand it. We can get along with our friends in French industry quite well."

The German industrialists' viewpoint seems to be shared to some extent by the same group in France, and is a serious drawback to plans for European federation, economic, political or military.

Then, almost as disheartening to interested Americans, there is the pitifully slow pace of actual progress toward federation. There is a good deal of talk when the European Consultative Assembly meets at Strasbourg about "the urgent need" for uniting Europe. The fact remains that although in 1947 the western European nations agreed to reduce trade barriers, rationalize investments and pool their resources, four years later at the end of 1951 little had been done to implement these pledges.

National rivalries and prides certainly have delayed progress even in countries whose salvation depends on the acceptance of federation. Oddly it is in these countries, France for instance, where the most outrageous forms of nationalism flourish.

Few critics of the European Army Concept or the North Atlantic Treaty system have been as harsh as General Charles de Gaulle, leader of the Rally of the French People, the largest single party in the French National Assembly.

De Gaulle—it is strange to think that some Americans once regarded him as "dangerously left"—now has returned to the reactionary surroundings in which former French generals are happiest.

The General is against the European Army because it will resurrect the German Army without guaranteeing the continued freedom of France to direct the French Army.

"We would be the only ones to surrender our army," De Gaulle complains. "And to whom? To Europe? But there is no such thing. Then to General Eisenhower? But for centuries our strength and prestige are one with the French Army. We cannot, we must not lose our army."

Of course, no one plans to take the French Army. What is planned is that France will contribute fourteen divisions or *groupements* to the European Army and will retain sufficient divisions to protect her overseas possessions.

De Gaulle goes further than most Frenchmen in asking the creation of a national German army. It was because the French government of M. Pleven could not accept a national army in Germany, that the Pleven concept of a European army including the Germans was accepted by the West. And the political record of General de Gaulle in the last few years is so uncertain that it seems likely that had the French government accepted a national army for Germany, he, as an opposition leader, would have opposed it.

The General's appeal in France, like that of Dr. Kurt Schumacher, the German socialist, in his country, is strongly nationalist. He is against handing over control of the French Army to a foreigner, i.e., Eisenhower. He opposes any alliance like the North Atlantic Treaty Organization which does not include guarantees to France on the amount of help to be sent her in the event of Soviet attack and other guarantees that there will be no interference with French possessions overseas.

Such elements flourish in every country in western Europe. Yet those who favor political federation and economic and military integration take heart from the fact that although these national desires are still strong and have an important effect on the popular mind, the idea of federation and integration has impressed itself upon men of intelligence in every European country as the best means by which Europe can attain a strong defensive position, both military and political, against the Soviet power.

To date, the pace has been terribly slow. But the project has been started. Each year more and more people learn about it. Like so many other great enterprises in world history, it depends on time. The current of history, sluggish though it may be, is flowing toward integration and federation in Europe.

Once it has been attained, the resulting confederation will not always be as sympathetic to American policy or as dependent on the economy of the United States as the individual nations are today. But Europe will have saved itself by our American example and the free world will be the stronger for that. This is a great conception, a truly revolutionary one. It is not surprising that a lady as old as Europe takes a long time to make up her mind.

American tourists abroad are shocked to learn that "there was a communist sitting next to us in the restaurant" or "the man who owned the garage said he was a communist." They also are unduly concerned over the lack of violent campaigns against communism in various European nations.

There have been no widely publicized government inquiries in Paris or London or Rome, nothing at any rate to compare with Washington's attacks on communist windmills. Although there is a bumper crop of disillusioned ex-communists in Europe, no Budenz has arisen. Nor has there been a European version of Senator McCarthy.

This is true. The nearest a western European state has come to copying United States methods of dealing with the communists occurred, naturally, in West Germany where the government asked the constitutional court to allow it to ban the Communist party and the Socialist Reichs party, a neo-Nazi organization. Being German, the Federal Government went further than anyone else, since not even in the United States has the government moved to ban the Communist party.

But we should not take European failure to copy American methods of handling communism as a sign that European governments are unaware of the dangers of communism or that communism, when it is measured in terms of party members, is gaining in western Europe.

We know that when the European rearmament program was first launched, there were a number of communists in important posts in the French civil service including some officials of the key ministries. Without a single investigation by legislators, these men were quietly eliminated. Without a single speech by a single general, a very thorough system of investigation was introduced into the French Army and the number of communists in important commands drastically reduced.

Similar measures have been taken in other NATO nations—Italy is an example—and although communist influence and Soviet espionage have not been completely eliminated from the government and fighting services of these countries (can this be said truly of any country?) the danger that everything the West does immediately is relayed to Moscow is much less than it was a year ago.

In this book I have frequently mentioned instances of Allied stupidity which have helped the communists in their fight against European rearmament. But this gratuitous assistance from western politicos has not restored the party to the influence and prestige it enjoyed in 1945.

There are in western Europe today, according to one shrewd intelligence officer, about 32% fewer members of the party than there were in 1945 in West Germany, France, the low countries, Italy and Scandinavia.

This does not mean that the electoral strength of the party has decreased to the same extent. Indeed it is rising in some areas, although there is no indication of an overall increase in communist voters, as opposed to party members, in these countries.

"As far as the question of defense against the Russians in time of war is concerned," the source quoted above said, "it is the regular party member who must be watched. Now a chap will go and vote communist, sometimes because he really believes in all their rot, sometimes because he doesn't like the foreman, but that doesn't mean that he will go out and blow a bridge because the local party leader tells him to. He may go out and demonstrate on party orders, but that's becoming unpopular because of police action. No, the real dirty work is left to the party member and, thank God, there are fewer of them than there were."

The reasons for the decline in party strength, which also is noticeable in Britain, are first, that the party has failed to deliver and second, Titoism.

The communists are not immune from such natural laws as politics can boast. Therefore after promising the moon to a great many eager young people in the dismal years immediately after the second World War, the party leaders should not be surprised today when these young people depart disillusioned after learning that it is not Russia that is helping France or Italy or Norway but the United States.

The average European is less afraid of communism than the average American but, with good reason, he is much more afraid of the physical power of Russia. Communism is familiar in Europe. The workers sympathize with some communist aims even though its methods are abhorred. Communism had its intellectual followers in Europe long before Lenin organized the Bolshevik state.

Americans must remember too that the Soviet armies and the communist underground bands in the West raised communist prestige during the war. Stalin's policy has almost completely destroyed this prestige, but the memory remains. Finally, those who fought the Germans in Europe were much closer emotionally to the Russians than Americans were; their lives literally depended on whether Russia stood or fell in 1941.

Unless the West is forced to fight within the next year, there are sound political and military reasons for believing that eventually a defense structure strong enough to deter Russia from attacking western Europe can be established. But the completion of that structure is far in the future.

Could the Russians be halted if they attacked today? Without German participation it is extremely doubtful if the western forces would be strong enough to halt the Soviet aggressors anywhere east of the Rhine. Certainly the day of the easy Soviet rush to the Atlantic is over. But we do not have the strength, now, to influence the Soviet General Staff against an attack in western Europe.

No one knows of course whether or not such a decision has been taken and the time set. If it has, and the Russians are hell-bent for war, will the present defense structure plus the expectation of atomic bombing deter them from aggression? My own belief is that it will not.

Of course, no one knows; the answer lies in the Russian character. During my stay in Moscow I was friendly with an elderly Scandinavian diplomat who had been born of a diplomatic family in St. Petersburg. Trouble was brewing then—it was 1947—and often we discussed the German and Russian totalitarianisms and their characteristics.

"One thing you must remember," he said once, "these people have a sense of the possible which the Germans lacked. If they come to a closed door they will not try to batter it down with their heads. They will halt and try something else, perhaps they will try to unlock the door or they will try the windows. But they are not like the Germans, stupider in many things, yes, but in what they can and cannot do, much more intelligent."

In this chapter we have been dealing with the more obvious physical strengths and favorable political aspects of western defense. The "door" to Europe seems very firm, very strong. If it is what it seems, will the Russians turn away and do something else? Perhaps. If it is as strong as it seems. Let us turn now to the weaknesses of the general European defense picture, in all its political, economic and military aspects, before we attempt a conclusion on whether Eisenhower's work will endure and Europe can be saved.

We should remember, I believe, that in discussions such as these it is realistic rather than unrealistic to assume that the Soviet Union is the enemy of the free world. Realism in political thinking today demands that we acknowledge, no matter how much we would like to forget it, that the Soviet Union has been rearming at top speed for the past four years, that it is bringing its forward divisions like those in Germany up to war strength, that it is arming and modernizing the organization of the satellite armies and that it is maintaining a constant propaganda attack on the United States. In other words, by every historical precedent, the Soviet Union is preparing for war.

Under those conditions weaknesses and deficiencies of little moment in periods of actual peace are terribly important now. Good intentions are not enough either on the part of our European allies or ourselves. Nor will expansive predictions of what American "know-how" can do in the future give the Russians pause now. If they are to be convinced that an attack in Europe would be national suicide then they must be confronted by something more than understrength European divisions and American divisions armed with obsolete tanks and relying on obsolete airplanes for their air support.

Europe has come a considerable distance. As this is written there are 3,100,000 men in the armies of the North Atlantic Treaty nations and there were only 1,800,000 in those armies in June of 1950. The American forces in Germany have been tripled, the British doubled. The façade is beginning to look imposing. Let's look behind it.

14. How Europe Sees Us

One of our national weaknesses is a tendency to confuse the adoption of a policy with the success of a policy. Hardly had the United States got the North Atlantic Treaty Organization started than American officials abroad began to assume that the rearmament policy, of which that organization is a symbol, was a success and that it had the wholehearted co-operation of the European peoples.

In one way the busy officials of the various NATO organizations in London and Paris were not to be blamed. For their acquaintance with the peoples of Europe, unless they are very unusual officials indeed, is slight. They depend for their ideas on European states of mind on a new genus of cabinet ministers. This species has developed in Europe since the war. Its members' portfolios vary but each could be called "the Minister for American Affairs." They are the men like Jean Monnet in France or Konrad Adenauer in Germany who can be depended upon to get along with the Americans and to get things from the Americans.

They know just where the Americans are vulnerable. They play with wonderful virtuosity on the average American official's fear of communism, and even more his fear of seeming to be assisting communism in any way. They understand that although United States officials are "briefed" from morning to night they really

294

know very little about the countries they have come
to assist, being immersed usually in the administration
of vast bureaucracies. They are, in short, a very intelligent, experienced group of Europeans doing the best
they can for their countries.

It is most unlikely however that they represent or
even understand the tides of public opinion which lie
just below the surface in each country. If, in this chapter, we are to make an honest assessment of whether
Europe will work and sacrifice to deter a Soviet attack or, if that effort fails, whether Europe will fight
a sustained war on our side against the Russians, these
aspects of public opinion are just as important to the
general picture as say the failure of United States industry to produce the needed aircraft or the shoddy
maintenance of French armor in the field.

There is a malaise in western continental Europe,
with the honorable exception of Norway, which cannot be identified precisely although, to be sure, we
call it loosely "neutrality" or "anti-Americanism."

In France I have heard it called Lavalism. It is an
attitude that is expressed in the idea that anything is
better than war, even occupation.

"Just consider what the thoughts of the ordinary
bourgeois Frenchman must be," an intelligent American official who lives in Paris said. "He looks around
at Paris, the restaurants are open, the shops are full,
the industrial and agricultural life of the country, from
his standpoint, is booming. But France was defeated
in 1940 and occupied for four years.

"He looks across the Channel at the British. They
were the winners. But Britain is perennially hard up,
so is France but it hasn't hit our Frenchman yet and

won't because he'll throw out any government that makes him feel the economic consequences of the war; in England there are no good restaurants, there is continued rationing, the cities still are shabby, life for the English is austere and grim.

"Can you wonder, then," the American asked, "why so many people here in this country are wondering if surrender and occupation don't pay after all? Four times lately, Frenchmen have said to me, 'Oh, of course, 1940 was terrible but after that, we got along.'"

I have encountered this state of mind in France and Belgium. Often it is connected with neutrality although neutrality, of course, presupposes the lack of occupation. Often it is tinged with anti-Americanism. Always it is connected with the fear of war so prevalent in Europe.

What has been the biggest political failure of the whole NATO policy? Simply that in two of the major nations of Europe, Germany and France, American and native spokesmen have failed to convince the people that rearmament is the one means remaining, save dishonorable surrender throughout the world to the ambitions of the Soviet Union, to save the peace.

On the contrary, in these nations and in others of western Europe there is profound apprehension among the people that rearmament is a step toward war. This is a perfectly logical development of a century of European rearmament races. They have always meant war in the past and no one in high position has been persuasive enough to change the minds of millions of Europeans.

The fear of war, therefore, is a strong psychological barrier that must be broken down before the North

Atlantic program receives the support of the people of Europe. We are deceiving ourselves if we think that such support exists today in the measure necessary to sacrifice and fight in war.

Anti-Americanism in the NATO nations is the morale factor which impresses Americans most and is responsible for the doubts, usually expressed in whispers, that officials have over Europe's ability to defend itself. Americanophobia is irritating, because usually it is based on ignorance, but I do not think we need regard it as a decisive morale factor.

Of course it is exaggerated by Americans. As a nation we still honor the fiction that everybody loves us. Therefore the colonel's wife in Paris or the Regional Commissioner in Hesse or the second secretary in Brussels is shocked to find that he or she is regarded with a sort of tolerant skepticism by the European intellectual.

"They treat us like children," an American woman told me in Munich. "All this hand kissing and bowing, but they really don't take us seriously. And they don't like us."

Of course, they don't like us. We are now receiving some of the animosity that the continent used to direct at the rich, powerful English in the 19th century and even before this last war. If we want to be liked in Europe we better blow up Pittsburgh and Detroit and go bankrupt.

Much of the anti-Americanism is the result of our own arrogance and ignorance.

"I love America," a Belgian said to me a year ago. "I studied there as a young man. I visit it whenever I can. But I am a Belgian and a European and proud of it. When the tourists come to Belgium I try to stay in my own house. How can people be so rude abroad and so polite and hospitable at home? The English? They were not as bad, I assure you. They were, what is their word, 'civil' to foreigners but most of them were people of education, our kind of education. And they didn't complain so much.

"Can no one explain to Americans that this is Europe, not the United States, and that it has been through two disastrous wars in a little more than three decades? If they want shower baths and movies at every corner, then let them stay home. Europe has finer things to offer but they will not accept them."

Exaggerated? Perhaps.

It is not this sort of anti-Americanism that is the most serious. It is that fostered by the fear that the United States wants to fight the Russians and will use the Europeans as cannon fodder and Europe as a battleground which hurts United States influence and prestige the most. We are foolish to think that this is all "communist inspired." A great deal of it is expressed by people who are violently anticommunist.

The general picture of the United States which has been constructed in European minds since the war is not totally black. We are admired for our generosity, for our willingness to assist Europe, for a million individual acts of kindness performed by Americans from soldiers on occupation duty to ambassadors. But we also represent to many millions of influential Europeans the type of reactionary capitalist power which they distrust.

This sentiment is strongest in areas where socialism has taken firm hold: Britain, Norway, West Germany and parts of Belgium. People there freely admit they do not know whether they have a system that can deal politically with the Soviets. But they are pretty sure we haven't either.

Finally there is neutrality, another important factor affecting European morale. This is not strong in its immediate sense. No reasonable European politician in the NATO nations is going to proclaim today his support for his country's neutrality in the event of war. But neutrality expressed in the desire to remain aloof from the great world conflict, to paint the barn, to go on holiday, to live a quiet life, has an important political potential for tomorrow.

We must ask ourselves what the answer would be of a small European state in the path of Russian aggression—and almost all European states are small compared to the Soviet Union—if it were offered neutrality by Russia in the event of war? Have the minor nations of Europe learned the lesson of 1940; that unless they hang together they will assuredly hang separately?

Here are the important political currents constantly affecting Europe's will to arm and, if need be, fight; neutrality, anti-Americanism, Lavalism. Each of them, it is important to note, runs counter to the main European political development, the movement toward integration in the economic and military fields and political federation.

These attitudes are the negation of the sacrifice and tolerance which progress toward unification demands. United States officials abroad have discounted them, largely as I mentioned before because of our national habit of believing that adoption of a policy means its success.

Inevitably in a program calling for revolutionary changes in outlook on the part of all Europeans, there are other continental conditions which must be altered if joint defense is to become possible.

One of these is the position of the national state in Europe. The modern concept of the state originated in the very area which is now moving to alter that concept almost beyond recognition. Americans impatient with the slow progress toward European federation sometimes compare what the national states of Europe are asked to do today with what the states of America were asked to do after the Revolutionary War.

The comparison is ridiculous. No one can compare the Virginia of 1789 with the France of 1951. In one case we had a new community, in the other we have a state with a national existence of over a thousand years. We are asking the individual European nations to discard national habits, customs and traditions far stronger than anything that gripped even the oldest of the thirteen American states.

The individuality of the European states is only part of the problem. The rivalries between nation and nation and between groups of nations presents an equally serious problem.

We have touched many times on the ancient enmity between Teuton and Gaul. And we have seen how irresponsible politicians in both Germany and France are willing to keep this enmity alive for political purposes, thus endangering the chances of political federation. Our problem in establishing Europe's political strength against Soviet political or military pressure is whether the bonds of European unity will be strong enough to hold France and Germany together despite this enmity.

The Soviet approach will be much more subtle than a mere sharpening of the Franco-German feud. We must expect that if the Russians become convinced that it is absolutely necessary to detach Federal Germany from the western European community, it will do so by offering Federal Germany not only union with East Germany but a promise of the return of some of the territory lost by Germany in the east at the end of World War II.

This sounds fantastic. Is it any more fantastic than the alliance the Soviet Union made with Nazi Germany in 1939 or, for that matter, more fantastic than the military agreement which is slowly being worked out between the United States and the communist state of Yugoslavia?

The national interests which must be plowed under if European union is to have any validity are not all connected with ancient enmities as in the case of France and Germany. A problem of a very different sort is Britain's aloofness from Europe and the reluctance of Norway and Denmark to join programs for European federation as long as Britain remains outside the Schuman Plan, the European Defense Force and any concrete scheme for political federation.

To United States planners, one of the most irritating aspects of British policy, whether the government is Labor or Conservative, is the stubborn British refusal to consider Britain as a part of Europe. They insist that Britain's role in the world conflict will be played more effectively if the United Kingdom remains at the head of the Commonwealth and what remains of the

Empire rather than as one of a league of European states.

Impatient Americans, dreaming of a United States of Europe, protest that "the damned British seem to think that their Commonwealth and these two-for-a-nickel colonies count as much as the idea of a federated Europe."

This is true, Britons do believe that the British Isles and Canada, Australia, New Zealand and South Africa count for as much as Europe in defense preparations and will weigh much more heavily in war.

"Don't go putting it about that I said so or I'll have the F.O. down on my neck, but here's the way I see the thing," a British general said to me when European rearmament was first taking shape.

"European federation is a damned fine thing; if we had plenty of time then the only thing to do is unite Europe and build her up. If we had the time. I think we might go in then. We may yet, your General Eisenhower is a persuasive fellow when he begins to talk.

"But look at it from our point of view. You're asking us to give up something we prize, our ties with the Commonwealth, to join a rather shaky lot on the continent. How could our country retain its present position with the Commonwealth if it were part of a European community? And after all, old chap, do you expect us to rely as much in war on the Italians or the French or the Dutch as on the Australians, Canadians and New Zealanders?"

This attitude may be stubborn, shortsighted and old-fashioned, as various American and continental advocates of a European union say it is. But it has one virtue. It represents the point of view of an international community whose record in the last war, and as far as Britain alone is concerned, in today's rearmament, is far better than that of the European states.

The reluctance of the Norwegians or the Danes to leap aboard the bandwagon of European unity is a backhanded tribute to the British. For the Scandinavians courteously explain that any European community without the British is not strong enough to accomplish its purpose of organizing Europe for its own defense.

"The North Atlantic Treaty Organization is as far as we want to go," a Norwegian told me. "We will not enter into the rights and wrongs of British aloofness from these plans for economic or military integration. All we can say is that we do not think they are worth much as long as the British are on the outside."

The problem of national rivalries and national ambitions plus the more deep-seated psychological problems inherent in the Lavalism, anti-Americanism and neutrality of large sections of the continental people directly affect European defense. But they are psychological or political issues which must be kept separate from the military and economic problems in any fair analysis of the European situation today.

The two are closely connected, it is hard to say where the problem of lack of sufficient armor ends and the problem of rising prices for raw materials begins. Remember, however, that the great black question mark of Europe's morale broods over both.

Let us begin by examining the question that a great many American officials would like to keep decently in the background: Are we arming the right people?

This question represents dozens of precise issues. Such as, should we rebuild the Italian air force or should we divert planes to the R.A.F. which, we can be confident, will put them to good use? Or, would not money spent for the equipment of French divisions be more gainfully used in Yugoslavia?

As this is written Turkey has not yet formally joined the Atlantic alliance although its adherence has been sought. But the question of whether exploitation of Turkey's singularly advantageous strategic position by an increased arms and training program for Turkey might not be a greater deterrent to Soviet military ambitions than the construction of western European divisions is one that we have to consider.

I know that the official answer is that Europe's security is only possible through a collective effort. But great contributions to that security are possible with-out lavish United States expenditure for field divisions in countries whose military record in the last war was not significant. Let those countries make a primarily economic contribution.

"If you put the St. Louis Browns in Yankee uni forms, they'd still be the Browns when they got out on the ball field," a somewhat unorthodox American diplomat said.

No one would suggest that the maximum effort should not be made to arm Europe. But the United States has a strategic as well as an economic interest in seeing that European rearmament is carried out in the most efficient possible manner.

The course taken thus far may lead, as General Eisenhower firmly believes, to a renaissance of European moral strength based on newly regained physical strength and to a military position which will deter the Soviet Union from aggression in Europe.

But completion of the course charted by NATO will take a long time and no one, barring Stalin, knows whether we have the time.

One of the reasons it will take a long time is the duplication of both civilian control groups and boards and military commands. At the Rome conference in November, 1951, a start was made on trimming down the loose-jointed, Hydra-headed body of NATO.

What is needed, it is plain, is one superior control group consisting of the Defense, finance and foreign ministers of the NATO nations. This group would operate as the only policy-making group in the field of political decisions, just as Eisenhower's SHAPE headquarters must be the only military body able to make decisions affecting the military side of defense in the area of NATO's responsibilities.

At SHAPE the national military points of view of the various nations contributing to European defense are made known to Eisenhower and his staff by representatives of the forces involved.

This streamlining of the North Atlantic political organization is essential. So is some reduction in the number of headquarters in the military fields.

Let us consider only the United States ground forces in central Europe. At the apex is SHAPE, the international headquarters which if war started tomorrow would direct the defense of Europe. Immediately below SHAPE is General Juin's headquarters commanding the ground forces of NATO between the Baltic and the Alps.

But existing side by side with Juin's headquarters is

European Command of the United States located at Heidelberg. Finally we get down to the headquarters at Stuttgart of the United States Seventh Army, the people who would do America's share of the fighting.

Our hopes for the erection of a permanent defensive shield in the European land mass rest ultimately on the organization of a primarily European force. But at the moment, January 1952, defense rests largely upon the United States and British divisions in Germany. Much stronger participation by the large European powers, especially Germany and France, is necessary, and this is to be done through the organization of a European army.

"Western European defense," says Eisenhower, "could never be anything but a stalemate established on the Rhine unless something is done to consolidate a European army. We have to attempt the impossible, and the European Defense Force is part of the impossible."

This is a timely warning that the Supreme Commander understands the difficulties ahead. His recognition of the difficulties and his confidence that they can be overcome is more reassuring than the easy optimism of civilian officials.

What are the difficulties that face the European Army?

The first is that one of its principal components, the German divisions, do not exist. The wholehearted cooperation of the government of Federal Germany, something which we cannot count upon if the coalition government of Chancellor Adenauer is overturned by the Socialists, and a readiness to make compromises on the part of the French, Belgians, Dutch, Italians and Luxembourgers, which has not been very evident up to now, will produce the start of concrete steps to raise a German army by the spring of 1952.

It may be 1954, however, before German units have reached a state of training and equipment enabling them to take their place in the defense of Europe.

As we have seen, one of the basic advantages of a European army lies in the opportunity for eventually standardizing weapons, organization, training and tactics in six European nations.

But as General Eisenhower pointed out before the planning for the European Army was completed, there were still misunderstandings among the principal contributors to European defense on four major points.

These are:

(1) Differences in methods of conscription.
(2) Differences in training methods.
(3) Differences in conception of the functions of reserve forces.
(4) Differences in the training of reserves.

"You can have all the new weapons in the world," Eisenhower said—"unless you get agreement on these basic problems, the weapons can't be used at top efficiency."

In his first year at SHAPE, Eisenhower has been extremely concerned over the competition for command posts. Himself a man who has learned to sublimate his robust Americanism to an international cause, he is irritated at the idea that possession of one command or another should be an objective of national rivalry. And he foresees more trouble along these lines when the European Army takes shape.

The 43 divisions of that army—eventually the number may be greater but that is the initial planning figure—are to be divided into armored divisions of 12,600 men, and infantry divisions of 13,000 men. In war, 2,000 reservists would be added to each division.

The force will be divided into corps of about 80,000 men, composed apparently of five divisions plus corps troops. The air arm will consist of formations of sixty-five aircraft with a ground force of about 12,000.

The organization seems sound enough although it is difficult to see how a *groupement* of 15,000 men is to be maneuvered tactically with an American division of 18,000 on one flank and a British division of 16,500 on the other.

The basic difficulty, however, is an old but very elementary one: the differences in language. There is no substitute in war for direct contact between commanders of units operating side by side. Such contact can be made swiftly and directly only when the two commanders speak each other's language. Earlier, I elaborated the difficulties which would arise in an army whose soldiers will speak French, German, Dutch, Italian and perhaps Flemish when the divisional and unit commanders confer.

Officers with service in Korea assert that there was no trouble in talking to officers of other nationalities there. They then deduce that there will be no trouble in a European army.

This strikes me as a deduction built on the shakiest evidence. It is a gross oversimplification to compare conditions in Korea where the largest non-American units were British with whom the language difficulty did not exist. In the European Army the problem will be complicated not only by the additional number of languages but by the fact that in each case, at the outset at any rate, the officer will be a man trained in the national army of his country and not as willing to make those concessions to the officer of another army that optimistic advocates of the idea expect.

But the elementary military difficulties of the North Atlantic powers today are more pressing than the probable difficulties that will arise tomorrow when the European Army is raised.

The difficulties which are to the fore as this is written will be with us for a long time. None of them are open to easy solution. Not necessarily in the order of their importance they are:

(1) The basic weakness of the military infrastructure—that is, the system of communications, depots, railheads and air fields on which armies contesting central Europe with the Russians would depend. Until this situation is improved, the military effectiveness of forces in Germany is suspect.

(2) The shortage of military equipment and the antiquity of much that is now in the hands of the troops.

(3) The inadequate defense production in all NATO nations not excepting the United States.

(4) The lag between promise of new divisions and their arrival on the scene, especially in the case of France, the largest NATO land power in Europe.

These are immediate difficulties affecting the ability of those forces thus far assembled in Europe to hold a Soviet attack. Our ability to deter Soviet aggression now rests on these forces, not on the promise of sixty or one hundred divisions plus atomic tactical weapons in the future.

Finally we return to the fundamental question, can Europe be defended?

The answer despite the many difficult problems that confront us is in the affirmative, *if* the West is given another year of peace. If the Soviet Union has not attacked by January 1, 1953, then it has lost its great military opportunity in Europe. If it attacks before then, the military odds on the continent still will favor the Soviet Union although the Russian advantage will decrease with every day's work by the West and no quick or easy victory will be possible for the Russians. This assessment does not cover, nor could it cover, military developments outside Europe such as the sustained atomic bombing of the centers of Soviet industrial production.

From the standpoint of world strategy Eisenhower and SHAPE already have done a great deal. There is no longer the possibility that at the outbreak of war the Russian steam roller could sweep unchallenged to the sea. Even if the Soviet divisions in eastern Germany are heavily reinforced by new divisions from the Soviet Union, they would face on the outbreak of any conflict strong opposition from good divisions well led and better armed than they were a year ago although not as well armed as they should be.

But if Europe is slowly achieving the strength to combat aggression it still falls far short of the strength to deter aggression.

The decisive combination in the struggle to deter aggression is European land and air forces plus American atomic power. But European strength still is too small to act as an effective deterrent to so strong a nation as the Soviet Union, once its rulers have begun to weigh the advantages of real war against the advantages of continuing the cold war.

Eisenhower tells the Europeans no more than the simple truth when he says they need sixty divisions by the end of 1952 and one hundred divisions by the end of 1954 if they wish to live in security.

But the defense of Europe, now or in the future, is not as we have seen merely a question of available divisions. The increase in military strength must be accompanied by a renaissance of European morale and by revolutionary changes in the political structure of Europe. These are not the price of strength, they are very definitely the price of survival.

The darkness to the east has no counterpart in the memory of western man. The fools who delude themselves with the idea that a Russian occupation would be similar to the German occupation do not understand the character of the Soviet state or the Russian people. The neutralists who toy with the pleasant idea of a neutral oasis in a sea of fire are almost as foolish. These ideas plus anti-Americanism, and Anglophobia or Francophobia or all the other phobias, are luxuries the West can no longer afford.

The United States has done a great deal. Not as much as it has promised to do, but if we are vouchsafed a year's time the shortages in deliveries of airplanes, tanks and guns may be made up. But the principal failure of the United States in Europe, oddly enough, has been in the spiritual rather than the material field.

Years ago, when I first began work as a correspondent, the central fact that impressed me most about the average European's attitude toward the United States was his belief that with all its imperfections the American system stood for a better life for the common man.

That idea still remains. But it is not as strong as it was. And if it dies completely, then the Communists have their great opportunity in Europe.

During the London conference of the Council of Foreign Ministers, John Foster Dulles was meditating upon what he had seen during a visit in France, then at the height of its postwar turbulence. Something, he admitted, had to be done by the United States.

"But," he added solemnly, "no country is so poor as the one that can give only money. There must be something else."

There is something else. It is time that the United States in Europe began to devote a little more political attention to those who, if the worst comes, will have to do the fighting and dying to preserve western civilization.

The path to Europe's strength does not lie through the chancellories of Europe but in the back lanes of the farming villages of France, in the huddled red brick homes of England's midlands, in the noisome tenements of Naples, in the shabby apartment houses of Essen. It is to them that our political appeal must be directed, it is to them that we must reassert our political beliefs.

We have come very close to losing these people. Partly because our representatives abroad, not even the best of them, ever have understood the manner in which the thinking members of the European proletariat have rejected the rulers of the 1930's. Partly it is because in so many instances from Algeria in 1942 to Germany in 1949, we have allied ourselves with those whose connections with the past are stronger than with the present.

The United States has lost its luster, it no longer represents the vision of political and economic freedom it did fifteen years ago.

Until that condition is altered, until Europeans freely accept the United States as the moral leader of the free world, the rearmament of Europe will be incomplete.

"Trust the people," said Lord Randolph Churchill. It is about time we did in Europe.

It will not be easy. The people of Europe do not fall into neat patterns. Their respect for the virtues of the soap opera and the advertising man is scanty. They seek the firm establishment on this continent of those fundamental truths we accept as our right. If we can guarantee those to the people, what allies they will be! And it is allies we must seek in this conflict with Russia. Let the Soviet Union have the vassals.

(²)